Mostly BASIC:

Applications for Your Apple® II

Book 2

Howard Berenbon is a graduate of Wayne State University with a Bachelor of Science in Electrical Engineering. He is a full-time free-lance technical writer, and spends much of his spare time developing new programs for microcomputers. He is the author of the companion to this volume, *Mostly BASIC: Applications for Your Apple® II, Book 1*; two similar books for the TRS-80®, *Mostly BASIC: Applications for Your TRS-80®*, Books 1 and 2; *Mostly BASIC: Applications for Your Atari;* and *Mostly BASIC: Applications for Your PET*. His articles have appeared in many of the popular electronics and microcomputer publications.

Mostly BASIC:

Applications for Your Apple® II
Book 2

by

Howard Berenbon

Howard W. Sams & Co., Inc.
4300 WEST 62ND ST. INDIANAPOLIS, INDIANA 46268 USA

Preface

This book is a companion volume to *Mostly BASIC: Applications for Your Apple® II, Book 1*. Written for the Apple* II computer hobbyist, it consists of 32 chapters, with 37 complete computer programs written in BASIC. It can help you learn history, budget your household expenses, analyze your utility costs, and aid in stock market investment, to mention a few.

As an added feature, two types of educational fantasy games are included. The first program is a single-level dungeon called The Time Dungeon. As you wander through the maze, you will be teleported to different dates in history, to answer questions relating to actual events from the past. You will receive gold for a correct response, and you will lose gold for an incorrect response. The second and similar program is called The Algebra Dungeon, where you must solve algebraic equations as you wander through a two-level dungeon.

Also included is a fantasy game called The Dungeon of Danger. Here, you must fight monsters that roam the chambers and corridors of the dungeon. Your goal is to find the way out, unharmed, with as much gold as possible.

The programs are written in BASIC for the Apple II Applesoft microcomputer. Also, many of the programs are easily modified to run in other microcomputer BASICs. In some cases the programs contain additional lines to ensure some compatibility with the many dialects of BASIC.

Note portions of some of the programs are identical. However, to avoid confusion, especially for the beginning operator, the complete program listing is given for each version. Thus, there is no need to input part of the program from one listing and then skip to another to complete the desired program.

I hope that this book will help stimulate your imagination and aid you in the development of some of your own applications for your home computer.

HOWARD BERENBON

---

* Apple is a registered trademark of Apple Computer, Inc.

*To my parents, Fay and Irving Berenbon.
To my family and friends who helped with their
encouragement and constructive criticism.*

Contents

SECTION IV

ESP Testing

SECTION V

A Fantasy Game

SECTION I

Educational Programs

An important application for the home computer is its use as an educational aid. This section consists of eleven chapters, with sixteen educational programs written in BASIC.

The section begins with an educational fantasy game called The Time Dungeon. Here, the player is teleported to different dates in history, to answer questions relating to actual events from the past. There are six separate programs including American History, 1607 to 1850; American History, 1848 to 1914; American History, 1916 to 1975; World History, World War I; World History, World War II; and Ancient History, Middle East, 4000 B.C. to 6 B.C. All six programs are identical except for the subject and date at line 100 and the question DATA sets at lines 483 to 532. After entering one complete program, you need only change line 100 and the DATA set to complete the entry of all six games. But each program is listed separately to avoid confusion.

Next is an algebra educational fantasy game called The Algebra Dungeon. The word association program is a test for children. The algebra test program generates simple algebra problems. There are two memory test games: one that generates random letters and another that displays words. There is the Presidents test program that tests for dates in office, and the State Capitals test that tests your knowledge of the capitals. The Student Grader is an aid for teachers. Finally, there is a Relativistic Mass Simulation for physics students.

CHAPTER 1

The Time Dungeon

The Time Dungeon is an educational fantasy game where you must answer history questions while wandering through the chambers and corridors of the 64-chamber dungeon. When you enter an active time portal, you will be teleported to an event in history. There, you will be asked a question. There are six complete programs in this chapter. They are written in BASIC for your microcomputer. See Program 1-1 for American History, 1607 to 1850; Program 1-2 for American History, 1848 to 1914; Program 1-3 for American History, 1916 to 1975; Program 1-4 for World History, World War I; Program 1-5 for World History, World War II; and Program 1-6 for Ancient History, Middle East, 4000 B.C. to 6 B.C.

THE PROGRAM

You are given 1000 gold pieces and then teleported to a random location in the dungeon. Your goal is to find your way out, with as much gold as possible. Gold pieces are acquired by correctly answering questions about events in history. When you enter a chamber that is an active time portal, you will be teleported to a specific year. Then a question relating to that year is displayed. You will receive a random amount of gold if a correct answer is entered, and you will lose gold for an incorrect response. See Fig. 1-1 for a sample run.

ACTIONS OR MOVES

In your trip through the dungeon you will encounter active time portals, alien travelers, inactive time portals, time traps, secret doors leading to north-south or east-west corridors, maps, a crystal key, and exit portals.

After you run the program, enter your name, or your favorite fantasy character's name, for your trip into history. Then enter the present year. In a few seconds you will be teleported to an inactive time portal, somewhere in the dungeon.

You now have a choice of six actions. Enter the letter in parentheses for the following actions or moves in the dungeon:

```
(N)ORTH movement   (up)
(E)AST movement    (right)
(S)OUTH movement   (down)
(W)EST movement    (left)
E(X)IT   (when you are at an exit portal and
          have the crystal key)
(G)OLD pieces left
```

Mapping the Dungeon

Before you proceed, it is a good idea to begin mapping out the dungeon. Find your way to a corner, to orient yourself. Draw an eight (8) by eight (8) checkerboard, and make a note of the contents of each square using the following symbols:

```
  0 = inactive portal
 AP = active portal
 NS = north-south corridor
 EW = east-west corridor
  A = alien traveler
  X = exit portal
  T = time trap
=P= = your location in the dungeon
```

It must be noted that after you answer a question correctly (in an active time portal) that portal becomes inactive. But an incorrect answer leaves the portal active for future use. Also, after encountering an alien traveler, that chamber becomes an inactive portal. But the alien can reappear elsewhere in the dungeon.

Mapping the dungeon will allow you to find all the active time portals, keep track of time traps (so you can avoid them), and identify exit portal locations. On occasion, maps can be found on glowing screens within corridors. But this will be discussed later in the text.

North Movement (UP)

Entering an N allows you to move north through the dungeon. You may not move north under the following conditions:

1. If you reach the North Wall, you cannot pass through it.

THE TIME DUNGEON: AMERICAN HISTORY
COPYRIGHT (C) 1980 BY HOWARD BERENBON

AN EDUCATIONAL FANTASY GAME

YOU WILL BE TELEPORTED TO . . .

THE TIME DUNGEON . . . .
TO STUDY AMERICAN HISTORY

ENTER YOUR CHARACTER'S NAME?
? SARGON
ENTER PRESENT YEAR
? 1981

SARGON . . . YOU ARE ON YOUR WAY

YOU HAVE ARRIVED AT . . . .

THE TIME DUNGEON: AMERICAN HISTORY
FOR THE YEARS: 1916 TO 1975

YOU CARRY 1000 GOLD PIECES

YOU WILL ENCOUNTER . . .
TIME PORTALS WHICH TELEPORT
YOU TO EVENTS IN AMERICAN HISTORY

YOU ARE IN A GLOWING TIME PORTAL

THE LIGHT FADES . . . . . .
THE PORTAL IS INACTIVE . . . .

SARGON,   WHAT IS YOUR ACTION OR MOVE?

(N)ORTH, (E)AST, (S)OUTH
(W)EST, E(X)IT, (G)OLD
? N

YOU ENTER INTO A BLUE HAZY . . .
. . . . TIME PORTAL . . .

A PULSATING GLOW . . . .
. . . . INDICATES ACTIVATION

PRESENT YEAR . . .   1981

          P O R T A L   Y E A R . . .   1 9 7 4

          P O R T A L   Y E A R . . .   1 9 6 5
A R R I V A L . . . . A T
D E S T I N A T I O N   Y E A R 1 9 6 5

YOU HAVE ARRIVED AT THE YEAR 1965
. . . . . . IN AMERICAN HISTORY

YOU MUST ANSWER THIS QUESTION . . TO CONTINUE YOUR JOURNEY

THE YEAR IS: 1965

RACE RIOTS ERUPTED IN THE .... SECTION OF LOS ANGELES?:
WHITE   POOR
OLD   WATTS

QUESTION TYPE: xxx MULTIPLE CHOICE ?
ENTER CORRECT ANSWER?
? WATTS

CORRECT
YOU WIN 237 GOLD PIECES

SARGON,   WHAT IS YOUR ACTION OR MOVE?

(N)ORTH, (E)AST, (S)OUTH
(W)EST, E(X)IT, (G)OLD
? E

YOU ENTER INTO A BLUE HAZY . . .
. . . . TIME PORTAL . . .

A PULSATING GLOW . . . .
. . . . INDICATES ACTIVATION

PRESENT YEAR . . .   1965

          .. P O R T A L   Y E A R . . .   1 9 7 0

          .. P O R T A L   Y E A R . . .   1 9 7 0
A R R I V A L . . . . A T
D E S T I N A T I O N   Y E A R 1 9 7 0

YOU HAVE ARRIVED AT THE YEAR 1970
. . . . . . IN AMERICAN HISTORY

YOU MUST ANSWER THIS QUESTION . . TO CONTINUE YOUR JOURNEY

THE YEAR IS: 1970

U.S. AND S. VIETNAMESE TROOPS ENTERED WHAT CITY

QUESTION TYPE: PEOPLE, PLACES, OR THINGS ?
ENTER CORRECT ANSWER?
? CAMBODIA

CORRECT
YOU WIN 260 GOLD PIECES

SARGON,   WHAT IS YOUR ACTION OR MOVE?

(N)ORTH, (E)AST, (S)OUTH
(W)EST, E(X)IT, (G)OLD
? S

Fig. 1-1. The Time Dungeon

YOU ENTER A NORTH-SOUTH CORRIDOR
THRU A SECRET DOOR

THE DOOR CLOSES AND LOCKS BEHIND YOU

ON THE WALL IS A GLOWING SCREEN
BELOW THE SCREEN IS A RED BUTTON

DO YOU WISH TO PUSH THE BUTTON?
ENTER (Y)ES OR (N)O
? Y

THE TIME DUNGEON * * * MAP

```
?    AP   0    0    0    ?    0    ?
NS   0    0    ?    ?    AP   ?    AP
X    AP   NS   NS   AP   AP   AP   0
EW   EW   AP   X    ?    AP   NS   NS
0    0    AP   0    AP   0    AP
AP   NS   AP   ?    NS   EW   NS   AP
EW   0    AP   AP   0    0    0    0
EW   NS   0    0    0    0    =P=  AP
```

YOU ENTER INTO A BLUE HAZY . . .
. . . . TIME PORTAL . . .

A PULSATING GLOW . . . .
. . . . INDICATES ACTIVATION

PRESENT YEAR . . .   1942

.   P O R T A L   Y E A R 1 9 4 3

.   P O R T A L   Y E A R 1 9 4 4
A R R I V A L . . . . A T
D E S T I N A T I O N   Y E A R 1 9 4 4

YOU HAVE ARRIVED AT THE YEAR 1944
. . . . . . IN AMERICAN HISTORY

YOU MUST ANSWER THIS QUESTION . . TO CONTINUE YOUR JOURNEY

THE YEAR IS: 1944

THE .... INVADED EUROPE AND FREED FRANCE-BELGIUM-& LUXEMBOURG

QUESTION TYPE: PEOPLE, PLACES, OR THINGS ?
ENTER CORRECT ANSWER?
? ALLIES

CORRECT
YOU WIN 308 GOLD PIECES

SARGON, WHAT IS YOUR ACTION OR MOVE?

(N)ORTH, (E)AST, (S)OUTH
(W)EST, E(X)IT, (G)OLD
? N

YOU ENTER INTO A BLUE HAZY . . .
. . . . TIME PORTAL . . .

A PULSATING GLOW . . . .
. . . . INDICATES ACTIVATION

PRESENT YEAR . . .   1944

. P O R T A L   Y E A R . . .   1 9 4 1

. P O R T A L   Y E A R . .   1 9 4 1
A R R I V A L . . . . A T
D E S T I N A T I O N   Y E A R . . . 1 9 4 1

YOU HAVE ARRIVED AT THE YEAR 1941
. . . . IN AMERICAN HISTORY

YOU MUST ANSWER THIS QUESTION . . TO CONTINUE YOUR JOURNEY

THE YEAR IS: 1941

ROOSEVELT AND CHURCHILL ISSUED THE .... CHARTER OF POSTWAR ARMS?
:
PACIFIC   FREEDOM
ATLANTIC   WESTERN

QUESTION TYPE: *** MULTIPLE CHOICE ?
ENTER CORRECT ANSWER?
? ATLANTIC

CORRECT
YOU WIN 248 GOLD PIECES

YOU SEARCH THE CHAMBER . . . AND
FIND . . . . THE CRYSTAL KEY

SARGON, WHAT IS YOUR ACTION OR MOVE?

(N)ORTH, (E)AST, (S)OUTH
(W)EST, E(X)IT, (G)OLD
? W

YOU ARE AT AN EXIT PORTAL

(A KEY IS REQUIRED)

SARGON, WHAT IS YOUR ACTION OR MOVE?

(N)ORTH, (E)AST, (S)OUTH
(W)EST, E(X)IT, (G)OLD
? X

YOU ENTER THE EXIT PORTAL AND
INSERT THE CRYSTAL KEY INTO THE SLOT

THE MACHINE BEGINS TO HUM . . . .

. P O R T A L   Y E A R 1 9 5 2

sample run.

```
        .       .   .   .  .                       . .
          .        .    .    .      .             .     .
      .   .  ..          .          .       .       .
                  .          .              .     .    .
      P O R T A L   Y E A R  .  .  .  1 9 8 1
    A R R I V A L  .  .  .  . A T
    D E S T I N A T I O N   Y E A R  .  .  .  .  1 9 8 1
        .         .          . . . .  .       .  . ..
      .                .          .        .
            .                      . .   .
                      .   .  .    .       .
```
```
YOU FOUND YOUR WAY . . . . .
. . . . BACK TO THE PRESENT

YOU HAVE ACQUIRED  3511  GOLD PIECES

GAME RATING IS  447

YOU TOOK  57  TURNS TO FIND THE WAY OUT
AND ANSWERED  9  QUESTION(S) CORRECTLY,
OUT OF  9  QUESTIONS ASKED.

ANOTHER GAME?
ENTER '1'-YES  '0'-NO
? 1
```

Fig. 1-1—cont. The Time Dungeon sample run.

2. If you enter an east-west corridor (through a secret door), movement north is not allowed.

East Movement (RIGHT)

Entering an E allows you to move east. You may not move east under the following conditions:

1. If you reach the East Wall, you cannot pass through it.
2. If you enter a north-south corridor (through a secret door), movement east is not allowed.

South Movement (DOWN)

Entering an S allows you to move south. You may not move south under the following conditions:

1. If you reach the South Wall, you cannot pass through it.
2. If you enter an east-west corridor (through a secret door), movement south is not allowed.

West Movement (LEFT)

Entering a W allows you to move west. You may not move west under the following conditions:
1. If you reach the West Wall, you cannot pass through it.
2. If you enter a north-south corridor (through a secret door), movement west is not allowed.

Exiting the Dungeon

Entering an X, when you are at an exit portal and have the crystal key, allows you to be teleported back to the present. If you haven't found the key, or you are not at an exit portal, you may not exit the dungeon.

To find the crystal key, you must correctly answer a random number of history questions. But, on occasion, you may find the key when encountering unfriendly alien travelers.

Gold Pieces Left

Entering a G will display the number of gold pieces you have with you. You will start out with 1000 and can gain or lose gold during your trip. But if you lose all your gold pieces, you will lose the game.

Active Portals

When you encounter an active time portal, the year in which you currently are will be displayed, and then a star background will be generated, indicating activation. The portal year will be displayed at the center of the screen as it decrements or increments from the present year to your new destination year. When approaching the destination year this action will slow down, and it will stop when the year is reached.

The question is displayed along with the year that you were teleported to. It is chosen randomly from a list of 50 and will not be repeated until all other questions are asked (for at least two or three games).

A correct answer wins you a random amount of gold, up to 625 pieces, then the portal becomes inactive. If your answer is incorrect, then the correct answer is displayed and you lose a random amount of gold (up to 425 pieces). But the time portal remains active for future use.

The questions are high-school and college level.

Question Types

There are four types of questions possible:

1. People, places, or things.
2. True or false.
3. Who am I (name).
4. Multiple choice.

Type 1 questions may be on any subject relating to the portal destination year. Enter the word or group of words that apply. It can be a fill-in-the-blank type or just a question.

Type 2 requires a true or false response. Enter the letter T for true, or F for false, when requested.

Type 3 requires a last-name entry. Enter the last name only.

Type 4 is a multiple-choice question. It will display a question with four possible answers, one of which is correct. Enter the correct answer.

Question types 1, 3, and 4 require that your answer be spelled correctly, otherwise an incorrect response will be indicated.

The Crystal Key

You will find the crystal key after you answer a random number of questions correctly (you need the key to exit the dungeon).

ALIEN TRAVELERS

When you encounter an alien traveler, he may be friendly or unfriendly. The friendly alien will give you a random number of gold pieces as he leaves. The unfriendly alien will take some of your gold. In this encounter, however, there is a chance that you may find the crystal key.

When the alien leaves, the chamber becomes an inactive portal, but the alien may reappear elsewhere in the dungeon.

TIME TRAPS

Some of the chambers contain time traps, which may, or may not, activate. If they activate, then you will be teleported to an unknown location in the dungeon and lose all but 100 gold pieces. When you discover time traps, avoid them.

NORTH-SOUTH AND EAST-WEST CORRIDORS

North-south and east-west corridors may be entered from any direction (through secret doors), but will limit your next move to the corridor direction displayed.

Corridor Objects

It is possible to find maps or gold inside a corridor. On occasion you will discover a glowing screen on the wall, with a red button below the screen. Depressing this button will result in one of three happenings:

1. A map of the dungeon will be displayed for a random number of seconds. The following symbols will be printed for the 64-chamber dungeon:

     0 = inactive portal
    AP = active portal
    NS = north-south corridor
    EW = east-west corridor
     ? = unknown contents (either an alien traveler or time trap)
     X = exit portal
    =P= = your location in the dungeon

2. Nothing happens.
3. You will receive gold pieces each time you push the button, but the corridor narrows at the same time. There is a possibility of getting stuck in the corridor. If that happens, you lose the game.

See Fig. 1-2 for a sample map.

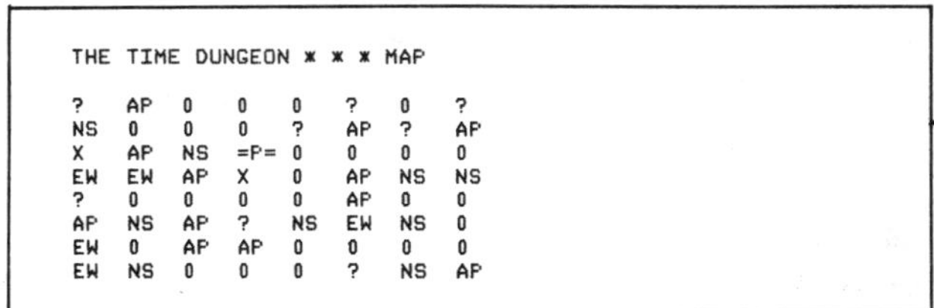

Fig. 1-2. The Time Dungeon sample map.

INACTIVE PORTALS

Inactive portals are, normally, empty chambers. Occasionally, however, you will find a door inside the chamber. Trying the door will result in one of three happenings:

1. The door opens, and you find gold inside the closet.
2. The door won't open.
3. The door opens, and the chamber begins to spin. You are teleported, momentarily, into another dimension, where you can lose up to half of your gold and waste up to 20 moves.

GAME RATING

After you complete the game, a game rating is displayed along with the number of gold pieces acquired, the number of history questions answered correctly out of the number of questions asked, and the number of turns (moves) taken. The rating is a number from approximately −600 to +2000, depending on the above statistics. The higher the rating number, the better is the game rating. A negative number indicates a poor rating.

```
100   HOME :BZ$ = "AMERICAN HISTORY":BW$ = "1607 TO 1850"
101   PRINT "THE TIME DUNGEON: ";BZ$
102   PRINT "COPYRIGHT (C) 1981 BY HOWARD BERENBON"
103   PRINT "APPLE II"
104   PRINT
105   PRINT "AN EDUCATIONAL FANTASY GAME"
106 GT = 5: GOSUB 134:Q3 = 0
107   HOME : DIM A(9,9),B(50): GOSUB 451
108   PRINT "YOU WILL BE TELEPORTED TO . . ."
109   PRINT
110   PRINT "THE TIME DUNGEON . . . ."
111   PRINT "TO STUDY ";BZ$
112   PRINT
114 CA = 0:G = 1000:M1 = 1:K = 0:KL = 1:TT = 0:TR = 0
115   PRINT "ENTER YOUR CHARACTER'S NAME?"
116   INPUT A$
117   PRINT "ENTER PRESENT YEAR"
118   INPUT Y2:YY = Y2: IF Y2 > 2000 THEN 117
119   PRINT : PRINT A$;" . . . YOU ARE ON YOUR WAY"
120 GT = 2: GOSUB 134
121   GOSUB 143
122   HOME
123   PRINT "YOU HAVE ARRIVED AT . . . ."
124   PRINT
125   PRINT "THE TIME DUNGEON: ";BZ$
126   PRINT "FOR THE YEARS:    ";BW$
127   PRINT
128   PRINT "YOU CARRY 1000 GOLD PIECES": PRINT
129   PRINT "YOU WILL ENCOUNTER . . ."
130   PRINT "TIME PORTALS WHICH TELEPORT"
131   PRINT "YOU TO EVENTS IN ";BZ$
132 GT = 8: GOSUB 134
133   GOTO 199
134   FOR ZZ = 1 TO 908 * GT
135   NEXT ZZ
136   RETURN
137   PRINT "O    ";: RETURN
138   PRINT "AP   ";: RETURN
139   PRINT "?    ";: RETURN
140   PRINT "NS   ";: RETURN
141   PRINT "EW   ";: RETURN
142   PRINT "X    ";: RETURN
143   REM  SET UP DUNGEON
144   FOR X = 1 TO 8
145   FOR Y = 1 TO 8
146 A(X,Y) =  INT ( RND (1) * 7 + 1)
147   NEXT Y
148   NEXT X
149   REM  TRAPS
150 H =  INT ( RND (1) * 3 + 1) + 1
151   FOR N = 1 TO H
152 X =  INT ( RND (1) * 8 + 1)
153 Y =  INT ( RND (1) * 8 + 1)
```

```
154 A(X,Y) = 8
155  NEXT N
156  REM  EXITS
157 S =  INT ( RND (1) * 4 + 1) + 1
158  FOR N = 1 TO S
159 X =  INT ( RND (1) * 8 + 1)
160 Y =  INT ( RND (1) * 8 + 1)
161 A(X,Y) = 9
162  NEXT N
163  RETURN
164 R6 =  INT ( RND (1) * 4 + 1): PRINT QD$;"?:": PRINT
165  ON R6 GOSUB 167,168,169,170
166  GOTO 433
167  PRINT AD$,I1$: PRINT I2$,I3$: RETURN
168  PRINT I2$,AD$: PRINT I1$,I3$: RETURN
169  PRINT I1$,I2$: PRINT AD$,I3$: RETURN
170  PRINT I3$,I1$: PRINT I2$,AD$: RETURN
171  HOME
173 GT = 1
174  GOSUB 134
175  FOR B = 1 TO 70:B4 =  INT ( RND (1) * 23 + 1)
176 B7 =  INT ( RND (1) * 39 + 1): VTAB B4: PRINT  TAB( B7)".";
177  PRINT : NEXT B: PRINT
178 GT = .005:Y5 = 25
179  IF Y3 = YY THEN  VTAB 1: PRINT "ALREADY AT . . . . ": GOTO 196
180  IF Y3 < YY THEN 188
181  IF (Y3 - YY) <  = 50 THEN 185
182 Y3 = Y3 - Y5
183  GOSUB 382
184  IF Y3 = YY THEN 195
185  IF (Y3 - YY) <  = 50 THEN Y5 = 1
186  IF (Y3 - YY) <  = 5 THEN GT = .4
187  GOTO 182
188  IF (YY - Y3) <  = 50 THEN 192
189 Y3 = Y3 + Y5
190  GOSUB 382
191  IF Y3 = YY THEN 195
192  IF (YY - Y3) <  = 50 THEN Y5 = 1
193  IF (YY - Y3) <  = 5 THEN GT = .4
194  GOTO 189
195  PRINT : PRINT "ARRIVAL . . . . AT"
196  PRINT "DESTINATION YEAR . . . . ";YY
197 GT = 4: GOSUB 134
198  HOME : RETURN
199 C =  INT ( RND (1) * 8 + 1):D =  INT ( RND (1) * 8 + 1):A(C,D) = 1
200 K4 =  INT ( RND (1) * 4 + 1) + 3
201  HOME :A = A(C,D):GT = 1: GOSUB 134
202  ON A GOSUB 292,300,410,410,306,330,335,338,362
203  IF KL = 0 THEN 567
204  PRINT : IF TT = 1 THEN TT = 0: GOTO 201
205  IF G <  = 0 THEN 264
206  PRINT A$;",  WHAT IS YOUR ACTION OR MOVE?"
207  PRINT
```

```
208   PRINT "(N)ORTH, (E)AST, (S)OUTH"
209   PRINT "(W)EST, E(X)IT, (G)OLD"
210   INPUT M1$
211 M1 = M1 + 1: IF K = 0 AND M1 > 70 THEN 371
212   IF M1$ = "N" THEN 220
213   IF M1$ = "E" THEN 225
214   IF M1$ = "S" THEN 230
215   IF M1$ = "W" THEN 235
216   IF M1$ = "X" THEN 240
217   IF M1$ = "G" THEN 251
218   PRINT
219   GOTO 204
220   REM  NORTH
221   IF A = 7 THEN 255
222   IF (D - 1) = 0 THEN 281
223 D = D - 1
224   GOTO 201
225   REM  EAST
226   IF A = 6 THEN 260
227   IF (C + 1) = 9 THEN 286
228 C = C + 1
229   GOTO 201
230   REM  SOUTH
231   IF A = 7 THEN 255
232   IF (D + 1) = 9 THEN 288
233 D = D + 1
234   GOTO 201
235   REM  WEST
236   IF A = 6 THEN 260
237   IF (C - 1) = 0 THEN 290
238 C = C - 1
239   GOTO 201
240   HOME
241   IF A < > 9 THEN 248
242   IF K = 1 THEN 387
243   PRINT "YOU CANNOT EXIT THE TIME DUNGEON"
244   PRINT "YOU DON'T HAVE THE CRYSTAL KEY"
245 GT = 2: GOSUB 134
246   PRINT
247   GOTO 204
248   PRINT "YOU ARE NOT AT AN EXIT PORTAL"
249 GT = 2: GOSUB 134
250   GOTO 204
251   REM  GOLD
252   HOME : PRINT "YOU HAVE ";G;" GOLD PIECES WITH YOU"
253   PRINT
254   GOTO 204
255   REM  EW
256   HOME : PRINT "YOU ARE IN AN EAST-WEST CORRIDOR"
257   PRINT "YOU CAN ONLY GO EAST OR WEST"
258   PRINT
259   GOTO 204
260   REM  NS
```

```
261  HOME : PRINT "YOU ARE IN A NORTH-SOUTH CORRIDOR"
262  PRINT "YOU CAN ONLY GO NORTH OR SOUTH"
263  GOTO 258
264  REM  GOLD ZERO
265 GT = 2: GOSUB 134
266  PRINT
267  PRINT "YOU LOST ALL YOUR GOLD AND YOU WERE"
268  PRINT " . . . UNABLE TO MEET THE DEMANDS OF"
269  PRINT " . . . THE TIME DUNGEON . . . . ."
270  PRINT
271  PRINT
272 T = 3: GOSUB 134
273  GOSUB 402
274  PRINT
275  PRINT "ANOTHER GAME?"
276  PRINT "ENTER '1'-YES  '0'-NO"
277  INPUT AA
278  IF AA <  > 1 THEN 280
279  HOME : GOTO 108
280  END
281  HOME : PRINT "YOU ARE AT THE NORTH WALL"
282  PRINT "YOU CANNOT PASS THROUGH"
283  PRINT
284  PRINT "TRY ANOTHER DIRECTION?"
285  GOTO 204
286  HOME : PRINT "YOU ARE AT THE EAST WALL"
287  GOTO 282
288  HOME : PRINT "YOU ARE AT THE SOUTH WALL"
289  GOTO 282
290  HOME : PRINT "YOU ARE AT THE WEST WALL"
291  GOTO 282
292 KT =  INT ( RND (1) * 9 + 1)
293  PRINT "YOU ARE IN A GLOWING TIME PORTAL"
294 GT = 1: GOSUB 134
295  PRINT
296  PRINT "THE LIGHT FADES . . . . . ."
297  PRINT "THE PORTAL IS INACTIVE . . . ."
298  IF A = 1 AND KT > 8 THEN 570
299  RETURN
300  PRINT "YOU ARE IN A DUST FILLED PORTAL"
301 GT = 1: GOSUB 134
302  PRINT
303  PRINT "A BRIGHT LIGHT IS ACTIVATED AND . ."
304  PRINT
305  GOTO 296
306  HOME
307  PRINT "AN ALIEN TRAVELER IS IN THIS CHAMBER"
308 A(C,D) =  INT ( RND (1) * 2 + 1): GOSUB 478
309 GT = 1: GOSUB 134
310 TD =  INT ( RND (1) * 10 + 1)
311 G4 =  INT ( RND (1) * 350 + 1)
312 Y =  INT ( RND (1) * 8 + 1)
313  IF Y <  = 5 THEN 320
```

```
314   PRINT : IF (G - G4) < 0 THEN G4 = G
315   PRINT "HE IS UNFRIENDLY . . . . AND AS HE"
316   PRINT "LEAVES . . . HE TAKES ";G4;" GOLD PIECES"
317   PRINT :G = G - G4
318   IF TD = 5 AND K = 0 THEN 325
319   RETURN
320   PRINT
321   PRINT "HE IS FRIENDLY . . . . . AND GIVES YOU"
322   PRINT ". . ";G4;" GOLD PIECES, WHICH YOU ACCEPT"
323   PRINT :G = G + G4
324   GOTO 318
325   PRINT :GT = 2: GOSUB 134
326   PRINT "YOU SEARCH THE CHAMBER . . . AND"
327 GT = 1: GOSUB 134
328   PRINT "FIND . . . . THE CRYSTAL KEY"
329 K = 1: RETURN
330   HOME
331   PRINT "YOU ENTER A NORTH-SOUTH CORRIDOR"
332   PRINT "THRU A SECRET DOOR": PRINT : GOSUB 380
333 KT =   INT ( RND (1) * 9 + 1): IF KT >  = 7 THEN 545
334   RETURN
335   HOME
336   PRINT "YOU ENTER AN EAST-WEST CORRIDOR"
337   GOTO 332
338   REM   TRAP
339   PRINT "YOU ENCOUNTER . . . A TIME TRAP"
340   PRINT ". . . . . . . . IN THIS CHAMBER":GT = 1: GOSUB 134
341 TD =   INT ( RND (1) * 9 + 1)
342   IF TD >  = 7 THEN 347
343   PRINT
344   PRINT "BUT YOU'RE LUCKY . . . . ."
345   PRINT ". . . IT DIDN'T ACTIVATE"
346   RETURN
347 TT = 1: PRINT "AND IT ACTIVATED . . . . .":GT = 2: GOSUB 134
348   FOR A = 1 TO 250
349   PRINT "*         %";
350   NEXT A
351 C =   INT ( RND (1) * 8 + 1):D =   INT ( RND (1) * 8 + 1)
352   PRINT
353   PRINT :G = 100
354   PRINT "YOU HAVE BEEN TELEPORTED TO . . . ."
355   PRINT ". . . . AN UNKNOWN LOCATION . . . ."
356   PRINT
357   PRINT "AND YOU LOST MOST OF YOUR GOLD"
358   PRINT
359   PRINT "YOU HAVE . . . ";G;" GOLD PIECES LEFT"
360 GT = 6: GOSUB 134
361   RETURN
362   PRINT "YOU ARE AT AN EXIT PORTAL"
363   PRINT
364   PRINT "(A KEY IS REQUIRED)"
365   PRINT
366   RETURN
```

```
367 H = 1:O = 9:W = 8
368 B = 0:E = 5:R = 14
369 C = 0:PR = 0
370  GOTO 216
371  PRINT :GT = 2: GOSUB 134
372  PRINT "BUT BEFORE YOU PROCEED . ."
373  PRINT "YOU LOOK TO THE GROUND AND . . ."
374  PRINT ". . . FIND THE CRYSTAL KEY . .":K = 1
375 GT = 3: GOSUB 134
376  GOTO 212
377  PRINT "YOU ANSWERED ";CA;" QUESTION(S) CORRECTLY"
378  PRINT " . . . . . IN ";M1;" TURNS,"
379  GOTO 409
380  PRINT "THE DOOR CLOSES AND LOCKS BEHIND YOU":GT = 1: GOSUB 134
381  RETURN
382  REM  TIME DISPLAY
383  VTAB 12: PRINT "PORTAL YEAR . . . ";Y3
385  GOSUB 134
386  RETURN
387  HOME : REM  EXIT PORTAL
388  PRINT "YOU ENTER THE EXIT PORTAL AND"
389  PRINT "INSERT THE CRYSTAL KEY INTO THE SLOT"
390  PRINT :GT = 4: GOSUB 134
391  PRINT "THE MACHINE BEGINS TO HUM . . . ."
392  PRINT :GT = 2: GOSUB 134
393 YY = Y2: GOSUB 171
394  PRINT
395  PRINT "YOU FOUND YOUR WAY . . . . ."
396  PRINT ". . . . BACK TO THE PRESENT"
397  PRINT
398  PRINT "YOU HAVE ACQUIRED ";G;" GOLD PIECES"
399  PRINT
400  GOSUB 402
401  GOTO 274
402 GG = G + 100
403 R =  INT ((GG * CA - 7000 + 1) / M1)
404  PRINT
405  PRINT "GAME RATING IS ";R
406  PRINT : IF G <  = 0 OR KL = 0 THEN 377
407  PRINT "YOU TOOK ";M1;" TURNS TO FIND THE WAY OUT"
408  PRINT "AND ANSWERED ";CA;" QUESTION(S) CORRECTLY,"
409  PRINT "OUT OF ";TR;" QUESTIONS ASKED.": RETURN
410  HOME :Y3 = YY
411  GOSUB 444
412 Q3 = Q3 + 1
413  IF Q3 > 50 THEN Q3 = 0: GOTO 415
414  GOTO 416
415  GOSUB 451
416 Q =  INT ( RND (1) * 50 + 1)
417  IF B(Q) = 1 THEN 416
418 B(Q) = 1
419  PRINT
420  FOR AB = 1 TO Q
```

```
421  READ YY,QD$,ID,AD$,I1$,I2$,I3$
422  NEXT AB
423  RESTORE
424  GOSUB 171
425  HOME :TR = TR + 1
426  PRINT "YOU HAVE ARRIVED AT THE YEAR ";YY
427  PRINT ". . . . . . IN ";BZ$: PRINT
428  PRINT "YOU MUST ANSWER THIS QUESTION"
429  PRINT " . . TO CONTINUE YOUR JOURNEY"
430  PRINT "------------------------------------------"
431  PRINT "THE YEAR IS: ";YY: PRINT : IF ID = 4 THEN 164
432  PRINT QD$
433  PRINT "------------------------------------------"
434  PRINT "QUESTION TYPE: "
435  ON ID GOSUB 455,456,457,458
436  GOSUB 459
437  IF E$ = AD$ THEN 441
438  PRINT "INCORRECT"
439  GOSUB 471
440  RETURN
441  PRINT "CORRECT"
442  GOSUB 463
443  RETURN
444  PRINT "YOU ENTER INTO A BLUE HAZY . . ."
445  PRINT ". . . . . . . TIME PORTAL . . ."
446  PRINT :GT = 1: GOSUB 134
447  PRINT "A PULSATING GLOW . . . . . . ."
448  PRINT ". . . . INDICATES ACTIVATION": PRINT
449  PRINT "PRESENT YEAR . . . "Y3:GT = 3: GOSUB 134
450  RETURN
451  FOR I = 1 TO 50
452  B(I) = 0
453  NEXT I
454  RETURN
455  PRINT "PEOPLE, PLACES, OR THINGS ?": RETURN
456  PRINT "*** (T)RUE OR (F)ALSE  ?": RETURN
457  PRINT "*** WHO AM I (LAST NAME) ?": RETURN
458  PRINT "*** MULTIPLE CHOICE ?": RETURN
459  PRINT "ENTER CORRECT ANSWER?"
460  INPUT E$
461  G4 =  INT ( RND (1) * 500 + 1) + 125
462  RETURN
463  G = G + G4
464  PRINT "YOU WIN ";G4;" GOLD PIECES"
465  A(C,D) =  INT ( RND (1) * 2 + 1)
466  CA = CA + 1: IF K = 1 THEN  RETURN
467  IF CA = K4 THEN 469
468  RETURN
469  GOSUB 325
470  RETURN
471  PRINT :G4 =  INT ( RND (1) * 400 + 1) + 25
472  PRINT "THE CORRECT ANSWER IS '";AD$;"'"
473  PRINT : IF (G - G4) < 0 THEN G4 = G
```

```
474 G = G - G4
475 GT = 1: GOSUB 134
476  PRINT "YOU LOSE ";G4;" GOLD PIECES"
477  RETURN
478 ZT = 5
479 X =  INT ( RND (1) * 8 + 1):Y =  INT ( RND (1) * 8 + 1)
480  IF A(X,Y) <  = 2 THEN A(X,Y) = 5: RETURN
481 ZT = ZT - 1: IF ZT = 0 THEN  RETURN
482  GOTO 479
483  DATA  1619,IN WHAT COLONY BEGAN THE SALE OF SLAVES FROM AFRICA,4,VIR
     GINIA,NEW HAMPSHIRE,PLYMOUTH,CONNECTICUT
484  DATA  1620,WHAT GROUP OF PEOPLE FOUNDED THE PLY-    MOUTH COLONY,4,S
     EPARATISTS,MORMONS,ENGLISH,CONFORMISTS
485  DATA  1607,THE LONDON CO. EXPEDITION SENT 3 SHIPS- GODSPEED-SARAH CO
     NSTANT-& .....,4,DISCOVERY,ENTERPRISE,BRITAIN,NEW WORLD
486  DATA  1607,CAPT. CHRISTOPHER .... COMMANDED THE 1ST LONDON CO. EXPED
     ITION,4,NEWPORT,PIKE,SMITH,WILLIAMS
487  DATA  1607,JAMESTOWN IS NAMED AFTER THE ENGLISH    KING-JAMES I,2,T,
     0,0,0
488  DATA  1630,WHAT GROUP BEGAN THE COLONY OF MASSACHU- SETTS BAY,4,PURI
     TANS,SEPARATISTS,MORMONS,LOYALISTS
489  DATA  1630,THE PURITANS WERE NOT WELL EQUIPPED TO  SETTLE IN MASSACH
     USETTS,2,F,0,0,0
490  DATA  1635,WHAT COLONY DID REVEREND THOMAS HOOK    HELP ESTABLISH,4,
     CONNECTICUT,VIRGINIA,PLYMOUTH,MASSACHUSETTS
491  DATA  1635,I WAS BANISHED FROM MASSACHUSETTS BAY   FOR MY RELIGIOUS
     BELIEFS,3,WILLIAMS,0,0,0
492  DATA  1783,WHAT DOCUMENT ENDED THE WAR OF INDEPEN- DENCE?,1,TREATY O
     F PARIS,0,0,0
493  DATA  1781,I SURRENDERED MY ENTIRE ARMY DURING THE WAR OF INDEPENDEN
     CE,3,CORNWALLIS,0,0,0
494  DATA  1766,WHAT COLONIAL TAX DID THE BRITISH REPEAL,4,STAMP ACT,WOOL
     EN ACT,SHIP TAX,FOOD TAX
495  DATA  1690,BRITISH PASSED THE .... ACT TO STOP THE MANUFACTURE OF TE
     XTILES,4,WOOLEN,COTTON,RAYON,CLOTHS
496  DATA  1782,AT WHAT CITY WAS THE AMERICAN VICTORY   THAT SHOCKED THE
     BRITISH,4,YORKTOWN,JAMESTOWN,NEW YORK,SARATOGA
497  DATA  1786,AT WHAT CITY BEGAN THE ALTERING OF THE  ARTICLES OF CONFÆ
     DERATION,4,ANNAPOLIS,SARATOGA,NEW YORK,ALBANY
498  DATA  1636,I FOUNDED THE SETTLEMENT CALLED PROVI-  DENCE,3,WILLIAMS,
     0,0,0
499  DATA  1638,NEW HAMPSHIRE WAS BUILT BY OVERFLOW OF  PEOPLE FROM MASSA
     CHUSETTS,2,T,0,0,0
500  DATA  1679,IN 1679-WHAT COLONY RECEIVED A CHARTER  FROM THE KING,4,N
     EW HAMPSHIRE,PLYMOUTH,VIRGINIA,CONNECTICUT
501  DATA  1649,LORD BALTIMORE PERSUADED THE VIRGINIA   COLONY TO PASS A
     TOLERATION ACT,2,F,0,0,0
502  DATA  1649,.... AND WILLIAMS ESTABLISHED THE TOLER-ATION ACT,4,BALTI
     MORE,WASHINGTON,JEFFERSON,FRANKLIN
503  DATA  1649,TOLERATION ACT ALLOWS CATHOLICS & PROTE-STANTS RELIGIOUS
     FREEDOM,2,T,0,0,0
504  DATA  1624,NEW YORK HAD BEEN FOUNDED AS NEW NETHER-LAND-A DUTCH COLO
     NY,2,T,0,0,0
```

```
505  DATA   1760,I WAS KNOWN FOR MY EXPERIMENTS WITH ELEC-TRICITY,3,FRANKL
IN,0,0,0
506  DATA   1760,I WROTE THE BOOK CALLED 'NOTES ON VIR-  GINIA',3,JEFFERSO
N,0,0,0
507  DATA   1763,THE FRENCH & INDIAN WAR ENDED WITH THE  SIGNING OF WHAT D
OCUMENT,1,PEACE OF PARIS,0,0,0
508  DATA   1777,MAIN BATTLE BETWEEN CONTINENTALS & BUR- GOYNE'S FORCES WA
S NEAR,4,SARATOGA,NEW YORK,YORKTOWN,ANNAPOLIS
509  DATA   1785,CONFEDERATIONS 1ST LAND ORDINANCE WAS    CALLED-LAND ORDIN
ANCE OF 1785,2,T,0,0,0
510  DATA   1787,NORTHWEST ORDINANCE ALLOWED CREATION OF NEW STATES IN THE
 WEST,2,T,0,0,0
511  DATA   1787,THE CONSTITUTION OF THE UNITED STATES   WAS COMPLETED IN
1785,2,F,0,0,0
512  DATA   1791,WHAT WERE THE 1ST 10 AMENDMENTS TO THE  CONSTITUTION CALL
ED,1,BILL OF RIGHTS,0,0,0
513  DATA   1790,THOMAS JEFFERSON AND JAMES MADISON FOUND-ED THE .... PART
Y,1,REPUBLICAN,0,0,0
514  DATA   1812,WAR OF 1812 RESULTED FROM BRITISH VIOLA-TING AMERICAN TRA
DE RIGHTS,2,T,0,0,0
515  DATA   1807,WHAT AMERICAN SHIP DID THE BRITISH OPEN FIRE UPON,4,CHESA
PEAKE,SARATOGA,DISCOVERY,GODSPEED
516  DATA   1812,WHO COMMANDED THE BATTLE OF NEW ORLEANS,4,JACKSON,BALTIMO
RE,LINCOLN,WASHINGTON
517  DATA   1806,HE FOLLOWED THE MISSISSIPPI RIVER NORTH-WARD TO ITS SOURC
E,4,PIKE,SMITH,ROGERS,JAMES
518  DATA   1845,WHAT GROUP OF PEOPLE MIGRATED TO THE    GREAT SALT LAKE,4
,MORMONS,SEPARATISTS,LOYALISTS,INDIANS
519  DATA   1845,I LEAD THE MORMON MIGRATION TO THE UTAH TERRITORY,3,YOUNG
,0,0,0
520  DATA   1850,BETWEEN 1830 AND 1850-2 MILLION EUROPEON-S IMMIGRATED TO
THE U.S.,2,T,0,0,0
521  DATA   1807,I INVENTED THE STEAMBOAT-WHICH MADE     WATER TRANSPORTAT
ION EASIER,3,FULTON,0,0,0
522  DATA   1812,BY 1812-STEAMBOATS SERVED ON THE OHIO   AND MISSISSIPPI R
IVERS,2,T,0,0,0
523  DATA 1816,I CREATED THE 'ERA OF GOOD FEELING' IN  POLITICS,3,MONROE,
0,0,0
524  DATA   1832,I FEARED THE BANK OF THE UNITED STATES  AS TOO POWERFUL,3
,JACKSON,0,0,0
525  DATA   1830,I SPOKE BEFORE THE SENATE IN SUPPORT OF 'UNIONS',3,WEBSTE
R,0,0,0
526  DATA   1812,THE WAR OF 1812 WAS OFTEN CALLED THE    SECOND WAR FOR IN
DEPENDENCE,2,T,0,0,0
527  DATA   1803,.... PURCHASE WAS AN ACHIEVEMENT OF     JEFFERSON'S ADMIN
ISTRATION,4,LOUISIANA,NORTHWEST,SOUTHERN,VIRGINIAN
528  DATA   1825,THE GREATEST NUMBER OF PEOPLE MIGRATED  TO NORTHERN-MOHAW
K VALLEY,2,T,0,0,0
529  DATA   1790,IN 1790-THERE WERE 8 MILLION PEOPLE IN  THE UNITED STATES
,2,F,0,0,0
530  DATA   1850,THERE WERE 8 MILLION PEOPLE BEYOND THE  APPALACHIAN MOUNT
AINS,2,T,0,0,0
```

```
531   DATA  1825,THE .... CANAL-CONNECTING ALBANY WITH   THE GREAT LAKES-W
      AS OPENED,4,ERIE,NEW YORK,MICHIGAN,ST CLARE
532   DATA  1810,THE MACON BILL NO. 2 ALLOWED TRADE WITH FRANCE AND ENGLAN
      D,2,T,0,0,0
533   HOME : PRINT "THE TIME DUNGEON * * * MAP"
534   PRINT
535   FOR Q = 1 TO 8
536   FOR N = 1 TO 8
537   IF C = N AND D = Q THEN  PRINT "=P= ";: GOTO 540
538 S1 = A(N,Q)
539   ON S1 GOSUB 137,137,138,138,139,140,141,139,142
540   NEXT N
541   PRINT
542   NEXT Q
543 GT =  INT ( RND (1) * 8 + 1) +  INT ( RND (1) * (CA + 5) + 1)
544   GOSUB 134: HOME : RETURN
545   PRINT : PRINT "ON THE WALL IS A GLOWING SCREEN"
546   PRINT "BELOW THE SCREEN IS A RED BUTTON": PRINT
547 KT =  INT ( RND (1) * 9 + 1):KL =  INT ( RND (1) * 15 + 1) + 2
548   GOSUB 565
549   INPUT K$
550   IF K$ = "Y" THEN 552
551   RETURN
552   IF KT >  = 6 THEN 533
553   IF KT <  = 4 THEN 562
554   PRINT :G4 =  INT ( RND (1) * 100 + 1) + 25:G = G + G4
555   PRINT "YOU RECEIVE ";G4;" GOLD PIECES . . ."
556   PRINT "BUT . . . . . . THE CORRIDOR NARROWS":GT = 3: GOSUB 134
557 KL = KL - 1: IF KL = 0 THEN  RETURN
558   GOSUB 565
559   INPUT K$
560   IF K$ = "Y" THEN 554
561   RETURN
562   PRINT : PRINT "NOTHING HAPPENS"
563 GT = 1: GOSUB 134
564   RETURN
565   PRINT : PRINT "DO YOU WISH TO PUSH THE BUTTON?"
566   PRINT "ENTER  (Y)ES  OR  (N)O": RETURN
567   HOME : PRINT "YOU ARE STUCK IN THE NARROW CORRIDOR"
568   PRINT ". . . . . . . . . . AND . . .": PRINT :GT = 3: GOSUB 134
569   GOTO 264
570   PRINT : PRINT "YOU NOTICE A DOOR TO YOUR RIGHT"
571   PRINT
572 KT =  INT ( RND (1) * 9 + 1)
573   PRINT "DO YOU WISH TO OPEN THE DOOR?"
574   PRINT "ENTER  (Y)ES  OR  (N)O"
575   INPUT K$
576   IF K$ = "Y" THEN 578
577   RETURN
578   PRINT : PRINT "YOU TRY THE DOOR . . . . .":GT = 1: GOSUB 134
579   IF KT >  = 7 THEN 589
580   IF KT <  = 4 THEN 587
581   PRINT :G4 =  INT ( RND (1) * 100 + 1) + 25
```

```
582  PRINT "THE DOOR OPENS . . . . . . ."
583  PRINT "REVEALING A CLOSET . . . ."
584  PRINT :G = G + G4
585  PRINT "WHERE YOU FIND ";G4;" GOLD PIECES"
586  PRINT : RETURN
587  PRINT "BUT THE DOOR WON'T OPEN . . . ."
588  PRINT ". . . . IT MUST BE LOCKED": RETURN
589  PRINT : PRINT "THE DOOR OPENS . . . AND SUDDENLY"
590  PRINT "THE CHAMBER BEGINS TO . . . SPIN"
591 G7 =  INT (G / 2):G4 =  INT ( RND (1) * G7 + 1):MM =  INT ( RND (1) *
    20 + 1)
592 GT = 4: GOSUB 134:G = G - G4
593  FOR K9 = 1 TO 250
594  PRINT "+     =     +";: NEXT K9
596  HOME : PRINT "YOU WERE TELEPORTED INTO . . . ."
597  PRINT ". . . . ANOTHER DIMENSION . . . ."
598  PRINT ". . AND RETURNED IN AN INSTANT . ."
599  PRINT : PRINT "BUT YOU DROPPED ";G4;" GOLD PIECES"
600  PRINT ". . . AND WASTED ";MM;" MOVES . . ."
601 M1 = M1 + MM
602 GT = 4: GOSUB 134
603  RETURN
```

```
100   HOME :BZ$ = "AMERICAN HISTORY":BW$ = "1848 TO 1914"
101   PRINT "THE TIME DUNGEON: ";BZ$
102   PRINT "COPYRIGHT (C) 1981 BY HOWARD BERENBON"
103   PRINT "APPLE II"
104   PRINT
105   PRINT "AN EDUCATIONAL FANTASY GAME"
106 GT = 5: GOSUB 134:Q3 = 0
107   HOME : DIM A(9,9),B(50): GOSUB 451
108   PRINT "YOU WILL BE TELEPORTED TO . . ."
109   PRINT
110   PRINT "THE TIME DUNGEON . . . ."
111   PRINT "TO STUDY ";BZ$
112   PRINT
114 CA = 0:G = 1000:M1 = 1:K = 0:KL = 1:TT = 0:TR = 0
115   PRINT "ENTER YOUR CHARACTER'S NAME?"
116   INPUT A$
117   PRINT "ENTER PRESENT YEAR"
118   INPUT Y2:YY = Y2: IF Y2 > 2000 THEN 117
119   PRINT : PRINT A$;" . . . YOU ARE ON YOUR WAY"
120 GT = 2: GOSUB 134
121   GOSUB 143
122   HOME
123   PRINT "YOU HAVE ARRIVED AT . . . ."
124   PRINT
125   PRINT "THE TIME DUNGEON: ";BZ$
126   PRINT "FOR THE YEARS:    ";BW$
127   PRINT
128   PRINT "YOU CARRY 1000 GOLD PIECES": PRINT
129   PRINT "YOU WILL ENCOUNTER . . ."
130   PRINT "TIME PORTALS WHICH TELEPORT"
131   PRINT "YOU TO EVENTS IN ";BZ$
132 GT = 8: GOSUB 134
133   GOTO 199
134   FOR ZZ = 1 TO 908 * GT
135   NEXT ZZ
136   RETURN
137   PRINT "O    ";: RETURN
138   PRINT "AP   ";: RETURN
139   PRINT "?    ";: RETURN
140   PRINT "NS   ";: RETURN
141   PRINT "EW   ";: RETURN
142   PRINT "X    ";: RETURN
143   REM  SET UP DUNGEON
144   FOR X = 1 TO 8
145   FOR Y = 1 TO 8
146 A(X,Y) =  INT ( RND (1) * 7 + 1)
147   NEXT Y
148   NEXT X
149   REM  TRAPS
150 H =  INT ( RND (1) * 3 + 1) + 1
151   FOR N = 1 TO H
152 X =  INT ( RND (1) * 8 + 1)
153 Y =  INT ( RND (1) * 8 + 1)
```

```
154 A(X,Y) = 8
155  NEXT N
156  REM  EXITS
157 S =  INT ( RND (1) * 4 + 1) + 1
158  FOR N = 1 TO S
159 X =  INT ( RND (1) * 8 + 1)
160 Y =  INT ( RND (1) * 8 + 1)
161 A(X,Y) = 9
162  NEXT N
163  RETURN
164 R6 =  INT ( RND (1) * 4 + 1): PRINT QD$;"?:": PRINT
165  ON R6 GOSUB 167,168,169,170
166  GOTO 433
167  PRINT AD$,I1$: PRINT I2$,I3$: RETURN
168  PRINT I2$,AD$: PRINT I1$,I3$: RETURN
169  PRINT I1$,I2$: PRINT AD$,I3$: RETURN
170  PRINT I3$,I1$: PRINT I2$,AD$: RETURN
171  HOME
173 GT = 1
174  GOSUB 134
175  FOR B = 1 TO 70:B4 =  INT ( RND (1) * 23 + 1)
176 B7 =  INT ( RND (1) * 39 + 1): VTAB B4: PRINT  TAB( B7)".";
177  PRINT : NEXT B: PRINT
178 GT = .005:Y5 = 25
179  IF Y3 = YY THEN  VTAB 1: PRINT "ALREADY AT . . . . ": GOTO 196
180  IF Y3 < YY THEN 188
181  IF (Y3 - YY) <  = 50 THEN 185
182 Y3 = Y3 - Y5
183  GOSUB 382
184  IF Y3 = YY THEN 195
185  IF (Y3 - YY) <  = 50 THEN Y5 = 1
186  IF (Y3 - YY) <  = 5 THEN GT = .4
187  GOTO 182
188  IF (YY - Y3) <  = 50 THEN 192
189 Y3 = Y3 + Y5
190  GOSUB 382
191  IF Y3 = YY THEN 195
192  IF (YY - Y3) <  = 50 THEN Y5 = 1
193  IF (YY - Y3) <  = 5 THEN GT = .4
194  GOTO 189
195  PRINT : PRINT "ARRIVAL . . . . AT"
196  PRINT "DESTINATION YEAR . . . . ";YY
197 GT = 4: GOSUB 134
198  HOME : RETURN
199 C =  INT ( RND (1) * 8 + 1):D =  INT ( RND (1) * 8 + 1):A(C,D) = 1
200 K4 =  INT ( RND (1) * 4 + 1) + 3
201  HOME :A = A(C,D):GT = 1: GOSUB 134
202  ON A GOSUB 292,300,410,410,306,330,335,338,362
203  IF KL = 0 THEN 567
204  PRINT : IF TT = 1 THEN TT = 0: GOTO 201
205  IF G <  = 0 THEN 264
206  PRINT A$;",  WHAT IS YOUR ACTION OR MOVE?"
207  PRINT
```

```
208  PRINT "(N)ORTH, (E)AST, (S)OUTH"
209  PRINT "(W)EST, E(X)IT, (G)OLD"
210  INPUT M1$
211 M1 = M1 + 1: IF K = 0 AND M1 > 70 THEN 371
212  IF M1$ = "N" THEN 220
213  IF M1$ = "E" THEN 225
214  IF M1$ = "S" THEN 230
215  IF M1$ = "W" THEN 235
216  IF M1$ = "X" THEN 240
217  IF M1$ = "G" THEN 251
218  PRINT
219  GOTO 204
220  REM  NORTH
221  IF A = 7 THEN 255
222  IF (D - 1) = 0 THEN 281
223 D = D - 1
224  GOTO 201
225  REM  EAST
226  IF A = 6 THEN 260
227  IF (C + 1) = 9 THEN 286
228 C = C + 1
229  GOTO 201
230  REM  SOUTH
231  IF A = 7 THEN 255
232  IF (D + 1) = 9 THEN 288
233 D = D + 1
234  GOTO 201
235  REM  WEST
236  IF A = 6 THEN 260
237  IF (C - 1) = 0 THEN 290
238 C = C - 1
239  GOTO 201
240  HOME
241  IF A < > 9 THEN 248
242  IF K = 1 THEN 387
243  PRINT "YOU CANNOT EXIT THE TIME DUNGEON"
244  PRINT "YOU DON'T HAVE THE CRYSTAL KEY"
245 GT = 2: GOSUB 134
246  PRINT
247  GOTO 204
248  PRINT "YOU ARE NOT AT AN EXIT PORTAL"
249 GT = 2: GOSUB 134
250  GOTO 204
251  REM  GOLD
252  HOME : PRINT "YOU HAVE ";G;" GOLD PIECES WITH YOU"
253  PRINT
254  GOTO 204
255  REM  EW
256  HOME : PRINT "YOU ARE IN AN EAST-WEST CORRIDOR"
257  PRINT "YOU CAN ONLY GO EAST OR WEST"
258  PRINT
259  GOTO 204
260  REM  NS
```

```
261   HOME : PRINT "YOU ARE IN A NORTH-SOUTH CORRIDOR"
262   PRINT "YOU CAN ONLY GO NORTH OR SOUTH"
263   GOTO 258
264   REM  GOLD ZERO
265 GT = 2: GOSUB 134
266   PRINT
267   PRINT "YOU LOST ALL YOUR GOLD AND YOU WERE"
268   PRINT " . . . UNABLE TO MEET THE DEMANDS OF"
269   PRINT " . . . THE TIME DUNGEON . . . . ."
270   PRINT
271   PRINT
272 T = 3: GOSUB 134
273   GOSUB 402
274   PRINT
275   PRINT "ANOTHER GAME?"
276   PRINT "ENTER '1'-YES  '0'-NO"
277   INPUT AA
278   IF AA < > 1 THEN 280
279   HOME : GOTO 108
280   END
281   HOME : PRINT "YOU ARE AT THE NORTH WALL"
282   PRINT "YOU CANNOT PASS THROUGH"
283   PRINT
284   PRINT "TRY ANOTHER DIRECTION?"
285   GOTO 204
286   HOME : PRINT "YOU ARE AT THE EAST WALL"
287   GOTO 282
288   HOME : PRINT "YOU ARE AT THE SOUTH WALL"
289   GOTO 282
290   HOME : PRINT "YOU ARE AT THE WEST WALL"
291   GOTO 282
292 KT =  INT ( RND (1) * 9 + 1)
293   PRINT "YOU ARE IN A GLOWING TIME PORTAL"
294 GT = 1: GOSUB 134
295   PRINT
296   PRINT "THE LIGHT FADES . . . . . ."
297   PRINT "THE PORTAL IS INACTIVE . . . ."
298   IF A = 1 AND KT > 8 THEN 570
299   RETURN
300   PRINT "YOU ARE IN A DUST FILLED PORTAL"
301 GT = 1: GOSUB 134
302   PRINT
303   PRINT "A BRIGHT LIGHT IS ACTIVATED AND . ."
304   PRINT
305   GOTO 296
306   HOME
307   PRINT "AN ALIEN TRAVELER IS IN THIS CHAMBER"
308 A(C,D) =  INT ( RND (1) * 2 + 1): GOSUB 478
309 GT = 1: GOSUB 134
310 TD =  INT ( RND (1) * 10 + 1)
311 G4 =  INT ( RND (1) * 350 + 1)
312 Y =  INT ( RND (1) * 8 + 1)
313  IF Y < = 5 THEN 320
```

```
314  PRINT : IF (G - G4) < 0 THEN G4 = G
315  PRINT "HE IS UNFRIENDLY . . . . AND AS HE"
316  PRINT "LEAVES . . . HE TAKES ";G4;" GOLD PIECES"
317  PRINT :G = G - G4
318  IF TD = 5 AND K = 0 THEN 325
319  RETURN
320  PRINT
321  PRINT "HE IS FRIENDLY . . . . . AND GIVES YOU"
322  PRINT ". . ";G4;" GOLD PIECES, WHICH YOU ACCEPT"
323  PRINT :G = G + G4
324  GOTO 318
325  PRINT :GT = 2: GOSUB 134
326  PRINT "YOU SEARCH THE CHAMBER . . . AND"
327 GT = 1: GOSUB 134
328  PRINT "FIND . . . . THE CRYSTAL KEY"
329 K = 1: RETURN
330  HOME
331  PRINT "YOU ENTER A NORTH-SOUTH CORRIDOR"
332  PRINT "THRU A SECRET DOOR": PRINT : GOSUB 380
333 KT =  INT ( RND (1) * 9 + 1): IF KT >  = 7 THEN 545
334  RETURN
335  HOME
336  PRINT "YOU ENTER AN EAST-WEST CORRIDOR"
337  GOTO 332
338  REM  TRAP
339  PRINT "YOU ENCOUNTER . . . A TIME TRAP"
340  PRINT ". . . . . . . . IN THIS CHAMBER":GT = 1: GOSUB 134
341 TD =  INT ( RND (1) * 9 + 1)
342  IF TD >  = 7 THEN 347
343  PRINT
344  PRINT "BUT YOU'RE LUCKY . . . . ."
345  PRINT ". . . IT DIDN'T ACTIVATE"
346  RETURN
347 TT = 1: PRINT "AND IT ACTIVATED . . . . .":GT = 2: GOSUB 134
348  FOR A = 1 TO 250
349  PRINT "*        %";
350  NEXT A
351 C =  INT ( RND (1) * 8 + 1):D =  INT ( RND (1) * 8 + 1)
352  PRINT
353  PRINT :G = 100
354  PRINT "YOU HAVE BEEN TELEPORTED TO . . . ."
355  PRINT ". . . . AN UNKNOWN LOCATION . . . ."
356  PRINT
357  PRINT "AND YOU LOST MOST OF YOUR GOLD"
358  PRINT
359  PRINT "YOU HAVE . . . ";G;" GOLD PIECES LEFT"
360 GT = 6: GOSUB 134
361  RETURN
362  PRINT "YOU ARE AT AN EXIT PORTAL"
363  PRINT
364  PRINT "(A KEY IS REQUIRED)"
365  PRINT
366  RETURN
```

```
367 H = 1:O = 9:W = 8
368 B = 0:E = 5:R = 14
369 C = 0:PR = 0
370  GOTO 216
371  PRINT :GT = 2: GOSUB 134
372  PRINT "BUT BEFORE YOU PROCEED . ."
373  PRINT "YOU LOOK TO THE GROUND AND . . . ."
374  PRINT ". . . FIND THE CRYSTAL KEY . .":K = 1
375 GT = 3: GOSUB 134
376  GOTO 212
377  PRINT "YOU ANSWERED ";CA;" QUESTION(S) CORRECTLY"
378  PRINT " . . . . . IN ";M1;" TURNS,"
379  GOTO 409
380  PRINT "THE DOOR CLOSES AND LOCKS BEHIND YOU":GT = 1: GOSUB 134
381  RETURN
382  REM  TIME DISPLAY
383  VTAB 12: PRINT "PORTAL YEAR . . . ";Y3
385  GOSUB 134
386  RETURN
387  HOME : REM  EXIT PORTAL
388  PRINT "YOU ENTER THE EXIT PORTAL AND"
389  PRINT "INSERT THE CRYSTAL KEY INTO THE SLOT"
390  PRINT :GT = 4: GOSUB 134
391  PRINT "THE MACHINE BEGINS TO HUM . . . ."
392  PRINT :GT = 2: GOSUB 134
393 YY = Y2: GOSUB 171
394  PRINT
395  PRINT "YOU FOUND YOUR WAY . . . . ."
396  PRINT ". . . . BACK TO THE PRESENT"
397  PRINT
398  PRINT "YOU HAVE ACQUIRED ";G;" GOLD PIECES"
399  PRINT
400  GOSUB 402
401  GOTO 274
402 GG = G + 100
403 R =  INT ((GG * CA - 7000 + 1) / M1)
404  PRINT
405  PRINT "GAME RATING IS ";R
406  PRINT : IF G <  = 0 OR KL = 0 THEN 377
407  PRINT "YOU TOOK ";M1;" TURNS TO FIND THE WAY OUT"
408  PRINT "AND ANSWERED ";CA;" QUESTION(S) CORRECTLY,"
409  PRINT "OUT OF ";TR;" QUESTIONS ASKED.": RETURN
410  HOME :Y3 = YY
411  GOSUB 444
412 Q3 = Q3 + 1
413  IF Q3 > 50 THEN Q3 = 0: GOTO 415
414  GOTO 416
415  GOSUB 451
416 Q =  INT ( RND (1) * 50 + 1)
417  IF B(Q) = 1 THEN 416
418 B(Q) = 1
419  PRINT
420  FOR AB = 1 TO Q
```

```
421  READ YY,QD$,ID,AD$,I1$,I2$,I3$
422  NEXT AB
423  RESTORE
424  GOSUB 171
425  HOME :TR = TR + 1
426  PRINT "YOU HAVE ARRIVED AT THE YEAR ";YY
427  PRINT ". . . . . . IN ";BZ$: PRINT
428  PRINT "YOU MUST ANSWER THIS QUESTION"
429  PRINT " . . TO CONTINUE YOUR JOURNEY"
430  PRINT "----------------------------------------"
431  PRINT "THE YEAR IS: ";YY: PRINT : IF ID = 4 THEN 164
432  PRINT QD$
433  PRINT "----------------------------------------"
434  PRINT "QUESTION TYPE: "
435  ON ID GOSUB 455,456,457,458
436  GOSUB 459
437  IF E$ = AD$ THEN 441
438  PRINT "INCORRECT"
439  GOSUB 471
440  RETURN
441  PRINT "CORRECT"
442  GOSUB 463
443  RETURN
444  PRINT "YOU ENTER INTO A BLUE HAZY . . ."
445  PRINT ". . . . . . . TIME PORTAL . . ."
446  PRINT :GT = 1: GOSUB 134
447  PRINT "A PULSATING GLOW . . . . . . ."
448  PRINT ". . . . INDICATES ACTIVATION": PRINT
449  PRINT "PRESENT YEAR . . .   "Y3:GT = 3: GOSUB 134
450  RETURN
451  FOR I = 1 TO 50
452 B(I) = 0
453  NEXT I
454  RETURN
455  PRINT "PEOPLE, PLACES, OR THINGS ?": RETURN
456  PRINT "*** (T)RUE OR (F)ALSE  ?": RETURN
457  PRINT "*** WHO AM I (LAST NAME) ?": RETURN
458  PRINT "*** MULTIPLE CHOICE ?": RETURN
459  PRINT "ENTER CORRECT ANSWER?"
460  INPUT E$
461 G4 =  INT ( RND (1) * 500 + 1) + 125
462  RETURN
463 G = G + G4
464  PRINT "YOU WIN ";G4;" GOLD PIECES"
465 A(C,D) =  INT ( RND (1) * 2 + 1)
466 CA = CA + 1: IF K = 1 THEN  RETURN
467  IF CA = K4 THEN 469
468  RETURN
469  GOSUB 325
470  RETURN
471  PRINT :G4 =  INT ( RND (1) * 400 + 1) + 25
472  PRINT "THE CORRECT ANSWER IS '";AD$;"'"
473  PRINT : IF (G - G4) < 0 THEN G4 = G
```

```
474 G = G - G4
475 GT = 1: GOSUB 134
476  PRINT "YOU LOSE ";G4;" GOLD PIECES"
477  RETURN
478 ZT = 5
479 X =  INT ( RND (1) * 8 + 1):Y =  INT ( RND (1) * 8 + 1)
480  IF A(X,Y) <  = 2 THEN A(X,Y) = 5: RETURN
481 ZT = ZT - 1: IF ZT = O THEN  RETURN
482  GOTO 479
483  DATA 1850,SLAVE TRADE WAS ABOLISHED IN WASHINGTON DC,2,T,0,0,0
484  DATA 1848,THE .... RUSH STARTED IN CALIFORNIA,4,GOLD,SILVER,TIN,BRAS
     S
485  DATA 1852,I PUBLISHED 'UNCLE TOMS'S CABIN',3,STOWE,0,0,0
486  DATA 1853,WHAT ALLOWED PURCHASE OF LAND FROM MEXI-CO,1,GADSDEN PURCH
     ASE,0,0,0
487  DATA 1854,I ENACTED THE KANSAS & NEBRASKA ACT,3,DOUGLAS,0,0,0
488  DATA 1856,WHAT POLITICAL PARTY WAS FORMED THIS    YEAR,4,REPUBLICAN,
     DEMOCRATIC,WHIGS,PROGRESSIVE
489  DATA 1857,THE SUPREME COURT RULED THE MISSOURI    COMPROMISE CONSTIT
     UTIONAL,2,F,0,0,0
490  DATA 1858,HE DEBATED SENATOR DOUGLAS ON SLAVERY,4,LINCOLN,PLESSY,STO
     WE,LEE
491  DATA 1859,I TRIED TO SEIZE THE FEDERAL ARSENAL AT HARPERS FERRY,3,BR
     OWN,0,0,0
492  DATA 1860,LINCOLN WAS ELECTED PRESIDENT IN THIS  YEAR,2,T,0,0,0
493  DATA  1861,WHO WAS PRESIDENTOF THE 'CONFEDERATE   STATESOF AMERICA',
     4,DAVIS,LEE,BROWN,LINCOLN
494  DATA 1861,S. CAROLINA TROOPS FIRED ON FORT ..... -STARTING THE CIVIL
      WAR,1,SUMTER,0,0,0
495  DATA 1861,NORTH CAROLINA WAS A CONFEDERATE STATE,2,T,0,0,0
496  DATA  1862,THE EMANCIPATION PROCLAMATION WAS TO    TAKE EFFECT IN JA
     NUARY-1863,2,T,0,0,0
497  DATA  1863,GENERAL MEADE'S UNION FORCES DEFEATS    GENERAL LEE'S AT?
     ,4,GETTYSBURG,NEW YORK,APPOMATTOX,WASHINGTON
498  DATA 1864,HE BECAME COMMANDER OF THE UNION ARMIES,4,GRANT,LEE,DAVIS,
     JACKSON
499  DATA 1865,THE .... AMENDMENT-ABOLISHING SLAVERY- WAS RATIFIED,4,13T
     H,2ND,20TH,5TH
500  DATA 1865,WHO ASSASSINATED LINCOLN-ON APRIL 14TH,1,BOOTH,0,0,0
501  DATA 1865,GENERAL LEE SURRENDERED AT ..... COURT HOUSE,1,APPOMATTOX,
     0,0,0
502  DATA 1866,IN WHAT STATE WAS THE KU KLUX KLAN FORM-ED,4,TENNESSEE,VIR
     GINIA,TEXAS,GEORGIA
503  DATA 1867,WHAT LAND WAS PURCHASED FROM RUSSIA THIS YEAR,4,ALASKA,HAW
     AII,OREGON,TEXAS
504  DATA 1867,WHAT WERE THE NORTHERNERS CALLED WHO    HELPED TO REBUILD
     THE SOUTH,1,CARPETBAGGERS,0,0,0
496  DATA  1862,THE EMANCIPATION PROCLAMATION WAS TO    TAKE EFFECT IN JA
     NUARY-1863,2,T,0,0,0
505  DATA 1870,THE 15TH AMENDMENT GAVE 'BACKS' THE     RIGHT TO ....,1,VO
     TE,0,0,0
506  DATA 1871,A DISASTROUS FIRE DESTROYED WHAT CITY,4,CHICAGO,DETROIT,NE
     W YORK,BOSTON
```

```
507  DATA 1875,CIVIL RIGHTS ACT PASSED AGAINST PUBLIC  DISCRIMINATION OF
     BLACKS,2,T,0,0,0
508  DATA 1876,MY TROOPS WERE MASSACRED BY SITTING BULL-AT LITTLE BIGHORN
     ,3,CUSTER,0,0,0
509  DATA 1881,WHAT PRESIDENT WAS SHOT THIS YEAR,4,GARFIELD,LINCOLN,TAFT,
     DAVIS
510  DATA 1886,HE WAS PRESIDENT OF THE AMERICAN FEDERA-TION OF LABOR,4,GO
     MPERS,MONROE,TAFT,FRICK
511  DATA 1883,THE ..... ACT ESTABLISHED THE CIVIL SER-VICE SYSTEM,4,PEND
     LETON,LABOR,TRADE,WORKERS
512  DATA 1890,THE ..... ANTI-TRUST ACT BECAME LAW THIS YEAR,4,SHERMAN,PU
     LLMAN,PENDLETON,TAFT
513  DATA 1894,WHAT STRIKE BROUGHT FEDERAL INTERVENTION,4,PULLMAN,COAL,FA
     RMERS,GRAIN
514  DATA 1895,SOUTHERN STATES USED .... CLAUSES-       DEPRIVE BLACKS VOT
     ING RIGHTS,1,GRANDFATHER,0,0,0
515  DATA 1896,SUPREME COURT-PLESSY V. FERGUSON-UPHELD LOUISIANA SEGREGAT
     ION LAW,2,T,0,0,0
516  DATA 1897,KLONDIKE .... RUSH BEGAN THIS YEAR,4,GOLD,SILVER,URANIUM,D
     IAMOND
517  DATA 1898,SPANISH-AMERICAN WAR BEGAN WHEN WHAT   SHIP EXPLODED-HAVA
     NA HARBOR,4,MAINE,UNION,YORK,ATLANTIC
518  DATA 1898,THE UNITED STATES ANNEXED THE .....     ISLANDS,1,HAWAIIAN
     ,0,0,0
519  DATA 1900,SAMOAN ISLANDS WERE DIVIDED BETWEEN THE UNITED STATES & ..
     ..,4,GERMANY,RUSSIA,FRANCE,ITALY
520  DATA 1901,I BECAME PRESIDENT AFTER MCKINLEY WAS   SHOT,3,ROOSEVELT,0
     ,0,0
521  DATA 1902,WHAT DID ROOSEVELT PLEDGE FOR BOTH LABOR & INDUSTRY,1,SQUA
     RE DEAL,0,0,0
522  DATA 1903,THE ..... BROTHERS FLEW THE 1ST SUCCESS-FUL AIRPLANE FLIGH
     T,1,WRIGHT,0,0,0
523  DATA 1906,EARTHQUAKE AND FIRE DESTROYED WHAT CITY,4,SAN FRANCISCO,CH
     ICAGO,BOSTON,RICHMOND
524  DATA 1907,GENTLEMANS AGREEMENT-WITH JAPAN-ALLOWED LABORERS TO MIGRAT
     E HERE,2,F,0,0,0
525  DATA 1899,THE UNITED STATES PARTICIPATED IN THE   1ST ..... CONFEREN
     CE,1,HAGUE,0,0,0
526  DATA 1909,HE DISCOVERED THE NORTH POLE THIS YEAR,4,PEARY,LOUIS,SMITH
     ,PIKE
527  DATA 1912,ROOSEVELT WAS WHAT PARTY'S CANDIDATE FOR PRESIDENT,1,PROGR
     ESSIVE, 0,0,0
528  DATA 1913,THE FEDERAL .... SYSTEM WAS ESTABLISHED THIS YEAR,1,RESERV
     E,0,0,0
529  DATA 1914,THE FEDERAL .... COMMISSION WAS ESTAB-  LISHED THIS YEAR,1
     ,TRADE,0,0,0
530  DATA 1908,I WAS ELECTED PRESIDENT THIS YEAR,3,TAFT,0,0,0
531  DATA 1914,THE UNITED STATES CLAIMED NEUTRALITY TO WORLD WAR I,2,T,0,
     0,0
532  DATA 1913,WILSON WON A REDUCTION OF THE .... AFTER A HARD FIGHT,1,TA
     RIFF,0,0,0
533  HOME : PRINT "THE TIME DUNGEON * * * MAP"
534  PRINT
```

```
535  FOR Q = 1 TO 8
536  FOR N = 1 TO 8
537   IF C = N AND D = Q THEN  PRINT "=P= ";: GOTO 540
538 S1 = A(N,Q)
539  ON S1 GOSUB 137,137,138,138,139,140,141,139,142
540  NEXT N
541  PRINT
542  NEXT Q
543 GT =  INT ( RND (1) * 8 + 1) +  INT ( RND (1) * (CA + 5) + 1)
544  GOSUB 134: HOME : RETURN
545  PRINT : PRINT "ON THE WALL IS A GLOWING SCREEN"
546  PRINT "BELOW THE SCREEN IS A RED BUTTON": PRINT
547 KT =  INT ( RND (1) * 9 + 1):KL =  INT ( RND (1) * 15 + 1) + 2
548  GOSUB 565
549  INPUT K$
550  IF K$ = "Y" THEN 552
551  RETURN
552  IF KT >  = 6 THEN 533
553  IF KT <  = 4 THEN 562
554  PRINT :G4 =  INT ( RND (1) * 100 + 1) + 25:G = G + G4
555  PRINT "YOU RECEIVE ";G4;" GOLD PIECES . . ."
556  PRINT "BUT . . . . . . THE CORRIDOR NARROWS":GT = 3: GOSUB 134
557 KL = KL - 1: IF KL = 0 THEN  RETURN
558  GOSUB 565
559  INPUT K$
560  IF K$ = "Y" THEN 554
561  RETURN
562  PRINT : PRINT "NOTHING HAPPENS"
563 GT = 1: GOSUB 134
564  RETURN
565  PRINT : PRINT "DO YOU WISH TO PUSH THE BUTTON?"
566  PRINT "ENTER  (Y)ES  OR  (N)O": RETURN
567  HOME : PRINT "YOU ARE STUCK IN THE NARROW CORRIDOR"
568  PRINT ". . . . . . . . . . AND . . .": PRINT :GT = 3: GOSUB 134
569  GOTO 264
570  PRINT : PRINT "YOU NOTICE A DOOR TO YOUR RIGHT"
571  PRINT
572 KT =  INT ( RND (1) * 9 + 1)
573  PRINT "DO YOU WISH TO OPEN THE DOOR?"
574  PRINT "ENTER  (Y)ES  OR  (N)O"
575  INPUT K$
576  IF K$ = "Y" THEN 578
577  RETURN
578  PRINT : PRINT "YOU TRY THE DOOR . . . . .":GT = 1: GOSUB 134
579  IF KT >  = 7 THEN 589
580  IF KT <  = 4 THEN 587
581  PRINT :G4 =  INT ( RND (1) * 100 + 1) + 25
582  PRINT "THE DOOR OPENS . . . . . . ."
583  PRINT "REVEALING A CLOSET . . . ."
584  PRINT :G = G + G4
585  PRINT "WHERE YOU FIND ";G4;" GOLD PIECES"
586  PRINT : RETURN
587  PRINT "BUT THE DOOR WON'T OPEN . . . ."
```

```
588  PRINT ". . . . IT MUST BE LOCKED": RETURN
589  PRINT : PRINT "THE DOOR OPENS . . . AND SUDDENLY"
590  PRINT "THE CHAMBER BEGINS TO . . . SPIN"
591 G7 =  INT (G / 2):G4 =  INT ( RND (1) * G7 + 1):MM =  INT ( RND (1) *
    20 + 1)
592 GT = 4: GOSUB 134:G = G - G4
593  FOR K9 = 1 TO 250
594  PRINT "+     =     +";: NEXT K9
596  HOME : PRINT "YOU WERE TELEPORTED INTO . . . ."
597  PRINT ". . . . ANOTHER DIMENSION . . . ."
598  PRINT ". . AND RETURNED IN AN INSTANT . ."
599  PRINT : PRINT "BUT YOU DROPPED ";G4;" GOLD PIECES"
600  PRINT ". . . AND WASTED ";MM;" MOVES . . ."
601 M1 = M1 + MM
602 GT = 4: GOSUB 134
603  RETURN
```

```
100  HOME :BZ$ = "AMERICAN HISTORY":BW$ = "1916 TO 1975"
101  PRINT "THE TIME DUNGEON: ";BZ$
102  PRINT "COPYRIGHT (C) 1981 BY HOWARD BERENBON"
103  PRINT "APPLE II"
104  PRINT
105  PRINT "AN EDUCATIONAL FANTASY GAME"
106 GT = 5: GOSUB 134:Q3 = 0
107  HOME : DIM A(9,9),B(50): GOSUB 451
108  PRINT "YOU WILL BE TELEPORTED TO . . ."
109  PRINT
110  PRINT "THE TIME DUNGEON . . . ."
111  PRINT "TO STUDY ";BZ$
112  PRINT
114 CA = 0:G = 1000:M1 = 1:K = 0:KL = 1:TT = 0:TR = 0
115  PRINT "ENTER YOUR CHARACTER'S NAME?"
116  INPUT A$
117  PRINT "ENTER PRESENT YEAR"
118  INPUT Y2:YY = Y2: IF Y2 > 2000 THEN 117
119  PRINT : PRINT A$;" . . . YOU ARE ON YOUR WAY"
120 GT = 2: GOSUB 134
121  GOSUB 143
122  HOME
123  PRINT "YOU HAVE ARRIVED AT . . . ."
124  PRINT
125  PRINT "THE TIME DUNGEON: ";BZ$
126  PRINT "FOR THE YEARS:     ";BW$
127  PRINT
128  PRINT "YOU CARRY 1000 GOLD PIECES": PRINT
129  PRINT "YOU WILL ENCOUNTER . . ."
130  PRINT "TIME PORTALS WHICH TELEPORT"
131  PRINT "YOU TO EVENTS IN ";BZ$
132 GT = 8: GOSUB 134
133  GOTO 199
134  FOR ZZ = 1 TO 908 * GT
135  NEXT ZZ
136  RETURN
137  PRINT "O    ";: RETURN
138  PRINT "AP   ";: RETURN
139  PRINT "?    ";: RETURN
140  PRINT "NS   ";: RETURN
141  PRINT "EW   ";: RETURN
142  PRINT "X    ";: RETURN
143  REM  SET UP DUNGEON
144  FOR X = 1 TO 8
145  FOR Y = 1 TO 8
146 A(X,Y) =  INT ( RND (1) * 7 + 1)
147  NEXT Y
148  NEXT X
149  REM  TRAPS
150 H =  INT ( RND (1) * 3 + 1) + 1
151  FOR N = 1 TO H
152 X =  INT ( RND (1) * 8 + 1)
153 Y =  INT ( RND (1) * 8 + 1)
```

```
154 A(X,Y) = 8
155  NEXT N
156  REM  EXITS
157 S =  INT ( RND (1) * 4 + 1) + 1
158  FOR N = 1 TO S
159 X =  INT ( RND (1) * 8 + 1)
160 Y =  INT ( RND (1) * 8 + 1)
161 A(X,Y) = 9
162  NEXT N
163  RETURN
164 R6 =  INT ( RND (1) * 4 + 1): PRINT QD$;"?:": PRINT
165  ON R6 GOSUB 167,168,169,170
166  GOTO 433
167  PRINT AD$,I1$: PRINT I2$,I3$: RETURN
168  PRINT I2$,AD$: PRINT I1$,I3$: RETURN
169  PRINT I1$,I2$: PRINT AD$,I3$: RETURN
170  PRINT I3$,I1$: PRINT I2$,AD$: RETURN
171  HOME
173 GT = 1
174  GOSUB 134
175  FOR B = 1 TO 70:B4 =  INT ( RND (1) * 23 + 1)
176 B7 =  INT ( RND (1) * 39 + 1): VTAB B4: PRINT  TAB( B7)".";
177  PRINT : NEXT B: PRINT
178 GT = .005:Y5 = 25
179  IF Y3 = YY THEN  VTAB 1: PRINT "ALREADY AT . . . . ": GOTO 196
180  IF Y3 < YY THEN 188
181  IF (Y3 - YY) <  = 50 THEN 185
182 Y3 = Y3 - Y5
183  GOSUB 382
184  IF Y3 = YY THEN 195
185  IF (Y3 - YY) <  = 50 THEN Y5 = 1
186  IF (Y3 - YY) <  = 5 THEN GT = .4
187  GOTO 182
188  IF (YY - Y3) <  = 50 THEN 192
189 Y3 = Y3 + Y5
190  GOSUB 382
191  IF Y3 = YY THEN 195
192  IF (YY - Y3) <  = 50 THEN Y5 = 1
193  IF (YY - Y3) <  = 5 THEN GT = .4
194  GOTO 189
195  PRINT : PRINT "ARRIVAL . . . . AT"
196  PRINT "DESTINATION YEAR . . . . ";YY
197 GT = 4: GOSUB 134
198  HOME : RETURN
199 C =  INT ( RND (1) * 8 + 1):D =  INT ( RND (1) * 8 + 1):A(C,D) = 1
200 K4 =  INT ( RND (1) * 4 + 1) + 3
201  HOME :A = A(C,D):GT = 1: GOSUB 134
202  ON A GOSUB 292,300,410,410,306,330,335,338,362
203  IF KL = 0 THEN 567
204  PRINT : IF TT = 1 THEN TT = 0: GOTO 201
205  IF G <  = 0 THEN 264
206  PRINT A$;",  WHAT IS YOUR ACTION OR MOVE?"
207  PRINT
```

```
208   PRINT "(N)ORTH, (E)AST, (S)OUTH"
209   PRINT "(W)EST, E(X)IT, (G)OLD"
210   INPUT M1$
211 M1 = M1 + 1: IF K = 0 AND M1 > 70 THEN 371
212   IF M1$ = "N" THEN 220
213   IF M1$ = "E" THEN 225
214   IF M1$ = "S" THEN 230
215   IF M1$ = "W" THEN 235
216   IF M1$ = "X" THEN 240
217   IF M1$ = "G" THEN 251
218   PRINT
219   GOTO 204
220   REM  NORTH
221   IF A = 7 THEN 255
222   IF (D - 1) = 0 THEN 281
223 D = D - 1
224   GOTO 201
225   REM  EAST
226   IF A = 6 THEN 260
227   IF (C + 1) = 9 THEN 286
228 C = C + 1
229   GOTO 201
230   REM  SOUTH
231   IF A = 7 THEN 255
232   IF (D + 1) = 9 THEN 288
233 D = D + 1
234   GOTO 201
235   REM  WEST
236   IF A = 6 THEN 260
237   IF (C - 1) = 0 THEN 290
238 C = C - 1
239   GOTO 201
240   HOME
241   IF A <  > 9 THEN 248
242   IF K = 1 THEN 387
243   PRINT "YOU CANNOT EXIT THE TIME DUNGEON"
244   PRINT "YOU DON'T HAVE THE CRYSTAL KEY"
245 GT = 2: GOSUB 134
246   PRINT
247   GOTO 204
248   PRINT "YOU ARE NOT AT AN EXIT PORTAL"
249 GT = 2: GOSUB 134
250   GOTO 204
251   REM  GOLD
252   HOME : PRINT "YOU HAVE ";G;" GOLD PIECES WITH YOU"
253   PRINT
254   GOTO 204
255   REM  EW
256   HOME : PRINT "YOU ARE IN AN EAST-WEST CORRIDOR"
257   PRINT "YOU CAN ONLY GO EAST OR WEST"
258   PRINT
259   GOTO 204
260   REM  NS
```

```
261  HOME : PRINT "YOU ARE IN A NORTH-SOUTH CORRIDOR"
262  PRINT "YOU CAN ONLY GO NORTH OR SOUTH"
263  GOTO 258
264  REM  GOLD ZERO
265 GT = 2: GOSUB 134
266  PRINT
267  PRINT "YOU LOST ALL YOUR GOLD AND YOU WERE"
268  PRINT " . . . UNABLE TO MEET THE DEMANDS OF"
269  PRINT " . . . THE TIME DUNGEON . . . . ."
270  PRINT
271  PRINT
272 T = 3: GOSUB 134
273  GOSUB 402
274  PRINT
275  PRINT "ANOTHER GAME?"
276  PRINT "ENTER '1'-YES  '0'-NO"
277  INPUT AA
278  IF AA < > 1 THEN 280
279  HOME : GOTO 108
280  END
281  HOME : PRINT "YOU ARE AT THE NORTH WALL"
282  PRINT "YOU CANNOT PASS THROUGH"
283  PRINT
284  PRINT "TRY ANOTHER DIRECTION?"
285  GOTO 204
286  HOME : PRINT "YOU ARE AT THE EAST WALL"
287  GOTO 282
288  HOME : PRINT "YOU ARE AT THE SOUTH WALL"
289  GOTO 282
290  HOME : PRINT "YOU ARE AT THE WEST WALL"
291  GOTO 282
292 KT =  INT ( RND (1) * 9 + 1)
293  PRINT "YOU ARE IN A GLOWING TIME PORTAL"
294 GT = 1: GOSUB 134
295  PRINT
296  PRINT "THE LIGHT FADES . . . . . ."
297  PRINT "THE PORTAL IS INACTIVE . . . ."
298  IF A = 1 AND KT > 8 THEN 570
299  RETURN
300  PRINT "YOU ARE IN A DUST FILLED PORTAL"
301 GT = 1: GOSUB 134
302  PRINT
303  PRINT "A BRIGHT LIGHT IS ACTIVATED AND . ."
304  PRINT
305  GOTO 296
306  HOME
307  PRINT "AN ALIEN TRAVELER IS IN THIS CHAMBER"
308 A(C,D) =  INT ( RND (1) * 2 + 1): GOSUB 478
309 GT = 1: GOSUB 134
310 TD =  INT ( RND (1) * 10 + 1)
311 G4 =  INT ( RND (1) * 350 + 1)
312 Y =  INT ( RND (1) * 8 + 1)
313  IF Y < = 5 THEN 320
```

```
314   PRINT : IF (G - G4) < 0 THEN G4 = G
315   PRINT "HE IS UNFRIENDLY . . . . AND AS HE"
316   PRINT "LEAVES . . . HE TAKES ";G4;" GOLD PIECES"
317   PRINT :G = G - G4
318   IF TD = 5 AND K = 0 THEN 325
319   RETURN
320   PRINT
321   PRINT "HE IS FRIENDLY . . . . . AND GIVES YOU"
322   PRINT ". . ";G4;" GOLD PIECES, WHICH YOU ACCEPT"
323   PRINT :G = G + G4
324   GOTO 318
325   PRINT :GT = 2: GOSUB 134
326   PRINT "YOU SEARCH THE CHAMBER . . . AND"
327 GT = 1: GOSUB 134
328   PRINT "FIND . . . . THE CRYSTAL KEY"
329 K = 1: RETURN
330   HOME
331   PRINT "YOU ENTER A NORTH-SOUTH CORRIDOR"
332   PRINT "THRU A SECRET DOOR": PRINT : GOSUB 380
333 KT =  INT ( RND (1) * 9 + 1): IF KT > = 7 THEN 545
334   RETURN
335   HOME
336   PRINT "YOU ENTER AN EAST-WEST CORRIDOR"
337   GOTO 332
338   REM  TRAP
339   PRINT "YOU ENCOUNTER . . . A TIME TRAP"
340   PRINT ". . . . . . . . IN THIS CHAMBER":GT = 1: GOSUB 134
341 TD =  INT ( RND (1) * 9 + 1)
342   IF TD > = 7 THEN 347
343   PRINT
344   PRINT "BUT YOU'RE LUCKY . . . . ."
345   PRINT ". . . IT DIDN'T ACTIVATE"
346   RETURN
347 TT = 1: PRINT "AND IT ACTIVATED . . . . .":GT = 2: GOSUB 134
348   FOR A = 1 TO 250
349   PRINT "*        %";
350   NEXT A
351 C =  INT ( RND (1) * 8 + 1):D =  INT ( RND (1) * 8 + 1)
352   PRINT
353   PRINT :G = 100
354   PRINT "YOU HAVE BEEN TELEPORTED TO . . . ."
355   PRINT ". . . . AN UNKNOWN LOCATION . . . ."
356   PRINT
357   PRINT "AND YOU LOST MOST OF YOUR GOLD"
358   PRINT
359   PRINT "YOU HAVE . . . ";G;" GOLD PIECES LEFT"
360 GT = 6: GOSUB 134
361   RETURN
362   PRINT "YOU ARE AT AN EXIT PORTAL"
363   PRINT
364   PRINT "(A KEY IS REQUIRED)"
365   PRINT
366   RETURN
```

```
367 H = 1:O = 9:W = 8
368 B = O:E = 5:R = 14
369 C = O:PR = 0
370  GOTO 216
371  PRINT :GT = 2: GOSUB 134
372  PRINT "BUT BEFORE YOU PROCEED . ."
373  PRINT "YOU LOOK TO THE GROUND AND . . .."
374  PRINT ". . . FIND THE CRYSTAL KEY . .":K = 1
375 GT = 3: GOSUB 134
376  GOTO 212
377  PRINT "YOU ANSWERED ";CA;" QUESTION(S) CORRECTLY"
378  PRINT " . . . . . IN ";M1;" TURNS,"
379  GOTO 409
380  PRINT "THE DOOR CLOSES AND LOCKS BEHIND YOU":GT = 1: GOSUB 134
381  RETURN
382  REM   TIME DISPLAY
383  VTAB 12: PRINT "PORTAL YEAR . . . ";Y3
385  GOSUB 134
386  RETURN
387  HOME : REM  EXIT PORTAL
388  PRINT "YOU ENTER THE EXIT PORTAL AND"
389  PRINT "INSERT THE CRYSTAL KEY INTO THE SLOT"
390  PRINT :GT = 4: GOSUB 134
391  PRINT "THE MACHINE BEGINS TO HUM . . . ."
392  PRINT :GT = 2: GOSUB 134
393 YY = Y2: GOSUB 171
394  PRINT
395  PRINT "YOU FOUND YOUR WAY . . . . ."
396  PRINT ". . . . BACK TO THE PRESENT"
397  PRINT
398  PRINT "YOU HAVE ACQUIRED ";G;" GOLD PIECES"
399  PRINT
400  GOSUB 402
401  GOTO 274
402 GG = G + 100
403 R =  INT ((GG * CA - 7000 + 1) / M1)
404  PRINT
405  PRINT "GAME RATING IS ";R
406  PRINT : IF G <  = 0 OR KL = 0 THEN 377
407  PRINT "YOU TOOK ";M1;" TURNS TO FIND THE WAY OUT"
408  PRINT "AND ANSWERED ";CA;" QUESTION(S) CORRECTLY,"
409  PRINT "OUT OF ";TR;" QUESTIONS ASKED.": RETURN
410  HOME :Y3 = YY
411  GOSUB 444
412 Q3 = Q3 + 1
413  IF Q3 > 50 THEN Q3 = O: GOTO 415
414  GOTO 416
415  GOSUB 451
416 Q =  INT ( RND (1) * 50 + 1)
417  IF B(Q) = 1 THEN 416
418 B(Q) = 1
419  PRINT
420  FOR AB = 1 TO Q
421  READ YY,QD$,ID,AD$,I1$,I2$,I3$
```

```
422   NEXT AB
423   RESTORE
424   GOSUB 171
425   HOME :TR = TR + 1
426   PRINT "YOU HAVE ARRIVED AT THE YEAR ";YY
427   PRINT ". . . . . . IN ";BZ$: PRINT
428   PRINT "YOU MUST ANSWER THIS QUESTION"
429   PRINT " . . TO CONTINUE YOUR JOURNEY"
430   PRINT "------------------------------------------"
431   PRINT "THE YEAR IS: ";YY: PRINT : IF ID = 4 THEN 164
432   PRINT QD$
433   PRINT "------------------------------------------"
434   PRINT "QUESTION TYPE: "
435   ON ID GOSUB 455,456,457,458
436   GOSUB 459
437   IF E$ = AD$ THEN 441
438   PRINT "INCORRECT"
439   GOSUB 471
440   RETURN
441   PRINT "CORRECT"
442   GOSUB 463
443   RETURN
444   PRINT "YOU ENTER INTO A BLUE HAZY . . ."
445   PRINT ". . . . . . . TIME PORTAL . . ."
446   PRINT :GT = 1: GOSUB 134
447   PRINT "A PULSATING GLOW . . . . . . ."
448   PRINT ". . . . INDICATES ACTIVATION": PRINT
449   PRINT "PRESENT YEAR . . .  "Y3:GT = 3: GOSUB 134
450   RETURN
451   FOR I = 1 TO 50
452 B(I) = 0
453   NEXT I
454   RETURN
455   PRINT "PEOPLE, PLACES, OR THINGS ?": RETURN
456   PRINT "*** (T)RUE OR (F)ALSE  ?": RETURN
457   PRINT "*** WHO AM I (LAST NAME) ?": RETURN
458   PRINT "*** MULTIPLE CHOICE ?": RETURN
459   PRINT "ENTER CORRECT ANSWER?"
460   INPUT E$
461 G4 =  INT ( RND (1) * 500 + 1) + 125
462   RETURN
463 G = G + G4
464   PRINT "YOU WIN ";G4;" GOLD PIECES"
465 A(C,D) =  INT ( RND (1) * 2 + 1)
466 CA = CA + 1: IF K = 1 THEN  RETURN
467   IF CA = K4 THEN 469
468   RETURN
469   GOSUB 325
470   RETURN
471   PRINT :G4 =  INT ( RND (1) * 400 + 1) + 25
472   PRINT "THE CORRECT ANSWER IS '";AD$;"'"
473   PRINT : IF (G - G4) < 0 THEN G4 = G
474 G = G - G4
```

```
475 GT = 1: GOSUB 134
476  PRINT "YOU LOSE ";G4;" GOLD PIECES"
477  RETURN
478 ZT = 5
479 X =  INT ( RND (1) * 8 + 1):Y =  INT ( RND (1) * 8 + 1)
480  IF A(X,Y) <  = 2 THEN A(X,Y) = 5: RETURN
481 ZT = ZT - 1: IF ZT = 0 THEN  RETURN
482  GOTO 479
483  DATA 1917,UNITED STATES SEVERED RELATIONS WITH    WHAT COUNTRY,4,GER
     MANY,CANADA,RUSSIA,FRANCE
484  DATA 1916,HE PURSUED PANCHO VILLA INTO MEXICO-    WITHOUT SUCCESS,4,
     PERSHING,YORK,HILL,SINCLAIR
485  DATA 1917,CONGRESS DECLARED WAR ON GERMANY-APRIL 6-1917,2,T,0,0,0
486  DATA  1920,HE ORDERED MASS ARRESTS DURING THE 'RED SCARE' PERIOD,4,P
     ALMER,SCOPES,MARSHALL,MCCARTHY
487  DATA 1920,THE 19TH AMENDMENT-WOMEN'S ....-WAS     RATIFIED THIS YEAR
     ,1,SUFFRAGE,0,0,0
488  DATA 1923,I BECAME PRESIDENT AFTER HARDING DIED,3,COOLIDGE,0,0,0
489  DATA 1925,I WAS CONVICTED FOR TEACHING EVOLUTION  IN TENNESSEE,3,SCO
     PES,0,0,0
490  DATA 1923,WHAT SWINDLE ENVOLVED OIL RESERVES LEAS-ED TO SINCLAIR BY
     SEC. FALL,1,TEAPOT DOME,0,0,0
491  DATA 1927,I MADE THE 1ST NONSTOP SOLO FLIGHT FROM NEW YORK TO PARIS,
     3,LINDBERGH,0,0,0
492  DATA 1929,WHAT CRASH GREW INTO THE 'GREAT DEPRES- SION,1,STOCK MARKE
     T,0,0,0
493  DATA 1933,ROOSEVELT ADOPTED WHAT POLICIES FOR     ECONOMIC & SOCIAL
     WELFARE,1,NEW DEAL,0,0,0
494  DATA 1933,A SEVERE DROUGHT CONVERTED THE GREAT    PLAINS INTO WHAT,1
     ,DUST BOWL,0,0,0
495  DATA 1934,THE FBI KILLED WHAT WELL KNOWN GANGSTER-IN CHICAGO,1,DILLI
     NGER,0,0,0
496  DATA 1939,SCIENTISTS-INCLUDING EINSTEIN-TOLD ROO- SEVELT THAT AN ATO
     MIC BOMB WAS POSSIBLE,2,T,0,0,0
497  DATA 1939,U.S. PLEDGED NEUTRALITY AFTER THE WAR   BEGAN IN EUROPE,2,
     T,0,0,0
498  DATA 1940,THE .... ACT MADE IT UNLAWFUL TO ADVO-  CATE THE OVERTHROW
      OF THE U.S.,4,SMITH,TRUMAN,TAFT,GUN
499  DATA 1941,JAPANESE ATTACKED .... HARBOR-ON DECEM- BER 7-1941,1,PEARL
     ,0,0,0
500  DATA 1941,ROOSEVELT AND CHURCHILL ISSUED THE .... CHARTER OF POSTWAR
      ARMS,4,ATLANTIC,PACIFIC,FREEDOM,WESTERN
501  DATA 1941,THE UNITED STATES DECLARED WAR ON WHAT  COUNTRY,1,JAPAN,0,
     0,0
502  DATA 1942,JAPANESE-AMERICANS WERE RELOCATED TO    WESTERN .... CAMPS
      IN 1942,4,DETENTION,SAFETY,SECURITY,FREEDOM
503  DATA 1944,THE .... INVADED EUROPE AND FREED FRANCE-BELGIUM-& LUXEMBO
     URG,1,ALLIES,0,0,0
504  DATA 1945,THE U.S. DROPPED ATOMIC BOMBS ON HIRO-  SHIMA AND ....,1,N
     AGASKI,0,0,0
505  DATA 1947,I PROPOSED A PLAN FOR EUROPEAN RECOVERY THIS YEAR,3,MARSHA
     LL,0,0,0
```

```
506  DATA 1948,HE ACCUSED ALGER HISS OF GIVING DOCU-   MENTS TO THE RUSSI
     ANS,4,CHAMBERS,TRUMAN,MCCARTHY,ROOSEVELT
507  DATA 1947,THE ....-HARTLY ACT LIMITED POWER OF    LABOR,4,TAFT,SMITH
     ,SHERMAN,BROWN
508  DATA 1949,THE NORTH .... TREATY ORGANIZATION WAS  APPROVED THIS YEAR
     ,4,ATLANTIC,PACIFIC,WEST,AMERICAN
509  DATA 1950,TRUMAN SENT U.S. TROOPS TO WHAT COUNTRY,4,KOREA,ISRAEL,TUR
     KEY,ITALY
510  DATA 1950,SENATOR .... CHARGED THAT THE STATE DEPT WAS INFILTRATED B
     Y COMMUNISTS,4,MCCARTHY,BROWN,MARSHALL,TAFT
511  DATA 1954,THE SUPREME COURT OUTLAWED .... SEGREGA-TION IN THE PUBLIC
       SCHOOLS,1,RACIAL,0,0,0
512  DATA 1955,THE AFL AND .... MERGED INTO ONE LABOR  ORGANIZATION,4,CIO
     ,NRA,CIA,FBI
513  DATA 1956,I REFUSED TO GIVE MY BUS SEAT TO A WHITE MAN-IN MONTGOMERY
     ,3,PARKS,0,0,0
514  DATA 1957,THE TRUMAN DOCTRINE WAS EXTENDED TO AID WHAT MIDDLE EAST C
     OUNTRY,4,JORDAN,ISRAEL,IRAN,EGYPT
515  DATA 1957,THE .... RIGHTS ACT WAS PASSED-DEALING  WITH MINORITIES,1,
     CIVIL,0,0,0
516  DATA 1959,THE STATES OF .... AND HAWII WERE ADMIT-ED TO THE UNION,1,
     ALASKA,0,0,0
517  DATA 1960,I FLEW THE U-2 SPY PLANE THAT WAS SHOT  DOWN OVER RUSSIA,3
     ,POWERS,0,0,0
518  DATA 1961,THE ANTI-CASTRO INVASION AT BAY OF PIGS WAS SUCCESSFUL,2,F
     ,0,0,0
519  DATA 1962,HE WAS THE 1ST AMERICAN TO ORBIT THE    EARTH,4,GLENN,POWE
     RS,ARMSTRONG,ALDRIN
520  DATA 1963,IN WHAT CITY WAS PRESIDENT KENNEDY      ASSASSINATED,4,DAL
     LAS,WASHINGTON,BOSTON,CHICAGO
521  DATA 1964,WHAT AMENDMENT-ABOLISHING POLL TAX-WAS  RATIFIED,4,24TH,20
     TH,31ST,29TH
522  DATA 1965,U.S. TROOP BUILD-UP IN VIETNAM CAUSED   ANTI-WAR DEMONSTRA
     TIONS,2,T,0,0,0
523  DATA 1965,RACE RIOTS ERUPTED IN THE .... SECTION  OF LOS ANGELES,4,W
     ATTS,POOR,OLD,WHITE
524  DATA 1968,REV. MARTIN LUTHER .... WAS ASSASSINATED THIS YEAR,1,KING,
     0,0,0
525  DATA 1968,SENATOR ROBERT F. .... WAS ASSASSINATED THIS YEAR,1,KENNED
     Y,0,0,0
526  DATA 1967,HE WAS THE 1ST BLACK ELECTED TO THE     SUPREME COURT,3,MA
     RSHALL,COSBY,CARVER,KING
527  DATA 1969,ARMSTRONG AND ALDRIN WERE THE 1ST TO    LAND ON THE MOON,2
     ,T,0,0,0
528  DATA 1970,U.S. AND S. VIETNAMESE TROOPS ENTERED   WHAT CITY,1,CAMBOD
     IA,0,0,0
529  DATA 1971,THE 26TH AMENDMENT ALLOWED VOTING RIGHTS TO .... YEAR OLDS
     ,4,18,20,17,16
530  DATA 1972,WHAT SCANDLE WAS 'COVERED UP' BY NIXON,1,WATERGATE,0,0,0
531  DATA 1975,THE WAR IN .... ENDED THIS YEAR,1,VIETNAM,0,0,0
532  DATA 1974,PRESIDENT NIXON RESIGNED BECAUSE OF THE .... SCANDLE,1,WAT
     ERGATE,0,0,0
533  HOME : PRINT "THE TIME DUNGEON * * * MAP"
```

```
534   PRINT
535   FOR Q = 1 TO 8
536   FOR N = 1 TO 8
537   IF C = N AND D = Q THEN  PRINT "=P= ";: GOTO 540
538 S1 = A(N,Q)
539   ON S1 GOSUB 137,137,138,138,139,140,141,139,142
540   NEXT N
541   PRINT
542   NEXT Q
543 GT =  INT ( RND (1) * 8 + 1) +  INT ( RND (1) * (CA + 5) + 1)
544   GOSUB 134: HOME : RETURN
545   PRINT : PRINT "ON THE WALL IS A GLOWING SCREEN"
546   PRINT "BELOW THE SCREEN IS A RED BUTTON": PRINT
547 KT =  INT ( RND (1) * 9 + 1):KL =  INT ( RND (1) * 15 + 1) + 2
548   GOSUB 565
549   INPUT K$
550   IF K$ = "Y" THEN 552
551   RETURN
552   IF KT >  = 6 THEN 533
553   IF KT <  = 4 THEN 562
554   PRINT :G4 =  INT ( RND (1) * 100 + 1) + 25:G = G + G4
555   PRINT "YOU RECEIVE ";G4;" GOLD PIECES . . ."
556   PRINT "BUT . . . . . . THE CORRIDOR NARROWS":GT = 3: GOSUB 134
557 KL = KL - 1: IF KL = 0 THEN  RETURN
558   GOSUB 565
559   INPUT K$
560   IF K$ = "Y" THEN 554
561   RETURN
562   PRINT : PRINT "NOTHING HAPPENS"
563 GT = 1: GOSUB 134
564   RETURN
565   PRINT : PRINT "DO YOU WISH TO PUSH THE BUTTON?"
566   PRINT "ENTER  (Y)ES  OR  (N)O": RETURN
567   HOME : PRINT "YOU ARE STUCK IN THE NARROW CORRIDOR"
568   PRINT ". . . . . . . . . . AND . . .": PRINT :GT = 3: GOSUB 134
569   GOTO 264
570   PRINT : PRINT "YOU NOTICE A DOOR TO YOUR RIGHT"
571   PRINT
572 KT =  INT ( RND (1) * 9 + 1)
573   PRINT "DO YOU WISH TO OPEN THE DOOR?"
574   PRINT "ENTER  (Y)ES  OR  (N)O"
575   INPUT K$
576   IF K$ = "Y" THEN 578
577   RETURN
578   PRINT : PRINT "YOU TRY THE DOOR . . . . .":GT = 1: GOSUB 134
579   IF KT >  = 7 THEN 589
580   IF KT <  = 4 THEN 587
581   PRINT :G4 =  INT ( RND (1) * 100 + 1) + 25
582   PRINT "THE DOOR OPENS . . . . . . ."
583   PRINT "REVEALING A CLOSET . . . ."
584   PRINT :G = G + G4
585   PRINT "WHERE YOU FIND ";G4;" GOLD PIECES"
586   PRINT : RETURN
```

```
587  PRINT "BUT THE DOOR WON'T OPEN . . . ."
588  PRINT ". . . . IT MUST BE LOCKED": RETURN
589  PRINT : PRINT "THE DOOR OPENS . . . AND SUDDENLY"
590  PRINT "THE CHAMBER BEGINS TO . . . SPIN"
591 G7 =  INT (G / 2):G4 =  INT ( RND (1) * G7 + 1):MM =  INT ( RND (1) *
    20 + 1)
592 GT = 4: GOSUB 134:G = G - G4
593  FOR K9 = 1 TO 250
594  PRINT "+     =     +";: NEXT K9
596  HOME : PRINT "YOU WERE TELEPORTED INTO . . . ."
597  PRINT ". . . . ANOTHER DIMENSION . . . ."
598  PRINT ". . AND RETURNED IN AN INSTANT . ."
599  PRINT : PRINT "BUT YOU DROPPED ";G4;" GOLD PIECES"
600  PRINT ". . . AND WASTED ";MM;" MOVES . . ."
601 M1 = M1 + MM
602 GT = 4: GOSUB 134
603  RETURN
```

```
100  HOME :BZ$ = "WORLD HISTORY-WW I":BW$ = "1894 TO 1919"
101  PRINT "THE TIME DUNGEON: ";BZ$
102  PRINT "COPYRIGHT (C) 1981 BY HOWARD BERENBON"
103  PRINT "APPLE II"
104  PRINT
105  PRINT "AN EDUCATIONAL FANTASY GAME"
106 GT = 5: GOSUB 134:Q3 = 0
107  HOME : DIM A(9,9),B(50): GOSUB 451
108  PRINT "YOU WILL BE TELEPORTED TO . . ."
109  PRINT
110  PRINT "THE TIME DUNGEON . . . ."
111  PRINT "TO STUDY ";BZ$
112  PRINT
114 CA = 0:G = 1000:M1 = 1:K = 0:KL = 1:TT = 0:TR = 0
115  PRINT "ENTER YOUR CHARACTER'S NAME?"
116  INPUT A$
117  PRINT "ENTER PRESENT YEAR"
118  INPUT Y2:YY = Y2: IF Y2 > 2000 THEN 117
119  PRINT : PRINT A$;" . . . YOU ARE ON YOUR WAY"
120 GT = 2: GOSUB 134
121  GOSUB 143
122  HOME
123  PRINT "YOU HAVE ARRIVED AT . . . ."
124  PRINT
125  PRINT "THE TIME DUNGEON: ";BZ$
126  PRINT "FOR THE YEARS:     ";BW$
127  PRINT
128  PRINT "YOU CARRY 1000 GOLD PIECES": PRINT
129  PRINT "YOU WILL ENCOUNTER . . ."
130  PRINT "TIME PORTALS WHICH TELEPORT"
131  PRINT "YOU TO EVENTS IN ";BZ$
132 GT = 8: GOSUB 134
133  GOTO 199
134  FOR ZZ = 1 TO 908 * GT
135  NEXT ZZ
136  RETURN
137  PRINT "O    ";: RETURN
138  PRINT "AP   ";: RETURN
139  PRINT "?    ";: RETURN
140  PRINT "NS   ";: RETURN
141  PRINT "EW   ";: RETURN
142  PRINT "X    ";: RETURN
143  REM  SET UP DUNGEON
144  FOR X = 1 TO 8
145  FOR Y = 1 TO 8
146 A(X,Y) =  INT ( RND (1) * 7 + 1)
147  NEXT Y
148  NEXT X
149  REM  TRAPS
150 H =  INT ( RND (1) * 3 + 1) + 1
151  FOR N = 1 TO H
152 X =  INT ( RND (1) * 8 + 1)
153 Y =  INT ( RND (1) * 8 + 1)
```

```
154 A(X,Y) = 8
155  NEXT N
156  REM  EXITS
157 S =  INT ( RND (1) * 4 + 1) + 1
158  FOR N = 1 TO S
159 X =  INT ( RND (1) * 8 + 1)
160 Y =  INT ( RND (1) * 8 + 1)
161 A(X,Y) = 9
162  NEXT N
163  RETURN
164 R6 =  INT ( RND (1) * 4 + 1): PRINT QD$;"?:": PRINT
165  ON R6 GOSUB 167,168,169,170
166  GOTO 433
167  PRINT AD$,I1$: PRINT I2$,I3$: RETURN
168  PRINT I2$,AD$: PRINT I1$,I3$: RETURN
169  PRINT I1$,I2$: PRINT AD$,I3$: RETURN
170  PRINT I3$,I1$: PRINT I2$,AD$: RETURN
171  HOME
173 GT = 1
174  GOSUB 134
175  FOR B = 1 TO 70:B4 =  INT ( RND (1) * 23 + 1)
176 B7 =  INT ( RND (1) * 39 + 1): VTAB B4: PRINT  TAB( B7)".";
177  PRINT : NEXT B: PRINT
178 GT = .005:Y5 = 25
179  IF Y3 = YY THEN  VTAB 1: PRINT "ALREADY AT . . . . ": GOTO 196
180  IF Y3 < YY THEN 188
181  IF (Y3 - YY) <  = 50 THEN 185
182 Y3 = Y3 - Y5
183  GOSUB 382
184  IF Y3 = YY THEN 195
185  IF (Y3 - YY) <  = 50 THEN Y5 = 1
186  IF (Y3 - YY) <  = 5 THEN GT = .4
187  GOTO 182
188  IF (YY - Y3) <  = 50 THEN 192
189 Y3 = Y3 + Y5
190  GOSUB 382
191  IF Y3 = YY THEN 195
192  IF (YY - Y3) <  = 50 THEN Y5 = 1
193  IF (YY - Y3) <  = 5 THEN GT = .4
194  GOTO 189
195  PRINT : PRINT "ARRIVAL . . . . AT"
196  PRINT "DESTINATION YEAR . . . . ";YY
197 GT = 4: GOSUB 134
198  HOME : RETURN
199 C =  INT ( RND (1) * 8 + 1):D =  INT ( RND (1) * 8 + 1):A(C,D) = 1
200 K4 =  INT ( RND (1) * 4 + 1) + 3
201  HOME :A = A(C,D):GT = 1: GOSUB 134
202  ON A GOSUB 292,300,410,410,306,330,335,338,362
203  IF KL = 0 THEN 567
204  PRINT : IF TT = 1 THEN TT = 0: GOTO 201
205  IF G <  = 0 THEN 264
206  PRINT A$;",  WHAT IS YOUR ACTION OR MOVE?"
207  PRINT
```

```
208  PRINT "(N)ORTH, (E)AST, (S)OUTH"
209  PRINT "(W)EST, E(X)IT, (G)OLD"
210  INPUT M1$
211 M1 = M1 + 1: IF K = 0 AND M1 > 70 THEN 371
212  IF M1$ = "N" THEN 220
213  IF M1$ = "E" THEN 225
214  IF M1$ = "S" THEN 230
215  IF M1$ = "W" THEN 235
216  IF M1$ = "X" THEN 240
217  IF M1$ = "G" THEN 251
218  PRINT
219  GOTO 204
220  REM  NORTH
221  IF A = 7 THEN 255
222  IF (D - 1) = 0 THEN 281
223 D = D - 1
224  GOTO 201
225  REM  EAST
226  IF A = 6 THEN 260
227  IF (C + 1) = 9 THEN 286
228 C = C + 1
229  GOTO 201
230  REM  SOUTH
231  IF A = 7 THEN 255
232  IF (D + 1) = 9 THEN 288
233 D = D + 1
234  GOTO 201
235  REM  WEST
236  IF A = 6 THEN 260
237  IF (C - 1) = 0 THEN 290
238 C = C - 1
239  GOTO 201
240  HOME
241  IF A < > 9 THEN 248
242  IF K = 1 THEN 387
243  PRINT "YOU CANNOT EXIT THE TIME DUNGEON"
244  PRINT "YOU DON'T HAVE THE CRYSTAL KEY"
245 GT = 2: GOSUB 134
246  PRINT
247  GOTO 204
248  PRINT "YOU ARE NOT AT AN EXIT PORTAL"
249 GT = 2: GOSUB 134
250  GOTO 204
251  REM  GOLD
252  HOME : PRINT "YOU HAVE ";G;" GOLD PIECES WITH YOU"
253  PRINT
254  GOTO 204
255  REM  EW
256  HOME : PRINT "YOU ARE IN AN EAST-WEST CORRIDOR"
257  PRINT "YOU CAN ONLY GO EAST OR WEST"
258  PRINT
259  GOTO 204
260  REM  NS
```

```
261   HOME : PRINT "YOU ARE IN A NORTH-SOUTH CORRIDOR"
262   PRINT "YOU CAN ONLY GO NORTH OR SOUTH"
263   GOTO 258
264   REM  GOLD ZERO
265 GT = 2: GOSUB 134
266   PRINT
267   PRINT "YOU LOST ALL YOUR GOLD AND YOU WERE"
268   PRINT " . . . UNABLE TO MEET THE DEMANDS OF"
269   PRINT " . . . THE TIME DUNGEON . . . . ."
270   PRINT
271   PRINT
272 T = 3: GOSUB 134
273   GOSUB 402
274   PRINT
275   PRINT "ANOTHER GAME?"
276   PRINT "ENTER '1'-YES  '0'-NO"
277   INPUT AA
278   IF AA <  > 1 THEN 280
279   HOME : GOTO 108
280   END
281   HOME : PRINT "YOU ARE AT THE NORTH WALL"
282   PRINT "YOU CANNOT PASS THROUGH"
283   PRINT
284   PRINT "TRY ANOTHER DIRECTION?"
285   GOTO 204
286   HOME : PRINT "YOU ARE AT THE EAST WALL"
287   GOTO 282
288   HOME : PRINT "YOU ARE AT THE SOUTH WALL"
289   GOTO 282
290   HOME : PRINT "YOU ARE AT THE WEST WALL"
291   GOTO 282
292 KT =  INT ( RND (1) * 9 + 1)
293   PRINT "YOU ARE IN A GLOWING TIME PORTAL"
294 GT = 1: GOSUB 134
295   PRINT
296   PRINT "THE LIGHT FADES . . . . . ."
297   PRINT "THE PORTAL IS INACTIVE . . . ."
298   IF A = 1 AND KT > 8 THEN 570
299   RETURN
300   PRINT "YOU ARE IN A DUST FILLED PORTAL"
301 GT = 1: GOSUB 134
302   PRINT
303   PRINT "A BRIGHT LIGHT IS ACTIVATED AND . ."
304   PRINT
305   GOTO 296
306   HOME
307   PRINT "AN ALIEN TRAVELER IS IN THIS CHAMBER"
308 A(C,D) =  INT ( RND (1) * 2 + 1): GOSUB 478
309 GT = 1: GOSUB 134
310 TD =  INT ( RND (1) * 10 + 1)
311 G4 =  INT ( RND (1) * 350 + 1)
312 Y =  INT ( RND (1) * 8 + 1)
313   IF Y <  = 5 THEN 320
```

```
314  PRINT : IF (G - G4) < O THEN G4 = G
315  PRINT "HE IS UNFRIENDLY . . . . AND AS HE"
316  PRINT "LEAVES . . . HE TAKES ";G4;" GOLD PIECES"
317  PRINT :G = G - G4
318  IF TD = 5 AND K = O THEN 325
319  RETURN
320  PRINT
321  PRINT "HE IS FRIENDLY . . . . . AND GIVES YOU"
322  PRINT ". . ";G4;" GOLD PIECES, WHICH YOU ACCEPT"
323  PRINT :G = G + G4
324  GOTO 318
325  PRINT :GT = 2: GOSUB 134
326  PRINT "YOU SEARCH THE CHAMBER . . . AND"
327 GT = 1: GOSUB 134
328  PRINT "FIND . . . . THE CRYSTAL KEY"
329 K = 1: RETURN
330  HOME
331  PRINT "YOU ENTER A NORTH-SOUTH CORRIDOR"
332  PRINT "THRU A SECRET DOOR": PRINT : GOSUB 380
333 KT =  INT ( RND (1) * 9 + 1): IF KT >  = 7 THEN 545
334  RETURN
335  HOME
336  PRINT "YOU ENTER AN EAST-WEST CORRIDOR"
337  GOTO 332
338  REM  TRAP
339  PRINT "YOU ENCOUNTER . . . A TIME TRAP"
340  PRINT ". . . . . . . . IN THIS CHAMBER":GT = 1: GOSUB 134
341 TD =  INT ( RND (1) * 9 + 1)
342  IF TD >  = 7 THEN 347
343  PRINT
344  PRINT "BUT YOU'RE LUCKY . . . . ."
345  PRINT ". . . IT DIDN'T ACTIVATE"
346  RETURN
347 TT = 1: PRINT "AND IT ACTIVATED . . . . .":GT = 2: GOSUB 134
348  FOR A = 1 TO 250
349  PRINT "*         %";
350  NEXT A
351 C =  INT ( RND (1) * 8 + 1):D =  INT ( RND (1) * 8 + 1)
352  PRINT
353  PRINT :G = 100
354  PRINT "YOU HAVE BEEN TELEPORTED TO . . . ."
355  PRINT ". . . . AN UNKNOWN LOCATION . . . ."
356  PRINT
357  PRINT "AND YOU LOST MOST OF YOUR GOLD"
358  PRINT
359  PRINT "YOU HAVE . . . ";G;" GOLD PIECES LEFT"
360 GT = 6: GOSUB 134
361  RETURN
362  PRINT "YOU ARE AT AN EXIT PORTAL"
363  PRINT
364  PRINT "(A KEY IS REQUIRED)"
365  PRINT
366  RETURN
```

```
367 H = 1:O = 9:W = 8
368 B = O:E = 5:R = 14
369 C = O:PR = 0
370   GOTO 216
371   PRINT :GT = 2: GOSUB 134
372   PRINT "BUT BEFORE YOU PROCEED . ."
373   PRINT "YOU LOOK TO THE GROUND AND . . . ."
374   PRINT ". . . FIND THE CRYSTAL KEY . .":K = 1
375 GT = 3: GOSUB 134
376   GOTO 212
377   PRINT "YOU ANSWERED ";CA;" QUESTION(S) CORRECTLY"
378   PRINT " . . . . . IN ";M1;" TURNS,"
379   GOTO 409
380   PRINT "THE DOOR CLOSES AND LOCKS BEHIND YOU":GT = 1: GOSUB 134
381   RETURN
382   REM  TIME DISPLAY
383   VTAB 12: PRINT "PORTAL YEAR . . . ";Y3
385   GOSUB 134
386   RETURN
387   HOME : REM  EXIT PORTAL
388   PRINT "YOU ENTER THE EXIT PORTAL AND"
389   PRINT "INSERT THE CRYSTAL KEY INTO THE SLOT"
390   PRINT :GT = 4: GOSUB 134
391   PRINT "THE MACHINE BEGINS TO HUM . . . ."
392   PRINT :GT = 2: GOSUB 134
393 YY = Y2: GOSUB 171
394   PRINT
395   PRINT "YOU FOUND YOUR WAY . . . . ."
396   PRINT ". . . . BACK TO THE PRESENT"
397   PRINT
398   PRINT "YOU HAVE ACQUIRED ";G;" GOLD PIECES"
399   PRINT
400   GOSUB 402
401   GOTO 274
402 GG = G + 100
403 R =  INT ((GG * CA - 7000 + 1) / M1)
404   PRINT
405   PRINT "GAME RATING IS ";R
406   PRINT : IF G <  = 0 OR KL = 0 THEN 377
407   PRINT "YOU TOOK ";M1;" TURNS TO FIND THE WAY OUT"
408   PRINT "AND ANSWERED ";CA;" QUESTION(S) CORRECTLY,"
409   PRINT "OUT OF ";TR;" QUESTIONS ASKED.": RETURN
410   HOME :Y3 = YY
411   GOSUB 444
412 Q3 = Q3 + 1
413   IF Q3 > 50 THEN Q3 = 0: GOTO 415
414   GOTO 416
415   GOSUB 451
416 Q =  INT ( RND (1) * 50 + 1)
417   IF B(Q) = 1 THEN 416
418 B(Q) = 1
419   PRINT
420   FOR AB = 1 TO Q
```

```
421  READ YY,QD$,ID,AD$,I1$,I2$,I3$
422  NEXT AB
423  RESTORE
424  GOSUB 171
425  HOME :TR = TR + 1
426  PRINT "YOU HAVE ARRIVED AT THE YEAR ";YY
427  PRINT ". . . . . . IN ";BZ$: PRINT
428  PRINT "YOU MUST ANSWER THIS QUESTION"
429  PRINT " . . TO CONTINUE YOUR JOURNEY"
430  PRINT "-------------------------------------------"
431  PRINT "THE YEAR IS: ";YY: PRINT : IF ID = 4 THEN 164
432  PRINT QD$
433  PRINT "-------------------------------------------"
434  PRINT "QUESTION TYPE: "
435  ON ID GOSUB 455,456,457,458
436  GOSUB 459
437  IF E$ = AD$ THEN 441
438  PRINT "INCORRECT"
439  GOSUB 471
440  RETURN
441  PRINT "CORRECT"
442  GOSUB 463
443  RETURN
444  PRINT "YOU ENTER INTO A BLUE HAZY . . ."
445  PRINT ". . . . . . . TIME PORTAL . . ."
446  PRINT :GT = 1: GOSUB 134
447  PRINT "A PULSATING GLOW . . . . . . ."
448  PRINT ". . . . INDICATES ACTIVATION": PRINT
449  PRINT "PRESENT YEAR . . .   "Y3:GT = 3: GOSUB 134
450  RETURN
451  FOR I = 1 TO 50
452 B(I) = 0
453  NEXT I
454  RETURN
455  PRINT "PEOPLE, PLACES, OR THINGS ?": RETURN
456  PRINT "*** (T)RUE OR (F)ALSE  ?": RETURN
457  PRINT "*** WHO AM I (LAST NAME) ?": RETURN
458  PRINT "*** MULTIPLE CHOICE ?": RETURN
459  PRINT "ENTER CORRECT ANSWER?"
460   INPUT E$
461 G4 =  INT ( RND (1) * 500 + 1) + 125
462  RETURN
463 G = G + G4
464  PRINT "YOU WIN ";G4;" GOLD PIECES"
465 A(C,D) =  INT ( RND (1) * 2 + 1)
466 CA = CA + 1: IF K = 1 THEN  RETURN
467  IF CA = K4 THEN 469
468  RETURN
469  GOSUB 325
470  RETURN
471  PRINT :G4 =   INT ( RND (1) * 400 + 1) + 25
472  PRINT "THE CORRECT ANSWER IS '";AD$;"'"
473  PRINT : IF (G - G4) < 0 THEN G4 = G
```

```
474 G = G - G4
475 GT = 1: GOSUB 134
476  PRINT "YOU LOSE ";G4;" GOLD PIECES"
477  RETURN
478 ZT = 5
479 X =  INT ( RND (1) * 8 + 1):Y =  INT ( RND (1) * 8 + 1)
480  IF A(X,Y) <  = 2 THEN A(X,Y) = 5: RETURN
481 ZT = ZT - 1: IF ZT = 0 THEN  RETURN
482  GOTO 479
483  DATA 1894,FRANCE AND .... FORMED A MILITARY ALLI- ANCE,4,RUSSIA,ITAL
     Y,GERMANY,SPAIN
484  DATA 1904,THE AGREEMENT BETWEEN ENGLAND & FRANCE  WAS CALLED ....,4,
     ENTENTE CORDIALE,NEW EUROPE,FREE EUROPE,AMI ICI
485  DATA 1902,GREAT BRITAIN AND .... FORMED AN ALLI- ANCE THIS YEAR,4,J
     APAN,U.S.,CANADA,GERMANY
486  DATA 1905,ENGLAND BUILT THE .... BATTLESHIP THIS  YEAR,4,DREADNOUGHT
     ,DISCOVERY,FREEDOM,BRITAIN
487  DATA 1899,THE 1ST PEACE CONFERENCE WAS HELD AT THE ....,1,HAGUE,0,0,
     0
488  DATA 1907,THE HAGUE PEACE CONFERENCES WERE NOT    EFFECTIVE,2,T,0,0,
     0
489  DATA 1905,FRANCE TRIED TO OCCUPY .... THIS YEAR,4,MOROCCO,HOLLAND,TU
     RKEY,SPAIN
490  DATA 1911,ITALY DECLARED WAR ON ....-AND SEIZED   TRIPOLI,4,TURKEY,S
     PAIN,JAPAN,RUMANIA
491  DATA 1912,THE BALKAN WARS PREPARED EUROPE FOR WW I,2,T,0,0,0
492  DATA 1914,JUNE 28-THE ARCHDUKE FRANCIS .... WAS   ASSASSINATED,1,FER
     DINAND,0,0,0
493  DATA 1914,ARCHDUKE FERDINAND WAS SHOT IN WHAT CITY,1,SARAJEVO,0,0,0
494  DATA 1914,JULY 28-AUSTRIA-HUNGARY DECLARED WAR ON ....,4,SERBIA,U.S.
     ,SPAIN,ITALY
495  DATA 1914,AUG 1-GERMANY DECLARED WAR ON ....,1,RUSSIA,0,0,0
496  DATA 1914,AUG 4-ENGLAND DECLARED WAR ON ....,1,GERMANY,0,0,0
497  DATA 1914,AUG 3-GERMANY DECLARED WAR ON ....,1,FRANCE,0,0,0
498  DATA 1914,THE CENTRAL POWERS WERE STRONGER THAN   THE ALLIES,2,F,0,0
     ,0
499  DATA 1914,SEPT 6-THE 1ST BATTLE OF THE ....        RIVER,4,MARNE,SEIN
     E,TEMPS,HAGUE
500  DATA 1914,GERMANS TRY TO CAPTURE PARIS-BUT FAIL,2,T,0,0,0
501  DATA  1914,AUG-RUSSIANS LOST THE BATTLE OF ....,4,TANNENBERG,SEINE,H
     INDENBURG,AUSTR
502  DATA 1914,I COMMANDED THE GERMANS AT THE BATTLE OF TANNENBERG,3,HIND
     ENBURG,0,0,0
503  DATA 1915,ALLIES HOPED TO TIGHTEN THE ....-TO     LIMIT SUPPLIES TO
     THE ENEMY,1,BLOCKADE,0,0,0
504  DATA 1915,SPRING-GERMANS LAUNCHED A HEAVY OFFEN-  SIVE ON THE EASTER
     N FRONT,2,T,0,0,0
505  DATA 1915,THE BRITISH CAMPAIGN IN THE MIDDLE EAST WAS A SUCCESS,2,F,
     0,0,0
506  DATA 1916,RUSSIAN FORCES HIT AUSTRIA-& TOOK ABOUT 300000 PRISONERS,2
     ,T,0,0,0
507  DATA 1916,MOST OF RUMANIA WAS OCCUPIED BY THE     CENTRAL POWERS,2,T
     ,0,0,0
```

```
508  DATA 1915,GERMANS DECLARED THE SEAS AROUND THE      BRITISH ISLES A .
     ...,4,WAR ZONE,HAZARD,NEUTRAL ZONE,BOMB ZONE
509  DATA 1915,MAY-BRITISH LINER .... WAS TORPEDOED BY THE GERMANS,4,LUSI
     TANIA,CONCORD,BRITAIN,ALLENBY
510  DATA 1916,DEC 12-GERMANY CONTACTED THE ALLIES TO  SUGGEST PEACE TALK
     S,2,T,0,0,0
511  DATA 1918,NOV 3-AUSTRIA ASKED FOR AN ARMISTICE,2,T,0,0,0
512  DATA 1916,DEC 30-ALLIES AGREE TO MAKE PEACE WITH  GERMANY,2,F,0,0,0
513  DATA 1917,APRIL 6-U.S. DECLARED WAR ON ....,1,GERMANY,0,0,0
514  DATA 1916,MY SLOGAN WAS 'HE KEPT US OUT OF WAR',3,WILSON,0,0,0
515  DATA 1917,JAN 19-GERMANY BEGINS .... WARFARE-UN-  RESTRICTED,4,SUBMA
     RINE,LAND,AIR,ALL OUT
516  DATA 1917,I COMMANDED THE AMERICAN EXPEDITIONARY  FORCE,3,PERSHING,0
     ,0,0
517  DATA 1917,BRITISH GENERAL .... WON THE HOLY LAND,4,ALLENBY,THOMAS,SM
     YTH,ROGERS
518  DATA 1918,WILSON'S '14 POINTS' OUTLINED A LASTING PEACE,2,T,0,0,0
519  DATA 1918,THE AMERICAN 2ND DIVISION STOPPED THE   GERMANS AT ....-FR
     ANCE,4,CHATEAUTHIERRY,HAGUE,NICE,CANNES
520  DATA 1918,JULY-2ND BATTLE OF THE MARNE PUSHED BACK THE GERMANS,2,T,0
     ,0,0
521  DATA 1918,OCT-THE .... LINE WAS BROKEN IN MANY    PLACES,4,HINDENBUR
     G,EASTERN,FRONT,WESTERN
522  DATA 1918,OCT-GENERAL ALLENBY CONQUERED ....,4,TURKEY,IRAN,JORDAN,EG
     YPT
523  DATA 1919,JAN 18-THE .... PEACE CONFERENCE OPENED THIS DAY,4,PARIS,L
     ONDON,NEW YORK,HAGUE
524  DATA 1919,THE PARIS CONFERENCE PRODUCED FIVE PEACE ....,1,TREATIES,0
     ,0,0
525  DATA 1919,THE TREATY OF .... WAS SIGNED BETWEEN   GERMANY & THE ALLI
     ES,1,VERSAILLES,0,0,0
526  DATA 1919,TREATY OF VERSAILLES WAS SIGNED IN THE   ....,1,HALL OF MIR
     RORS,0,0,0
527  DATA 1918,NOV-KAISER WILLIAM II WAS FORCED TO ....,1,ABDICATE,0,0,0
528  DATA 1918,NOV 11-GERMANS SIGNED AN ARMISTICE IN A RAILROAD CAR,2,T,0
     ,0,0
529  DATA 1918,TOTAL COST OF THE WAR WAS ABOUT 300      BILLION DOLLARS,2,
     T,0,0,0
530  DATA 1919,ALL OF WILSON'S 14 POINTS WERE ACCEPTED,2,F,0,0,0
531  DATA 1919,CLEMINCEAU OF FRANCE WANTED TO KEEP      GERMANY ....,4,WEA
     K,UNDIVIDED,DIVIDED,STRONG
532  DATA 1919,WILSONS'S POINT 14 GAVE RISE TO THE      'LEAGUE OF NATIONS
     ',2,T,0,0,0
533  HOME : PRINT "THE TIME DUNGEON * * * MAP"
534  PRINT
535  FOR Q = 1 TO 8
536  FOR N = 1 TO 8
537  IF C = N AND D = Q THEN  PRINT "=P= ";: GOTO 540
538 S1 = A(N,Q)
539  ON S1 GOSUB 137,137,138,138,139,140,141,139,142
540  NEXT N
541  PRINT
542  NEXT Q
```

```
543 GT =  INT ( RND (1) * 8 + 1) +  INT ( RND (1) * (CA + 5) + 1)
544  GOSUB 134: HOME : RETURN
545  PRINT : PRINT "ON THE WALL IS A GLOWING SCREEN"
546  PRINT "BELOW THE SCREEN IS A RED BUTTON": PRINT
547 KT =  INT ( RND (1) * 9 + 1):KL =  INT ( RND (1) * 15 + 1) + 2
548  GOSUB 565
549  INPUT K$
550  IF K$ = "Y" THEN 552
551  RETURN
552  IF KT >  = 6 THEN 533
553  IF KT <  = 4 THEN 562
554  PRINT :G4 =  INT ( RND (1) * 100 + 1) + 25:G = G + G4
555  PRINT "YOU RECEIVE ";G4;" GOLD PIECES . . ."
556  PRINT "BUT . . . . . . THE CORRIDOR NARROWS":GT = 3: GOSUB 134
557 KL = KL - 1: IF KL = 0 THEN  RETURN
558  GOSUB 565
559  INPUT K$
560  IF K$ = "Y" THEN 554
561  RETURN
562  PRINT : PRINT "NOTHING HAPPENS"
563 GT = 1: GOSUB 134
564  RETURN
565  PRINT : PRINT "DO YOU WISH TO PUSH THE BUTTON?"
566  PRINT "ENTER  (Y)ES  OR  (N)O": RETURN
567  HOME : PRINT "YOU ARE STUCK IN THE NARROW CORRIDOR"
568  PRINT ". . . . . . . . . . AND . . .": PRINT :GT = 3: GOSUB 134
569  GOTO 264
570  PRINT : PRINT "YOU NOTICE A DOOR TO YOUR RIGHT"
571  PRINT
572 KT =  INT ( RND (1) * 9 + 1)
573  PRINT "DO YOU WISH TO OPEN THE DOOR?"
574  PRINT "ENTER  (Y)ES  OR  (N)O"
575  INPUT K$
576  IF K$ = "Y" THEN 578
577  RETURN
578  PRINT : PRINT "YOU TRY THE DOOR . . . . .":GT = 1: GOSUB 134
579  IF KT >  = 7 THEN 589
580  IF KT <  = 4 THEN 587
581  PRINT :G4 =  INT ( RND (1) * 100 + 1) + 25
582  PRINT "THE DOOR OPENS . . . . . . ."
583  PRINT "REVEALING A CLOSET . . . ."
584  PRINT :G = G + G4
585  PRINT "WHERE YOU FIND ";G4;" GOLD PIECES"
586  PRINT : RETURN
587  PRINT "BUT THE DOOR WON'T OPEN . . . ."
588  PRINT ". . . . IT MUST BE LOCKED": RETURN
589  PRINT : PRINT "THE DOOR OPENS . . . AND SUDDENLY"
590  PRINT "THE CHAMBER BEGINS TO . . . SPIN"
591 G7 =  INT (G / 2):G4 =  INT ( RND (1) * G7 + 1):MM =  INT ( RND (1) *
     20 + 1)
592 GT = 4: GOSUB 134:G = G - G4
593  FOR K9 = 1 TO 250
594  PRINT "+     =     +";: NEXT K9
```

```
596   HOME : PRINT "YOU WERE TELEPORTED INTO . . . ."
597   PRINT ". . . . ANOTHER DIMENSION . . . ."
598   PRINT ". . AND RETURNED IN AN INSTANT . ."
599   PRINT : PRINT "BUT YOU DROPPED ";G4;" GOLD PIECES"
600   PRINT ". . . AND WASTED ";MM;" MOVES . . ."
601 M1 = M1 + MM
602 GT = 4: GOSUB 134
603   RETURN
```

```
100   HOME :BZ$ = "WORLD HISTORY-WW II":BW$ = "1933 TO 1945"
101   PRINT "THE TIME DUNGEON: ";BZ$
102   PRINT "COPYRIGHT (C) 1981 BY HOWARD BERENBON"
103   PRINT "APPLE II"
104   PRINT
105   PRINT "AN EDUCATIONAL FANTASY GAME"
106 GT = 5: GOSUB 134:Q3 = 0
107   HOME : DIM A(9,9),B(50): GOSUB 451
108   PRINT "YOU WILL BE TELEPORTED TO . . ."
109   PRINT
110   PRINT "THE TIME DUNGEON . . . ."
111   PRINT "TO STUDY ";BZ$
112   PRINT
114 CA = 0:G = 1000:M1 = 1:K = 0:KL = 1:TT = 0:TR = 0
115   PRINT "ENTER YOUR CHARACTER'S NAME?"
116   INPUT A$
117   PRINT "ENTER PRESENT YEAR"
118   INPUT Y2:YY = Y2: IF Y2 > 2000 THEN 117
119   PRINT : PRINT A$;" . . . YOU ARE ON YOUR WAY"
120 GT = 2: GOSUB 134
121   GOSUB 143
122   HOME
123   PRINT "YOU HAVE ARRIVED AT . . . ."
124   PRINT
125   PRINT "THE TIME DUNGEON: ";BZ$
126   PRINT "FOR THE YEARS:     ";BW$
127   PRINT
128   PRINT "YOU CARRY 1000 GOLD PIECES": PRINT
129   PRINT "YOU WILL ENCOUNTER . . ."
130   PRINT "TIME PORTALS WHICH TELEPORT"
131   PRINT "YOU TO EVENTS IN ";BZ$
132 GT = 8: GOSUB 134
133   GOTO 199
134   FOR ZZ = 1 TO 908 * GT
135   NEXT ZZ
136   RETURN
137   PRINT "O    ";: RETURN
138   PRINT "AP   ";: RETURN
139   PRINT "?    ";: RETURN
140   PRINT "NS   ";: RETURN
141   PRINT "EW   ";: RETURN
142   PRINT "X    ";: RETURN
143   REM   SET UP DUNGEON
144   FOR X = 1 TO 8
145   FOR Y = 1 TO 8
146 A(X,Y) =  INT ( RND (1) * 7 + 1)
147   NEXT Y
148   NEXT X
149   REM   TRAPS
150 H =  INT ( RND (1) * 3 + 1) + 1
151   FOR N = 1 TO H
152 X =  INT ( RND (1) * 8 + 1)
153 Y =  INT ( RND (1) * 8 + 1)
```

```
154 A(X,Y) = 8
155  NEXT N
156  REM  EXITS
157 S =  INT ( RND (1) * 4 + 1) + 1
158  FOR N = 1 TO S
159 X =  INT ( RND (1) * 8 + 1)
160 Y =  INT ( RND (1) * 8 + 1)
161 A(X,Y) = 9
162  NEXT N
163  RETURN
164 R6 =  INT ( RND (1) * 4 + 1): PRINT QD$;"?:": PRINT
165  ON R6 GOSUB 167,168,169,170
166  GOTO 433
167  PRINT AD$,I1$: PRINT I2$,I3$: RETURN
168  PRINT I2$,AD$: PRINT I1$,I3$: RETURN
169  PRINT I1$,I2$: PRINT AD$,I3$: RETURN
170  PRINT I3$,I1$: PRINT I2$,AD$: RETURN
171  HOME
173 GT = 1
174  GOSUB 134
175  FOR B = 1 TO 70:B4 =  INT ( RND (1) * 23 + 1)
176 B7 =  INT ( RND (1) * 39 + 1): VTAB B4: PRINT  TAB( B7)".";
177  PRINT : NEXT B: PRINT
178 GT = .005:Y5 = 25
179  IF Y3 = YY THEN  VTAB 1: PRINT "ALREADY AT . . . . ": GOTO 196
180  IF Y3 < YY THEN 188
181  IF (Y3 - YY) <  = 50 THEN 185
182 Y3 = Y3 - Y5
183  GOSUB 382
184  IF Y3 = YY THEN 195
185  IF (Y3 - YY) <  = 50 THEN Y5 = 1
186  IF (Y3 - YY) <  = 5 THEN GT = .4
187  GOTO 182
188  IF (YY - Y3) <  = 50 THEN 192
189 Y3 = Y3 + Y5
190  GOSUB 382
191  IF Y3 = YY THEN 195
192  IF (YY - Y3) <  = 50 THEN Y5 = 1
193  IF (YY - Y3) <  = 5 THEN GT = .4
194  GOTO 189
195  PRINT : PRINT "ARRIVAL . . . . AT"
196  PRINT "DESTINATION YEAR . . . . ";YY
197 GT = 4: GOSUB 134
198  HOME : RETURN
199 C =  INT ( RND (1) * 8 + 1):D =  INT ( RND (1) * 8 + 1):A(C,D) = 1
200 K4 =  INT ( RND (1) * 4 + 1) + 3
201  HOME :A = A(C,D):GT = 1: GOSUB 134
202  ON A GOSUB 292,300,410,410,306,330,335,338,362
203  IF KL = 0 THEN 567
204  PRINT : IF TT = 1 THEN TT = 0: GOTO 201
205  IF G <  = 0 THEN 264
206  PRINT A$;",  WHAT IS YOUR ACTION OR MOVE?"
207  PRINT
```

```
208   PRINT "(N)ORTH, (E)AST, (S)OUTH"
209   PRINT "(W)EST, E(X)IT, (G)OLD"
210   INPUT M1$
211 M1 = M1 + 1: IF K = 0 AND M1 > 70 THEN 371
212   IF M1$ = "N" THEN 220
213   IF M1$ = "E" THEN 225
214   IF M1$ = "S" THEN 230
215   IF M1$ = "W" THEN 235
216   IF M1$ = "X" THEN 240
217   IF M1$ = "G" THEN 251
218   PRINT
219   GOTO 204
220   REM  NORTH
221   IF A = 7 THEN 255
222   IF (D - 1) = 0 THEN 281
223 D = D - 1
224   GOTO 201
225   REM  EAST
226   IF A = 6 THEN 260
227   IF (C + 1) = 9 THEN 286
228 C = C + 1
229   GOTO 201
230   REM  SOUTH
231   IF A = 7 THEN 255
232   IF (D + 1) = 9 THEN 288
233 D = D + 1
234   GOTO 201
235   REM  WEST
236   IF A = 6 THEN 260
237   IF (C - 1) = 0 THEN 290
238 C = C - 1
239   GOTO 201
240   HOME
241   IF A < > 9 THEN 248
242   IF K = 1 THEN 387
243   PRINT "YOU CANNOT EXIT THE TIME DUNGEON"
244   PRINT "YOU DON'T HAVE THE CRYSTAL KEY"
245 GT = 2: GOSUB 134
246   PRINT
247   GOTO 204
248   PRINT "YOU ARE NOT AT AN EXIT PORTAL"
249 GT = 2: GOSUB 134
250   GOTO 204
251   REM  GOLD
252   HOME : PRINT "YOU HAVE ";G;" GOLD PIECES WITH YOU"
253   PRINT
254   GOTO 204
255   REM  EW
256   HOME : PRINT "YOU ARE IN AN EAST-WEST CORRIDOR"
257   PRINT "YOU CAN ONLY GO EAST OR WEST"
258   PRINT
259   GOTO 204
260   REM  NS
```

```
261   HOME : PRINT "YOU ARE IN A NORTH-SOUTH CORRIDOR"
262   PRINT "YOU CAN ONLY GO NORTH OR SOUTH"
263   GOTO 258
264   REM  GOLD ZERO
265 GT = 2: GOSUB 134
266   PRINT
267   PRINT "YOU LOST ALL YOUR GOLD AND YOU WERE"
268   PRINT " . . . UNABLE TO MEET THE DEMANDS OF"
269   PRINT " . . . THE TIME DUNGEON . . . . ."
270   PRINT
271   PRINT
272 T = 3: GOSUB 134
273   GOSUB 402
274   PRINT
275   PRINT "ANOTHER GAME?"
276   PRINT "ENTER '1'-YES  '0'-NO"
277   INPUT AA
278   IF AA <  > 1 THEN 280
279   HOME : GOTO 108
280   END
281   HOME : PRINT "YOU ARE AT THE NORTH WALL"
282   PRINT "YOU CANNOT PASS THROUGH"
283   PRINT
284   PRINT "TRY ANOTHER DIRECTION?"
285   GOTO 204
286   HOME : PRINT "YOU ARE AT THE EAST WALL"
287   GOTO 282
288   HOME : PRINT "YOU ARE AT THE SOUTH WALL"
289   GOTO 282
290   HOME : PRINT "YOU ARE AT THE WEST WALL"
291   GOTO 282
292 KT =  INT ( RND (1) * 9 + 1)
293   PRINT "YOU ARE IN A GLOWING TIME PORTAL"
294 GT = 1: GOSUB 134
295   PRINT
296   PRINT "THE LIGHT FADES . . . . . ."
297   PRINT "THE PORTAL IS INACTIVE . . . ."
298   IF A = 1 AND KT > 8 THEN 570
299   RETURN
300   PRINT "YOU ARE IN A DUST FILLED PORTAL"
301 GT = 1: GOSUB 134
302   PRINT
303   PRINT "A BRIGHT LIGHT IS ACTIVATED AND . ."
304   PRINT
305   GOTO 296
306   HOME
307   PRINT "AN ALIEN TRAVELER IS IN THIS CHAMBER"
308 A(C,D) =  INT ( RND (1) * 2 + 1): GOSUB 478
309 GT = 1: GOSUB 134
310 TD =  INT ( RND (1) * 10 + 1)
311 G4 =  INT ( RND (1) * 350 + 1)
312 Y =  INT ( RND (1) * 8 + 1)
313   IF Y <  = 5 THEN 320
```

```
314  PRINT : IF (G - G4) < 0 THEN G4 = G
315  PRINT "HE IS UNFRIENDLY . . . . AND AS HE"
316  PRINT "LEAVES . . . HE TAKES ";G4;" GOLD PIECES"
317  PRINT :G = G - G4
318  IF TD = 5 AND K = 0 THEN 325
319  RETURN
320  PRINT
321  PRINT "HE IS FRIENDLY . . . . . AND GIVES YOU"
322  PRINT ". . ";G4;" GOLD PIECES, WHICH YOU ACCEPT"
323  PRINT :G = G + G4
324  GOTO 318
325  PRINT :GT = 2: GOSUB 134
326  PRINT "YOU SEARCH THE CHAMBER . . . AND"
327 GT = 1: GOSUB 134
328  PRINT "FIND . . . . THE CRYSTAL KEY"
329 K = 1: RETURN
330  HOME
331  PRINT "YOU ENTER A NORTH-SOUTH CORRIDOR"
332  PRINT "THRU A SECRET DOOR": PRINT : GOSUB 380
333 KT =  INT ( RND (1) * 9 + 1): IF KT > = 7 THEN 545
334  RETURN
335  HOME
336  PRINT "YOU ENTER AN EAST-WEST CORRIDOR"
337  GOTO 332
338  REM  TRAP
339  PRINT "YOU ENCOUNTER . . . A TIME TRAP"
340  PRINT ". . . . . . . . IN THIS CHAMBER":GT = 1: GOSUB 134
341 TD =  INT ( RND (1) * 9 + 1)
342  IF TD > = 7 THEN 347
343  PRINT
344  PRINT "BUT YOU'RE LUCKY . . . . ."
345  PRINT ". . . IT DIDN'T ACTIVATE"
346  RETURN
347 TT = 1: PRINT "AND IT ACTIVATED . . . . .":GT = 2: GOSUB 134
348  FOR A = 1 TO 250
349  PRINT "*          %";
350  NEXT A
351 C =  INT ( RND (1) * 8 + 1):D =  INT ( RND (1) * 8 + 1)
352  PRINT
353  PRINT :G = 100
354  PRINT "YOU HAVE BEEN TELEPORTED TO . . . ."
355  PRINT ". . . . AN UNKNOWN LOCATION . . . ."
356  PRINT
357  PRINT "AND YOU LOST MOST OF YOUR GOLD"
358  PRINT
359  PRINT "YOU HAVE . . . ";G;" GOLD PIECES LEFT"
360 GT = 6: GOSUB 134
361  RETURN
362  PRINT "YOU ARE AT AN EXIT PORTAL"
363  PRINT
364  PRINT "(A KEY IS REQUIRED)"
365  PRINT
366  RETURN
```

```
367 H = 1:O = 9:W = 8
368 B = 0:E = 5:R = 14
369 C = 0:PR = 0
370  GOTO 216
371  PRINT :GT = 2: GOSUB 134
372  PRINT "BUT BEFORE YOU PROCEED . ."
373  PRINT "YOU LOOK TO THE GROUND AND . . ."
374  PRINT ". . . FIND THE CRYSTAL KEY . .":K = 1
375 GT = 3: GOSUB 134
376  GOTO 212
377  PRINT "YOU ANSWERED ";CA;" QUESTION(S) CORRECTLY"
378  PRINT " . . . . . IN ";M1;" TURNS,"
379  GOTO 409
380  PRINT "THE DOOR CLOSES AND LOCKS BEHIND YOU":GT = 1: GOSUB 134
381  RETURN
382  REM  TIME DISPLAY
383  VTAB 12: PRINT "PORTAL YEAR . . . ";Y3
385  GOSUB 134
386  RETURN
387  HOME : REM  EXIT PORTAL
388  PRINT "YOU ENTER THE EXIT PORTAL AND"
389  PRINT "INSERT THE CRYSTAL KEY INTO THE SLOT"
390  PRINT :GT = 4: GOSUB 134
391  PRINT "THE MACHINE BEGINS TO HUM . . . ."
392  PRINT :GT = 2: GOSUB 134
393 YY = Y2: GOSUB 171
394  PRINT
395  PRINT "YOU FOUND YOUR WAY . . . . ."
396  PRINT ". . . . BACK TO THE PRESENT"
397  PRINT
398  PRINT "YOU HAVE ACQUIRED ";G;" GOLD PIECES"
399  PRINT
400  GOSUB 402
401  GOTO 274
402 GG = G + 100
403 R =  INT ((GG * CA - 7000 + 1) / M1)
404  PRINT
405  PRINT "GAME RATING IS ";R
406  PRINT : IF G <  = 0 OR KL = 0 THEN 377
407  PRINT "YOU TOOK ";M1;" TURNS TO FIND THE WAY OUT"
408  PRINT "AND ANSWERED ";CA;" QUESTION(S) CORRECTLY,"
409  PRINT "OUT OF ";TR;" QUESTIONS ASKED.": RETURN
410  HOME :Y3 = YY
411  GOSUB 444
412 Q3 = Q3 + 1
413  IF Q3 > 50 THEN Q3 = 0: GOTO 415
414  GOTO 416
415  GOSUB 451
416 Q =  INT ( RND (1) * 50 + 1)
417  IF B(Q) = 1 THEN 416
418 B(Q) = 1
419  PRINT
420  FOR AB = 1 TO Q
```

```
421  READ YY,QD$,ID,AD$,I1$,I2$,I3$
422  NEXT AB
423  RESTORE
424  GOSUB 171
425  HOME :TR = TR + 1
426  PRINT "YOU HAVE ARRIVED AT THE YEAR ";YY
427  PRINT ". . . . . . IN ";BZ$: PRINT
428  PRINT "YOU MUST ANSWER THIS QUESTION"
429  PRINT " . . TO CONTINUE YOUR JOURNEY"
430  PRINT "------------------------------------------"
431  PRINT "THE YEAR IS: ";YY: PRINT : IF ID = 4 THEN 164
432  PRINT QD$
433  PRINT "------------------------------------------"
434  PRINT "QUESTION TYPE: "
435  ON ID GOSUB 455,456,457,458
436  GOSUB 459
437  IF E$ = AD$ THEN 441
438  PRINT "INCORRECT"
439  GOSUB 471
440  RETURN
441  PRINT "CORRECT"
442  GOSUB 463
443  RETURN
444  PRINT "YOU ENTER INTO A BLUE HAZY . . ."
445  PRINT ". . . . . . . TIME PORTAL . . ."
446  PRINT :GT = 1: GOSUB 134
447  PRINT "A PULSATING GLOW . . . . . . ."
448  PRINT ". . . . INDICATES ACTIVATION": PRINT
449  PRINT "PRESENT YEAR . . .   "Y3:GT = 3: GOSUB 134
450  RETURN
451  FOR I = 1 TO 50
452 B(I) = 0
453  NEXT I
454  RETURN
455  PRINT "PEOPLE, PLACES, OR THINGS ?": RETURN
456  PRINT "*** (T)RUE OR (F)ALSE  ?": RETURN
457  PRINT "*** WHO AM I (LAST NAME) ?": RETURN
458  PRINT "*** MULTIPLE CHOICE ?": RETURN
459  PRINT "ENTER CORRECT ANSWER?"
460  INPUT E$
461 G4 =  INT ( RND (1) * 500 + 1) + 125
462  RETURN
463 G = G + G4
464  PRINT "YOU WIN ";G4;" GOLD PIECES"
465 A(C,D) =  INT ( RND (1) * 2 + 1)
466 CA = CA + 1: IF K = 1 THEN  RETURN
467  IF CA = K4 THEN 469
468  RETURN
469  GOSUB 325
470  RETURN
471  PRINT :G4 =  INT ( RND (1) * 400 + 1) + 25
472  PRINT "THE CORRECT ANSWER IS '";AD$;"'"
473  PRINT : IF (G - G4) < 0 THEN G4 = G
```

```
474 G = G - G4
475 GT = 1: GOSUB 134
476  PRINT "YOU LOSE ";G4;" GOLD PIECES"
477  RETURN
478 ZT = 5
479 X =  INT ( RND (1) * 8 + 1):Y =  INT ( RND (1) * 8 + 1)
480  IF A(X,Y) <  = 2 THEN A(X,Y) = 5: RETURN
481 ZT = ZT - 1: IF ZT = O THEN  RETURN
482  GOTO 479
483  DATA 1945,FROM 1939 TO 1945 NAZIS MURDERED 6       MILLION JEWS,2,T,O
     ,0,0
484  DATA 1933,HITLER AND HIS .... BECAME GERMANY'S     GOVERNMENT,4,NAZIS
     ,NATIONALS,DEMOCRATICS,COMMUNISTS
485  DATA 1933,HITLER BLAMED THE .... FOR MOST OF       GERMANY'S ILLS,4,J
     EWS,ENGLISH,CATHOLICS,PROTESTANTS
486  DATA 1935,THE .... LAWS DEPRIVED THE JEWS OF       CITIZENSHIP,1,NURE
     MBERG,0,0,0
487  DATA 1934,HITLER'S SECRET POLICE WAS CALLED THE    ....,4,GESTAPO,CIA
     ,KBG,SPO
488  DATA 1936,THE SPANISH .... WAR BEGINS,4,CIVIL,COLD,GERMAN,RUSSIAN
489  DATA 1938,HITLER'S TROOPS RODE INTO .... AUSTRIA   THIS YEAR,1,VIENNA
     ,0,0,0
490  DATA 1938,GERMANS WORKED ON FORTIFICATIONS CALLED THE .... LINE,4,SI
     EGFRIED,MGINOT,FRONT,WESTERN
491  DATA 1939,AUG 23-RUSSIA SIGNED A .... PACT WITH    GERMANY,1,NONAGGRE
     SSION,0,0,0
492  DATA 1939,SEPT 1-GERMAN FORCES INVADED ....,4,POLAND,FRANCE,RUSSIA,E
     NGLAND
493  DATA 1939,SEPT 3-GREAT BRITAIN AND .... DECLARED   WAR ON GERMANY,1,F
     RANCE,0,0,0
494  DATA 1939,GERMAN'S OCCUPYING POLAND KILLED 3       MILLION .... BY 19
     45,4,JEWS,COMMUNISTS,SOCIALISTS,TURKS
495  DATA 1945,THE NUREMBERG .... TRIED NAZIS LEADERS   FOR  WAR CRIMES,1,
     TRIALS,0,0,0
496  DATA 1940,MARCH-.... LOST SOME OF HER BEST LAND    TO RUSSIA,4,FINLAN
     D,HOLLAND,FRANCE,ITALY
497  DATA 1939,DEC-BRITISH SHIPS TRAPPED THE GERMAN     SHIP .... IN MONTE
     VIDEO HARBOR,4,GRAF SPEE,NUREMBERG,SIEGFRIED,LUFTWAFFE
498  DATA 1940,APRIL 9-THE NAZIS INVADED .... & NORWAY,1,DENMARK,0,0,0
499  DATA 1940,APRIL-I WAS A NAZIS SYMPATHIZER IN       NORWAY,3,QUISLING,
     0,0,0
500  DATA 1940,MAY-HITLER BEGAN THE INVASION OF THE     NETHERLANDS- LUXEM
     BERG- & ....,4,BELGIUM,NORWAY,DENMARK,FRANCE
501  DATA 1940,BY MAY 10-GERMANS BROKE THRU THE ....    -AT SEDAN,1,MAGINO
     T LINE,0,0,0
502  DATA 1940,JUNE-GERMAN TROOPS OCCUPIED ....,4,FRANCE,ENGLAND,EGYPT,RU
     SSIA
503  DATA 1940,JUNE 18-BATTLE OF .... BEGAN AFTER THE   FALL OF FRANCE,4,B
     RITAIN,FREEDOM,FRANCE,GERMANY
504  DATA 1941,HITLER LOST THE BATTLE OF BRITAIN,2,T,0,0,0
505  DATA 1940,THE GERMAN .... (AIR FORCE) GREATLY HURT BRITAIN,1,LUFTWAF
     FE,0,0,0
506  DATA 1940,OCT-ITALIAN TROOPS INVADED ....,1,GREECE,0,0,0
```

```
507  DATA 1941,JUNE 22-HITLER ATTACKED THE SOVIET UNION,2,T,0,0,0
508  DATA 1941,BY 1941-HITLER CONTROLLED THE .... AND  WESTERN EUROPE,1,B
     ALKANS,0,0,0
509  DATA 1941,DEC 7-THE JAPANESE ATTACKED .... HARBOR,1,PEARL,0,0,0
510  DATA 1941,NOV-CONGRESS REPEALED THE .... ACT,1,NEUTRALITY,0,0,0
511  DATA 1942,JAN 1-THE .... NATIONS WAS CREATED DUR- ING WW II,1,UNITED
     ,0,0,0
512  DATA 1942,JUNE-AMERICANS HELD OFF THE JAPANESE AT .... ISLAND,1,MIDW
     AY,0,0,0
513  DATA 1942,GERMANS FAILED TO TAKE ....-IN RUSSIA,1,STALINGRAD,0,0,0
514  DATA 1943,JAN-ROOSEVELT & CHURCHHILL MET IN ....  -MOROCCO,1,CASABLA
     NCA,0,0,0
515  DATA 1943,I WAS CALLED THE DESERT FOX (GERMAN),3,ROMMEL,0,0,0
516  DATA 1943,EARLY IN 1943-AMERICANS BEGAN AN OFFEN- SIVE IN THE ....,1
     ,ALEUTIANS,0,0,0
517  DATA 1944,JUNE 4-GENERAL CLARK'S AMERICAN TROOPS  MARCHED INTO ....,
     4,ROME,FLORENCE,VENICE,NAPLES
518  DATA 1944,GERMANS V-1 ROCKET WAS KNOWN IN BRITAIN AS THE ....,4,BUZZ
      BOMB,FLY BOMB,ROCKET BOMB,DEATH BOMB
519  DATA 1944,SEPT-ALLIES FREED BELGIUM-LUXEMBURG- &  MOST OF ....,1,FRA
     NCE,0,0,0
520  DATA 1944,SEPT 12-THE BATTLE OF .... BEGAN,4,GERMANY,FRANCE,OKINAWA,
     EGYPT
521  DATA 1945,MAY 7-GERMANS SIGNED A SURRENDER AGREE- MENT IN ....-CITY,
     4,REIMS,LONDON,PARIS,NICE
522  DATA 1944,JUNE 6-'D-DAY' WAS THE ALLIED INVASION  OF ....,4,FRANCE,G
     ERMANY,ITALY,SPAIN
523  DATA 1945,THE JAPANESE USED .... OR SUICIDE PLANES,1,KAMIKAZE,0,0,0
524  DATA 1945,JUNE-AMERICANS WON THE JAPANESE ISLAND  OF ....,4,OKINAWA,
     KAMIKAZE,NAGASAKI,HIROSHIMA
525  DATA 1945,JULY-ALLIES ISSUED THE .... DECLARATION,4,POTSDAM,FREEDOM,
     FINAL,LAST
526  DATA 1945,AUG 6-AN ATOMIC BOMB WAS DROPPED ON ....-CITY,1,HIROSHIMA,
     0,0,0
527  DATA 1945,AUG 9-AN ATOMIC BOMB WAS DROPPED ON ....-CITY,1,NAGASAKI,0
     ,0,0
528  DATA 1945,AUG 14-JAPAN SURRENDERED AFTER THE       ATOMIC DEVASTATION
     ,2,T,0,0,0
529  DATA 1945,SEPT 2-JAPAN FORMALLY SURRENDERED ON THE AMERICAN SHIP ...
     .,4,MISSOURI,MIDWAY,ENTERPRISE,OHIO
530  DATA 1944,THE INVASION OF FRANCE TOOK PLACE       BETWEEN CHERBOURG
     & ....,4,LE HARVE,NICE,CANNES,PARIS
531  DATA 1945,GENOCIDE OF THE JEWS-IN NAZIS CONCENTRA-TION CAMPS-WAS REV
     EALED,2,T,0,0,0
532  DATA 1944,DEC 16-GERMANS COUNTER OFFENSIVE WAS THE 'BATTLE OF THE ..
     ..',4,BULGE,BOLD,RHINE,SWINE
533  HOME : PRINT "THE TIME DUNGEON * * * MAP"
534  PRINT
535  FOR Q = 1 TO 8
536  FOR N = 1 TO 8
537  IF C = N AND D = Q THEN  PRINT "=P= ";: GOTO 540
538 S1 = A(N,Q)
539  ON S1 GOSUB 137,137,138,138,139,140,141,139,142
```

```
540   NEXT N
541   PRINT
542   NEXT Q
543 GT =  INT ( RND (1) * 8 + 1) +  INT ( RND (1) * (CA + 5) + 1)
544   GOSUB 134: HOME : RETURN
545   PRINT : PRINT "ON THE WALL IS A GLOWING SCREEN"
546   PRINT "BELOW THE SCREEN IS A RED BUTTON": PRINT
547 KT =  INT ( RND (1) * 9 + 1):KL =  INT ( RND (1) * 15 + 1) + 2
548   GOSUB 565
549   INPUT K$
550   IF K$ = "Y" THEN 552
551   RETURN
552   IF KT >  = 6 THEN 533
553   IF KT <  = 4 THEN 562
554   PRINT :G4 =  INT ( RND (1) * 100 + 1) + 25:G = G + G4
555   PRINT "YOU RECEIVE ";G4;" GOLD PIECES . . ."
556   PRINT "BUT . . . . . . THE CORRIDOR NARROWS":GT = 3: GOSUB 134
557 KL = KL - 1: IF KL = 0 THEN  RETURN
558   GOSUB 565
559   INPUT K$
560   IF K$ = "Y" THEN 554
561   RETURN
562   PRINT : PRINT "NOTHING HAPPENS"
563 GT = 1: GOSUB 134
564   RETURN
565   PRINT : PRINT "DO YOU WISH TO PUSH THE BUTTON?"
566   PRINT "ENTER  (Y)ES  OR  (N)O": RETURN
567   HOME : PRINT "YOU ARE STUCK IN THE NARROW CORRIDOR"
568   PRINT ". . . . . . . . . . AND . . .": PRINT :GT = 3: GOSUB 134
569   GOTO 264
570   PRINT : PRINT "YOU NOTICE A DOOR TO YOUR RIGHT"
571   PRINT
572 KT =  INT ( RND (1) * 9 + 1)
573   PRINT "DO YOU WISH TO OPEN THE DOOR?"
574   PRINT "ENTER  (Y)ES  OR  (N)O"
575   INPUT K$
576   IF K$ = "Y" THEN 578
577   RETURN
578   PRINT : PRINT "YOU TRY THE DOOR . . . . .":GT = 1: GOSUB 134
579   IF KT >  = 7 THEN 589
580   IF KT <  = 4 THEN 587
581   PRINT :G4 =  INT ( RND (1) * 100 + 1) + 25
582   PRINT "THE DOOR OPENS . . . . . . ."
583   PRINT "REVEALING A CLOSET . . . ."
584   PRINT :G = G + G4
585   PRINT "WHERE YOU FIND ";G4;" GOLD PIECES"
586   PRINT : RETURN
587   PRINT "BUT THE DOOR WON'T OPEN . . . ."
588   PRINT ". . . . IT MUST BE LOCKED": RETURN
589   PRINT : PRINT "THE DOOR OPENS . . . AND SUDDENLY"
590   PRINT "THE CHAMBER BEGINS TO . . . SPIN"
591 G7 =  INT (G / 2):G4 =  INT ( RND (1) * G7 + 1):MM =  INT ( RND (1) *
    20 + 1)
```

```
592 GT = 4: GOSUB 134:G = G - G4
593  FOR K9 = 1 TO 250
594  PRINT "+     =     +";: NEXT K9
596  HOME : PRINT "YOU WERE TELEPORTED INTO . . . ."
597  PRINT ". . . . ANOTHER DIMENSION . . . ."
598  PRINT ". . AND RETURNED IN AN INSTANT . ."
599  PRINT : PRINT "BUT YOU DROPPED ";G4;" GOLD PIECES"
600  PRINT ". . . AND WASTED ";MM;" MOVES . . ."
601 M1 = M1 + MM
602 GT = 4: GOSUB 134
603  RETURN
```

```
100   HOME :BZ$ = "ANCIENT HISTORY-MID EAST":BW$ = "4000 BC TO 6 BC"
101   PRINT "THE TIME DUNGEON:": PRINT BZ$
102   PRINT "COPYRIGHT (C) 1981 BY HOWARD BERENBON"
103   PRINT "APPLE II"
104   PRINT
105   PRINT "AN EDUCATIONAL FANTASY GAME"
106 GT = 5: GOSUB 134:Q3 = 0
107   HOME : DIM A(9,9),B(50): GOSUB 451
108   PRINT "YOU WILL BE TELEPORTED TO . . ."
109   PRINT
110   PRINT "THE TIME DUNGEON . . . ."
111   PRINT "TO STUDY ";BZ$
112   PRINT
114 CA = 0:G = 1000:M1 = 1:K = 0:KL = 1:TT = 0:TR = 0
115   PRINT "ENTER YOUR CHARACTER'S NAME?"
116   INPUT A$
117   PRINT "ENTER PRESENT YEAR"
118   INPUT Y2:YY = Y2: IF Y2 > 2000 THEN 117
119   PRINT : PRINT A$;" . . . YOU ARE ON YOUR WAY"
120 GT = 2: GOSUB 134
121   GOSUB 143
122   HOME
123   PRINT "YOU HAVE ARRIVED AT . . . ."
124   PRINT
125   PRINT "THE TIME DUNGEON: ";BZ$
126   PRINT "FOR THE YEARS:     ";BW$
127   PRINT
128   PRINT "YOU CARRY 1000 GOLD PIECES": PRINT
129   PRINT "YOU WILL ENCOUNTER . . ."
130   PRINT "TIME PORTALS WHICH TELEPORT YOU TO"
131   PRINT "EVENTS IN ";BZ$
132 GT = 8: GOSUB 134
133   GOTO 199
134   FOR ZZ = 1 TO 908 * GT
135   NEXT ZZ
136   RETURN
137   PRINT "O    ";: RETURN
138   PRINT "AP   ";: RETURN
139   PRINT "?    ";: RETURN
140   PRINT "NS   ";: RETURN
141   PRINT "EW   ";: RETURN
142   PRINT "X    ";: RETURN
143   REM   SET UP DUNGEON
144   FOR X = 1 TO 8
145   FOR Y = 1 TO 8
146 A(X,Y) =   INT ( RND (1) * 7 + 1)
147   NEXT Y
148   NEXT X
149   REM   TRAPS
150 H =   INT ( RND (1) * 3 + 1) + 1
151   FOR N = 1 TO H
152 X =   INT ( RND (1) * 8 + 1)
153 Y =   INT ( RND (1) * 8 + 1)
```

```
154 A(X,Y) = 8
155  NEXT N
156  REM  EXITS
157 S =  INT ( RND (1) * 4 + 1) + 1
158  FOR N = 1 TO S
159 X =  INT ( RND (1) * 8 + 1)
160 Y =  INT ( RND (1) * 8 + 1)
161 A(X,Y) = 9
162  NEXT N
163  RETURN
164 R6 =  INT ( RND (1) * 4 + 1): PRINT QD$;"?:": PRINT
165  ON R6 GOSUB 167,168,169,170
166  GOTO 433
167  PRINT AD$,I1$: PRINT I2$,I3$: RETURN
168  PRINT I2$,AD$: PRINT I1$,I3$: RETURN
169  PRINT I1$,I2$: PRINT AD$,I3$: RETURN
170  PRINT I3$,I1$: PRINT I2$,AD$: RETURN
171  HOME
173 GT = 1
174  GOSUB 134
175  FOR B = 1 TO 70:B4 =  INT ( RND (1) * 23 + 1)
176 B7 =  INT ( RND (1) * 39 + 1): VTAB B4: PRINT  TAB( B7)".";
177  PRINT : NEXT B: PRINT
178 GT = .005:Y5 = 25
179  IF Y3 = YY THEN  VTAB 1: PRINT "ALREADY AT . . . . ": GOTO 196
180  IF Y3 < YY THEN 188
181  IF (Y3 - YY) <  = 50 THEN 185
182 Y3 = Y3 - Y5
183  GOSUB 382
184  IF Y3 = YY THEN 195
185  IF (Y3 - YY) <  = 50 THEN Y5 = 1
186  IF (Y3 - YY) <  = 5 THEN GT = .4
187  GOTO 182
188  IF (YY - Y3) <  = 50 THEN 192
189 Y3 = Y3 + Y5
190  GOSUB 382
191  IF Y3 = YY THEN 195
192  IF (YY - Y3) <  = 50 THEN Y5 = 1
193  IF (YY - Y3) <  = 5 THEN GT = .4
194  GOTO 189
195  PRINT : PRINT "ARRIVAL . . . . AT"
196  PRINT "DESTINATION YEAR . . . . ";YY
197 GT = 4: GOSUB 134
198  HOME : RETURN
199 C =  INT ( RND (1) * 8 + 1):D =  INT ( RND (1) * 8 + 1):A(C,D) = 1
200 K4 =  INT ( RND (1) * 4 + 1) + 3
201  HOME :A = A(C,D):GT = 1: GOSUB 134
202  ON A GOSUB 292,300,410,410,306,330,335,338,362
203  IF KL = 0 THEN 567
204  PRINT : IF TT = 1 THEN TT = 0: GOTO 201
205  IF G <  = 0 THEN 264
206  PRINT A$;",  WHAT IS YOUR ACTION OR MOVE?"
207  PRINT
```

```
208  PRINT "(N)ORTH, (E)AST, (S)OUTH"
209  PRINT "(W)EST, E(X)IT, (G)OLD"
210  INPUT M1$
211 M1 = M1 + 1: IF K = 0 AND M1 > 70 THEN 371
212  IF M1$ = "N" THEN 220
213  IF M1$ = "E" THEN 225
214  IF M1$ = "S" THEN 230
215  IF M1$ = "W" THEN 235
216  IF M1$ = "X" THEN 240
217  IF M1$ = "G" THEN 251
218  PRINT
219  GOTO 204
220  REM  NORTH
221  IF A = 7 THEN 255
222  IF (D - 1) = 0 THEN 281
223 D = D - 1
224  GOTO 201
225  REM  EAST
226  IF A = 6 THEN 260
227  IF (C + 1) = 9 THEN 286
228 C = C + 1
229  GOTO 201
230  REM  SOUTH
231  IF A = 7 THEN 255
232  IF (D + 1) = 9 THEN 288
233 D = D + 1
234  GOTO 201
235  REM  WEST
236  IF A = 6 THEN 260
237  IF (C - 1) = 0 THEN 290
238 C = C - 1
239  GOTO 201
240  HOME
241  IF A < > 9 THEN 248
242  IF K = 1 THEN 387
243  PRINT "YOU CANNOT EXIT THE TIME DUNGEON"
244  PRINT "YOU DON'T HAVE THE CRYSTAL KEY"
245 GT = 2: GOSUB 134
246  PRINT
247  GOTO 204
248  PRINT "YOU ARE NOT AT AN EXIT PORTAL"
249 GT = 2: GOSUB 134
250  GOTO 204
251  REM  GOLD
252  HOME : PRINT "YOU HAVE ";G;" GOLD PIECES WITH YOU"
253  PRINT
254  GOTO 204
255  REM  EW
256  HOME : PRINT "YOU ARE IN AN EAST-WEST CORRIDOR"
257  PRINT "YOU CAN ONLY GO EAST OR WEST"
258  PRINT
259  GOTO 204
260  REM  NS
```

```
261  HOME : PRINT "YOU ARE IN A NORTH-SOUTH CORRIDOR"
262  PRINT "YOU CAN ONLY GO NORTH OR SOUTH"
263  GOTO 258
264  REM  GOLD ZERO
265 GT = 2: GOSUB 134
266  PRINT
267  PRINT "YOU LOST ALL YOUR GOLD AND YOU WERE"
268  PRINT " . . . UNABLE TO MEET THE DEMANDS OF"
269  PRINT " . . . THE TIME DUNGEON . . . . ."
270  PRINT
271  PRINT
272 T = 3: GOSUB 134
273  GOSUB 402
274  PRINT
275  PRINT "ANOTHER GAME?"
276  PRINT "ENTER '1'-YES  '0'-NO"
277  INPUT AA
278  IF AA <  > 1 THEN 280
279  HOME : GOTO 108
280  END
281  HOME : PRINT "YOU ARE AT THE NORTH WALL"
282  PRINT "YOU CANNOT PASS THROUGH"
283  PRINT
284  PRINT "TRY ANOTHER DIRECTION?"
285  GOTO 204
286  HOME : PRINT "YOU ARE AT THE EAST WALL"
287  GOTO 282
288  HOME : PRINT "YOU ARE AT THE SOUTH WALL"
289  GOTO 282
290  HOME : PRINT "YOU ARE AT THE WEST WALL"
291  GOTO 282
292 KT =  INT ( RND (1) * 9 + 1)
293  PRINT "YOU ARE IN A GLOWING TIME PORTAL"
294 GT = 1: GOSUB 134
295  PRINT
296  PRINT "THE LIGHT FADES . . . . . ."
297  PRINT "THE PORTAL IS INACTIVE . . . ."
298  IF A = 1 AND KT > 8 THEN 570
299  RETURN
300  PRINT "YOU ARE IN A DUST FILLED PORTAL"
301 GT = 1: GOSUB 134
302  PRINT
303  PRINT "A BRIGHT LIGHT IS ACTIVATED AND . ."
304  PRINT
305  GOTO 296
306  HOME
307  PRINT "AN ALIEN TRAVELER IS IN THIS CHAMBER"
308 A(C,D) =  INT ( RND (1) * 2 + 1): GOSUB 478
309 GT = 1: GOSUB 134
310 TD =  INT ( RND (1) * 10 + 1)
311 G4 =  INT ( RND (1) * 350 + 1)
312 Y =  INT ( RND (1) * 8 + 1)
313  IF Y <  = 5 THEN 320
```

```
314   PRINT : IF (G - G4) < 0 THEN G4 = G
315   PRINT "HE IS UNFRIENDLY . . . . AND AS HE"
316   PRINT "LEAVES . . . HE TAKES ";G4;" GOLD PIECES"
317   PRINT :G = G - G4
318   IF TD = 5 AND K = 0 THEN 325
319   RETURN
320   PRINT
321   PRINT "HE IS FRIENDLY . . . . . AND GIVES YOU"
322   PRINT ". . ";G4;" GOLD PIECES, WHICH YOU ACCEPT"
323   PRINT :G = G + G4
324   GOTO 318
325   PRINT :GT = 2: GOSUB 134
326   PRINT "YOU SEARCH THE CHAMBER . . . AND"
327 GT = 1: GOSUB 134
328   PRINT "FIND . . . . THE CRYSTAL KEY"
329 K = 1: RETURN
330   HOME
331   PRINT "YOU ENTER A NORTH-SOUTH CORRIDOR"
332   PRINT "THRU A SECRET DOOR": PRINT : GOSUB 380
333 KT =  INT ( RND (1) * 9 + 1): IF KT >  = 7 THEN 545
334   RETURN
335   HOME
336   PRINT "YOU ENTER AN EAST-WEST CORRIDOR"
337   GOTO 332
338   REM  TRAP
339   PRINT "YOU ENCOUNTER . . . A TIME TRAP"
340   PRINT ". . . . . . . . IN THIS CHAMBER":GT = 1: GOSUB 134
341 TD =  INT ( RND (1) * 9 + 1)
342   IF TD >  = 7 THEN 347
343   PRINT
344   PRINT "BUT YOU'RE LUCKY . . . . ."
345   PRINT ". . . IT DIDN'T ACTIVATE"
346   RETURN
347 TT = 1: PRINT "AND IT ACTIVATED . . . . .":GT = 2: GOSUB 134
348   FOR A = 1 TO 250
349   PRINT "*         %";
350   NEXT A
351 C =  INT ( RND (1) * 8 + 1):D =  INT ( RND (1) * 8 + 1)
352   PRINT
353   PRINT :G = 100
354   PRINT "YOU HAVE BEEN TELEPORTED TO . . . ."
355   PRINT ". . . . AN UNKNOWN LOCATION . . . ."
356   PRINT
357   PRINT "AND YOU LOST MOST OF YOUR GOLD"
358   PRINT
359   PRINT "YOU HAVE . . . ";G;" GOLD PIECES LEFT"
360 GT = 6: GOSUB 134
361   RETURN
362   PRINT "YOU ARE AT AN EXIT PORTAL"
363   PRINT
364   PRINT "(A KEY IS REQUIRED)"
365   PRINT
366   RETURN
```

```
367 H = 1:O = 9:W = 8
368 B = 0:E = 5:R = 14
369 C = 0:PR = 0
370  GOTO 216
371  PRINT :GT = 2: GOSUB 134
372  PRINT "BUT BEFORE YOU PROCEED . ."
373  PRINT "YOU LOOK TO THE GROUND AND . . . ."
374  PRINT ". . . FIND THE CRYSTAL KEY . .":K = 1
375 GT = 3: GOSUB 134
376  GOTO 212
377  PRINT "YOU ANSWERED ";CA;" QUESTION(S) CORRECTLY"
378  PRINT " . . . . . IN ";M1;" TURNS,"
379  GOTO 409
380  PRINT "THE DOOR CLOSES AND LOCKS BEHIND YOU":GT = 1: GOSUB 134
381  RETURN
382  REM  TIME DISPLAY
383  VTAB 12: PRINT "PORTAL YEAR . . . ";Y3;" "
385  GOSUB 134
386  RETURN
387  HOME : REM  EXIT PORTAL
388  PRINT "YOU ENTER THE EXIT PORTAL AND"
389  PRINT "INSERT THE CRYSTAL KEY INTO THE SLOT"
390  PRINT :GT = 4: GOSUB 134
391  PRINT "THE MACHINE BEGINS TO HUM . . . ."
392  PRINT :GT = 2: GOSUB 134
393 YY = Y2: GOSUB 171
394  PRINT
395  PRINT "YOU FOUND YOUR WAY . . . . ."
396  PRINT ". . . . BACK TO THE PRESENT"
397  PRINT
398  PRINT "YOU HAVE ACQUIRED ";G;" GOLD PIECES"
399  PRINT
400  GOSUB 402
401  GOTO 274
402 GG = G + 100
403 R =  INT ((GG * CA - 7000 + 1) / M1)
404  PRINT
405  PRINT "GAME RATING IS ";R
406  PRINT : IF G <  = 0 OR KL = 0 THEN 377
407  PRINT "YOU TOOK ";M1;" TURNS TO FIND THE WAY OUT"
408  PRINT "AND ANSWERED ";CA;" QUESTION(S) CORRECTLY,"
409  PRINT "OUT OF ";TR;" QUESTIONS ASKED.": RETURN
410  HOME :Y3 = YY
411  GOSUB 444
412 Q3 = Q3 + 1
413  IF Q3 > 50 THEN Q3 = 0: GOTO 415
414  GOTO 416 .
415  GOSUB 451
416 Q =  INT ( RND (1) * 50 + 1)
417  IF B(Q) = 1 THEN 416
418 B(Q) = 1
419  PRINT
420  FOR AB = 1 TO Q
```

```
421  READ YY,QD$,ID,AD$,I1$,I2$,I3$
422  NEXT AB
423  RESTORE
424  GOSUB 171
425  HOME :TR = TR + 1
426  PRINT "YOU HAVE ARRIVED AT THE YEAR ";YY
427  PRINT ". . . . . . IN ";BZ$: PRINT
428  PRINT "YOU MUST ANSWER THIS QUESTION"
429  PRINT " . . TO CONTINUE YOUR JOURNEY"
430  PRINT "----------------------------------------"
431  PRINT "THE YEAR IS: ";YY: PRINT : IF ID = 4 THEN 164
432  PRINT QD$
433  PRINT "----------------------------------------"
434  PRINT "QUESTION TYPE: "
435  ON ID GOSUB 455,456,457,458
436  GOSUB 459
437  IF E$ = AD$ THEN 441
438  PRINT "INCORRECT"
439  GOSUB 471
440  RETURN
441  PRINT "CORRECT"
442  GOSUB 463
443  RETURN
444  PRINT "YOU ENTER INTO A BLUE HAZY . . ."
445  PRINT ". . . . . . . TIME PORTAL . . ."
446  PRINT :GT = 1: GOSUB 134
447  PRINT "A PULSATING GLOW . . . . . . ."
448  PRINT ". . . . INDICATES ACTIVATION": PRINT
449  PRINT "PRESENT YEAR . . .  "Y3:GT = 3: GOSUB 134
450  RETURN
451  FOR I = 1 TO 50
452 B(I) = 0
453  NEXT I
454  RETURN
455  PRINT "PEOPLE, PLACES, OR THINGS ?": RETURN
456  PRINT "*** (T)RUE OR (F)ALSE  ?": RETURN
457  PRINT "*** WHO AM I (LAST NAME) ?": RETURN
458  PRINT "*** MULTIPLE CHOICE ?": RETURN
459  PRINT "ENTER CORRECT ANSWER?"
460  INPUT E$
461 G4 =  INT ( RND (1) * 500 + 1) + 125
462  RETURN
463 G = G + G4
464  PRINT "YOU WIN ";G4;" GOLD PIECES"
465 A(C,D) =  INT ( RND (1) * 2 + 1)
466 CA = CA + 1: IF K = 1 THEN  RETURN
467  IF CA = K4 THEN 469
468  RETURN
469  GOSUB 325
470  RETURN
471  PRINT :G4 =  INT ( RND (1) * 400 + 1) + 25
472  PRINT "THE CORRECT ANSWER IS '";AD$;"'"
473  PRINT : IF (G - G4) < 0 THEN G4 = G
```

```
474 G = G - G4
475 GT = 1: GOSUB 134
476  PRINT "YOU LOSE ";G4;" GOLD PIECES"
477  RETURN
478 ZT = 5
479 X =  INT ( RND (1) * 8 + 1):Y =  INT ( RND (1) * 8 + 1)
480  IF A(X,Y) < = 2 THEN A(X,Y) = 5: RETURN
481 ZT = ZT - 1: IF ZT = O THEN  RETURN
482  GOTO 479
483  DATA -4000,THE SIGHT OF BABYLON WAS SETTLED BY THE SUMERIANS,2,T,0,0
    ,0
484  DATA -3700,1ST USE OF WRITING WAS IN ....-A        SUMERIAN CITY,4,U
    RUK,ERECH,KISH,AGADE
485  DATA -3500,THE .... SETTLED ALONG THE EUPHRATES,1,SUMERIANS,0,0,0
486  DATA -3000,.... WAS THE LEADING SUMERIAN CITY      UNDER KING ETANA,
    4,KISH,URUK,ERECH,AGADE
487  DATA -2800,MESKIAGGASHER FOUNDED DYNASTY IN ....- CITY,4,ERECH,URUK
    ,GIZEH,SUMER
488  DATA -2686,BEGINNING OF THE .... KINGDOM OF EGYPT,4,OLD,2ND,MIDDLE,N
    EW
489  DATA -2600,THE GREAT .... FOR PHARAOH KHUFU WAS     COMPLETED,4,PYRAM
    ID,BATHS,FOUNTAIN,FORTRESS
490  DATA -2600,GREAT PYRAMID FOR PHARAOH KHUFU WAS      BUILT AT GIZEH,2,
    T,0,0,0
491  DATA -2650,.... REIGNED AS KING OF ERECH-SUMERIAN,1,GILGAMESH,0,0,0
492  DATA -2325,.... THE GREAT RULED OVER MESOPOTAMIA,4,SARGON,URUK,ETANA
    , KISH
493  DATA -2200,GUTIANS CONQUERED SUMERIA AND DESTROYED ....,4,AGADE,GIZE
    H,URUK,KISH
494  DATA -2133,BEGINNING OF THE .... KINGDOM OF EGYPT,4,MIDDLE,2ND,OLD,N
    EW
495  DATA -2100,UR-NAMMAU FOUNDED THE LAST SUMERIAN      DYNASTY,2,T,0,0,0

496  DATA -3200,UPPER AND .... EGYPT UNITED BY PHARAOH   MENES,4,LOWER,NEW
    ,MIDDLE,OLD
497  DATA -3200,.... WAS THE 1ST PHARAOH-BUILT MEMPHIS,4,MENES,SARGON,PIL
    SER,ABRAHAM
498  DATA -2000,THE .... DESTROYED UR IN MESOPOTAMIA,4,ELAMITES,HITTITES,
    HEBREWS,EGYPTIANS
499  DATA -2000,I WAS THE FOUNDER OF JUDAISM,3,ABRAHAM,0,0,0
500  DATA -2000,THE .... LIVED AS NOMADIC SHEPHERDS IN   CANAAN,4,HEBREWS,
    TURKS,EGYPTIANS,SUMERIANS
501  DATA -1786,EGYPT RULED BY .... KINGS,4,HYKSOS,HEBREW,ELAMITE,HITTITE

502  DATA -1750,HAMMURABI RULED BABYLONIA-HAD CODE OF    LAWS,2,T,0,0,0
503  DATA -1600,BABYLONIAN DYNASTY DESTROYED BY THE ....,4,HITTITES,HEBRE
    WS,SUMERIANS,EGYPTIANS
504  DATA -1567,BEGINNING OF THE .... KINGDOM IN EGYPT,4,NEW,OLD,MIDDLE,U
    PPER
505  DATA -1468,EGYPTIANS CONQUERED SYRIA-BATTLE OF ....,1,MEGIDDO,0,0,0
506  DATA -1250,I LED THE HEBREWS OUT OF BONDAGE IN      EGYPT,3,MOSES,0,0
    ,0
```

```
507  DATA -1250,PHOENICIANS ESTABLISHED THE CITY STATES OF TYRE & ....,4,
     SIDON,URUK,BABYLON,CANAAN
508  DATA -1250,THE HEBREWS ENTERED ....,4,CANAAN,EGYPT,BABYLON,URUK
509  DATA -1020,.... BECAME KING OF THE HEBREWS,4,SAUL,MOSES,ABRAHAM,DAVI
     D
510  DATA -910,BEGINNING OF THE .... EMPIRE,4,ASSYRIAN,EGYPTIAN,TURKISH,H
     EBREW
511  DATA -747,TIGLATH-.... III RULED ASSYRIA,1,PILSER,0,0,0
512  DATA -705,SENNACHERIB OF ASSYRIA DESTROYED ....,4,BABYLON,EGYPT,PERS
     IA,SUMERIA
513  DATA -705,SENNACHERIB OF ASSYRIA BUILT A PALACE AT ....,1,NINEVEH,0,
     0,0
514  DATA -705,SARGON II OF ASSYRIA COMPLETED CONQUEST OF ....,4,ISRAEL,E
     GYPT,TURKEY,BABYLON
515  DATA -625,BEGINNING OF THE .... EMPIRE OF MESOPO- TAMIA,1,CHALDEAN,0
     ,0,0
516  DATA -606,BATTLE OF .... ENDED THE ASSYRIAN EMPIRE,1,CARCHEMISH,0,0,
     0
517  DATA -605,BEGINS THE REIGN OF KING ....-II OF       BABYLONIA,4,NEBUCH
     ADNEZZAR,SARGON,HAMMURABI,PILSER
518  DATA -550,BEGINNING OF THE PERSIAN EMPIRE,2,T,0,0,0
519  DATA -550,PERSIAN EMPIRE FOUNDED BY .... THE GREAT,4,CYRUS,HAMMURABI
     ,PILSER,DARIUS
520  DATA -538,CYRUS THE GREAT CONQUERED ....,4,BABYLON,EGYPT,TURKEY,ISRA
     EL
521  DATA -538,PERSIANS CONQUERED BABYLON & RETURNED   HEBREWS TO ....,1,
     JERUSALEM,0,0,0
522  DATA -525,PERSIANS CONQUERED AND RULED ....,4,EGYPT,IRAN,JORDAN,SYRI
     A
523  DATA -490,1ST PERSIAN EXPEDITION TO GREECE UNDER   DARIUS I,2,T,0,0,0

524  DATA -480,2ND PERSIAN EXPEDITION TO GREECE UNDER   ....-I,1,XERXES,0,
     0,0
525  DATA -334,.... THE GREAT FOUNDED THE CITY          ALEXANDRIA,1,ALEXA
     NDER,0,0,0
526  DATA -300,ALEXANDRIA ....-BECAME AN INTELLECTUAL   CENTER,4,EGYPT,ISR
     AEL,TURKEY,PERSIA
527  DATA -250,THE .... EMPIRE SUCCEEDED THE PERSIAN    EMPIRE,1,PARTHIAN,
     0,0,0
528  DATA -280,.....-II BUILT A LIGHTHOUSE ON PHAROS-   ALEXANDRIA,1,PTOLE
     MY,0,0,0
529  DATA -192,BEGINS .... WAR BETWEEN ROME AND         SELEUCIDS,4,SYRIAN
     ,MACCABEES,SELEUCID,PERSIAN
530  DATA -167,HEBREW .... REVOLTED AGAINST ANTIOCHUS- IV OF SYRIA,1,MACC
     ABEES,0,0,0
531  DATA -48,AIDED BY CAESAR-I BECAME THE QUEEN OF    EGYPT,3,CLEOPATRA,0
     ,0,0
532  DATA -6,.... CHRIST WAS BORN IN BETHLEHEM,1,JESUS,0,0,0
533  HOME : PRINT "THE TIME DUNGEON * * * MAP"
534  PRINT
535  FOR Q = 1 TO 8
536  FOR N = 1 TO 8
537  IF C = N AND D = Q THEN  PRINT "=P= ";: GOTO 540
```

```
538 S1 = A(N,Q)
539  ON S1 GOSUB 137,137,138,138,139,140,141,139,142
540  NEXT N
541  PRINT
542  NEXT Q
543 GT =  INT ( RND (1) * 8 + 1) +  INT ( RND (1) * (CA + 5) + 1)
544  GOSUB 134: HOME : RETURN
545  PRINT : PRINT "ON THE WALL IS A GLOWING SCREEN"
546  PRINT "BELOW THE SCREEN IS A RED BUTTON": PRINT
547 KT =  INT ( RND (1) * 9 + 1):KL =  INT ( RND (1) * 15 + 1) + 2
548  GOSUB 565
549  INPUT K$
550  IF K$ = "Y" THEN 552
551  RETURN
552  IF KT >  = 6 THEN 533
553  IF KT <  = 4 THEN 562
554  PRINT :G4 =  INT ( RND (1) * 100 + 1) + 25:G = G + G4
555  PRINT "YOU RECEIVE ";G4;" GOLD PIECES . . ."
556  PRINT "BUT . . . . . . THE CORRIDOR NARROWS":GT = 3: GOSUB 134
557 KL = KL - 1: IF KL = 0 THEN  RETURN
558  GOSUB 565
559  INPUT K$
560  IF K$ = "Y" THEN 554
561  RETURN
562  PRINT : PRINT "NOTHING HAPPENS"
563 GT = 1: GOSUB 134
564  RETURN
565  PRINT : PRINT "DO YOU WISH TO PUSH THE BUTTON?"
566  PRINT "ENTER  (Y)ES  OR  (N)O": RETURN
567  HOME : PRINT "YOU ARE STUCK IN THE NARROW CORRIDOR"
568  PRINT ". . . . . . . . . AND . . .": PRINT :GT = 3: GOSUB 134
569  GOTO 264
570  PRINT : PRINT "YOU NOTICE A DOOR TO YOUR RIGHT"
571  PRINT
572 KT =  INT ( RND (1) * 9 + 1)
573  PRINT "DO YOU WISH TO OPEN THE DOOR?"
574  PRINT "ENTER  (Y)ES  OR  (N)O"
575  INPUT K$
576  IF K$ = "Y" THEN 578
577  RETURN
578  PRINT : PRINT "YOU TRY THE DOOR . . . . .":GT = 1: GOSUB 134
579  IF KT >  = 7 THEN 589
580  IF KT <  = 4 THEN 587
581  PRINT :G4 =  INT ( RND (1) * 100 + 1) + 25
582  PRINT "THE DOOR OPENS . . . . . . ."
583  PRINT "REVEALING A CLOSET . . . ."
584  PRINT :G = G + G4
585  PRINT "WHERE YOU FIND ";G4;" GOLD PIECES"
586  PRINT : RETURN
587  PRINT "BUT THE DOOR WON'T OPEN . . . ."
588  PRINT ". . . . IT MUST BE LOCKED": RETURN
589  PRINT : PRINT "THE DOOR OPENS . . . AND SUDDENLY"
590  PRINT "THE CHAMBER BEGINS TO . . . SPIN"
```

```
591 G7 =  INT (G / 2):G4 =  INT ( RND (1) * G7 + 1):MM =  INT ( RND (1) *
    20 + 1)
592 GT = 4: GOSUB 134:G = G - G4
593  FOR K9 = 1 TO 250
594  PRINT "+     =     +";: NEXT K9
596  HOME : PRINT "YOU WERE TELEPORTED INTO . . . ."
597  PRINT ". . . . ANOTHER DIMENSION . . . ."
598  PRINT ". . AND RETURNED IN AN INSTANT . ."
599  PRINT : PRINT "BUT YOU DROPPED ";G4;" GOLD PIECES"
600  PRINT ". . . AND WASTED ";MM;" MOVES . . ."
601 M1 = M1 + MM
602 GT = 4: GOSUB 134
603  RETURN
```

The Algebra Dungeon

The Algebra Dungeon is an educational fantasy game where the player must solve algebraic equations as he or she wanders through the chambers and corridors of the dungeon. It's a two-level dungeon, based on the fantasy role playing game Dungeons and Dragons.* It's written in BASIC for your microcomputer. See Program 2-1 for the program listing.

THE PROGRAM

You are given 1000 gold pieces and are then teleported to a random location in the lower level of this 128-chamber, two-level dungeon (64 chambers per level). Your goal is to find your way out, with as much gold as possible. Gold pieces are acquired by solving algebraic equations given by monsters that occupy the dungeon. Each time an equation is solved correctly, a random amount of gold is given as a reward. If your answer is incorrect, then a random amount of gold is taken away. The level of math is beginning algebra. See Fig. 2-1 for a sample run.

The Algebra Problems

The problems are generated randomly using program lines 3240 through 3480 and 4360 through 4470. A random number generator subroutine at line 3840 is used to generate the X, Y, P, and Q components of the problems. The following equations are used to generate random problems. In all cases, X must be solved for:

$$Y = PX \qquad Y = PX - Q \qquad Y = PX + Q$$
$$X = PY \qquad X = PY - Q \qquad X = PY + Q$$

---

* Dungeons and Dragons is a registered trademark of TSR Hobbies, Inc.

In any case where division is required to solve for X, the division will result in an integer.

In the lower level of the dungeon, level two, the problems are generally less difficult than those at level one. The maximum value generated for X, Y, P, and Q is 50 for level one, and 25 for level two. The values in the random-number generator subroutine may be changed for different difficulty levels.

ACTIONS OR MOVES

In your trip into the dungeon, you will encounter algebra monsters, thieves, empty chambers, trap doors, secret doors leading to north-south or east-west corridors, maps, and enchanted keys.

Enter the letter in parentheses for the following actions or moves in the dungeon:

    (N)ORTH movement   (up)
    (E)AST movement   (right)
    (S)OUTH movement   (down)
    (W)EST movement   (left)
    (U)P movement   (when at a stairway, and
                           have the enchanted key)
    (M)AP display   (if found—when encounter-
                           ing thieves)
    (G)OLD pieces left

North Movement

Entering an N allows you to move north through the dungeon. You may not move north under the following conditions:

1. If you reach the North Wall, you cannot pass through it.
2. If you enter an east-west corridor (through a secret door), movement north is not allowed.

```
YOU WILL BE TELEPORTED TO . . .

THE ALGEBRA DUNGEON

ENTER YOUR CHARACTER'S NAME?
? ERIC THE BOLD

YOU CARRY 1000 GOLD PIECES WITH YOU

ERIC THE BOLD . . . YOU ARE ON YOUR WAY


YOU HAVE ARRIVED AT . . . .

THE ALGEBRA DUNGEON . . . LEVEL 2

YOU WILL ENCOUNTER MONSTERS AND
THIEVES, AND GOLD . . . BUT WATCH
YOUR STEP . . . . . . . . .
TRAP DOORS CAN BE COSTLY . . . .


YOU ARE IN A COLD AND DARK
 . . . . . . EMPTY CHAMBER


ERIC THE BOLD,  WHAT IS YOUR ACTION OR MOVE?

(N)ORTH, (E)AST, (S)OUTH, (W)EST
(U)P, (M)AP, (G)OLD
? N

YOU DISTURBED A MONSTER IN THIS CHAMBER
AND HE SPEAKS . . . . . . . . .

HALT . . . I AM THE KEEPER
OF . . . . . . . . ALGEBRA

YOU MAY NOT PASS THRU UNTIL
YOU SOLVE THIS EQUATION FOR X

Y =  19 X

IF Y =  133   THEN SOLVE FOR X

? 7


CORRECT
YOU WIN  59  GOLD PIECES

ERIC THE BOLD,  WHAT IS YOUR ACTION OR MOVE?

(N)ORTH, (E)AST, (S)OUTH, (W)EST
(U)P, (M)AP, (G)OLD
? N

YOU ARE IN A DAMP AND MISTY
 . . . . . . . EMPTY CHAMBER


ERIC THE BOLD,  WHAT IS YOUR ACTION OR MOVE?

(N)ORTH, (E)AST, (S)OUTH, (W)EST
(U)P, (M)AP, (G)OLD
? E

YOU DISTURBED A MONSTER IN THIS CHAMBER
AND HE SPEAKS . . . . . . . . .

HALT . . . I AM THE KEEPER
OF . . . . . . . . ALGEBRA

YOU MAY NOT PASS THRU UNTIL
YOU SOLVE THIS EQUATION FOR X

Y =  13 X  -  7

IF Y =  149   THEN SOLVE FOR X

? 12


12
CORRECT
YOU WIN  70  GOLD PIECES

YOU HAVE FOUND THE ENCHANTED KEY . . .


ERIC THE BOLD,  WHAT IS YOUR ACTION OR MOVE?

(N)ORTH, (E)AST, (S)OUTH, (W)EST
(U)P, (M)AP, (G)OLD
? S


YOU DISTURBED A MONSTER IN THIS CHAMBER
AND HE SPEAKS . . . . . . . .

HALT . . . I AM THE KEEPER
OF . . . . . . . . ALGEBRA

YOU MAY NOT PASS THRU UNTIL
YOU SOLVE THIS EQUATION FOR X

X =  10 Y +  4

IF Y =  16   THEN SOLVE FOR X

? 164


CORRECT
YOU WIN  312  GOLD PIECES


ERIC THE BOLD,  WHAT IS YOUR ACTION OR MOVE?

(N)ORTH, (E)AST, (S)OUTH, (W)EST
(U)P, (M)AP, (G)OLD
? E




YOU ACTIVATED A . . . TRAP DOOR

BUT . . . YOU CAUGHT YOURSELF
FROM FALLING

ERIC THE BOLD,  WHAT IS YOUR ACTION OR MOVE?

(N)ORTH, (E)AST, (S)OUTH, (W)EST
(U)P, (M)AP, (G)OLD
? E



YOU DISTURBED A MONSTER IN THIS CHAMBER
AND HE SPEAKS . . . . . . . . .

HALT . . . I AM THE KEEPER
OF . . . . . . . . ALGEBRA

YOU MAY NOT PASS THRU UNTIL
YOU SOLVE THIS EQUATION FOR X

X =  15 Y

IF Y =  40   THEN SOLVE FOR X

? 600


600
CORRECT
YOU WIN  382  GOLD PIECES


ERIC THE BOLD,  WHAT IS YOUR ACTION OR MOVE?

(N)ORTH, (E)AST, (S)OUTH, (W)EST
(U)P, (M)AP, (G)OLD
? E




YOU ARE AT A STAIRWAY
 . . . . . . . GOING UP


ERIC THE BOLD,  WHAT IS YOUR ACTION OR MOVE?

(N)ORTH, (E)AST, (S)OUTH, (W)EST
(U)P, (M)AP, (G)OLD
? U




YOU WALK UP THE STAIRWAY
THE ENCHANTED KEY . . . OPENS THE LOCK
YOU FOUND YOUR WAY . . .
 . . . OUT OF THE ALGEBRA DUNGEON

YOU HAVE ACQUIRED  4289  GOLD PIECES

GAME RATING IS  521

YOU TOOK  155  TURNS TO FIND THE WAY OUT,
AND ANSWERED  20  QUESTIONS CORRECTLY
OUT OF  20  QUESTIONS ASKED.

ANOTHER GAME?
ENTER '1'-YES  '0'-NO
? 1
```

Fig. 2-1. The Algebra Dungeon sample run.

East Movement

Entering an E allows you to move east. You may not move east under the following conditions:

1. If you reach the East Wall, you cannot pass through it.
2. If you enter a north-south corridor (through a secret door), movement east is not allowed.

South Movement

Entering an S allows you to move south. You may not move south under the following conditions:

1. If you reach the South Wall, you cannot pass through it.
2. If you enter an east-west corridor (through a secret door), movement south is not allowed.

West Movement

Entering a W allows you to move west. You may not move west under the following conditions:

1. If you reach the West Wall, you cannot pass through it.
2. If you enter a north-south corridor (through a secret door), movement west is not allowed.

Up Movement

Entering a U, when you are at a stairway and have found the Enchanted Key, allows you to go up to the next level. If you haven't found the key or you are not at a stairway, you cannot go up the stairway. To find the Enchanted Key, you must solve a random number of algebraic equations correctly, for each level. There is a different key for each level.

Map Display

Entering an M when you have found a map will display the map for that level. Each level has a different map, and the maps may be found when you are encountering thieves. The 64-chamber dungeon is displayed using the following symbols:

M = algebra monster
0 = empty chamber
? = unknown contents (either a thief or a trap door)
UP = stairway up

NS = north-south corridor (entered through secret doors)
EW = east-west corridor (entered through secret doors)
P1 = your location in the dungeon

See Fig. 2-2 for a sample map.

A question mark (?) indicates either a thief or a trap door. There is no way of knowing which it is unless you enter the chamber. If you encounter a thief, either you surprise him and he drops some of his gold pieces or he surprises you and steals some of your gold pieces. This is randomly determined, but it's in favor of the thief.

If you activate a trap door, you can either fall through or catch yourself from falling. If you fall through, you will lose most of your gold pieces. There is a 50-percent chance that you will fall through. If you are at level two, you will fall into a deep pit. If you are at level one, you will fall through to level two.

Gold Pieces Left

Entering a G will display the number of gold pieces you have with you. You will start out with 1000 and can gain or lose gold during your trip. But if you lose all your gold pieces, you will lose the game.

GAME RATING

After you complete the game, a game rating is displayed, along with the number of gold pieces acquired, the number of algebraic equations solved correctly out of the number of questions asked, and the number of turns taken. The rating is a number from approximately −600 to +2000, depending on the above statistics. The higher the rating number, the better is the game rating. A negative number indicates a poor rating.

```
THE ALGEBRA DUNGEON  *** MAP LEVEL  1 ***

EW   ?    UP   0    ?    0    NS   0
0    0    EW   M    0    0    EW   0
0    0    0    0    UP   UP   0    EW
EW   M    0    NS   EW   UP   NS   0
?    M    P1   M    M    0    UP   0
0    NS   0    0    M    0    0    0
M    M    M    EW   EW   0    0    0
M    UP   NS   NS   ?    0    NS   NS

ERIC THE BOLD,   WHAT IS YOUR ACTION OR MOVE?

(N)ORTH, (E)AST, (S)OUTH, (W)EST
(U)P, (M)AP, (G)OLD
? E
```

Fig. 2-2. The Algebra Dungeon sample map.

Program 2-1. The Algebra Dungeon Program Listing

```
100    HOME
110    PRINT "THE ALGEBRA DUNGEON"
120    PRINT "APPLE II"
130    PRINT "COPYRIGHT (C) 1980 BY HOWARD BERENBON"
140    PRINT
150    PRINT "AN EDUCATIONAL FANTASY GAME"
160    GOSUB 440
170    GOSUB 440
180    HOME : DIM A(9,9,2)
190    PRINT "YOU WILL BE TELEPORTED TO . . . "
200    PRINT
210    PRINT "THE ALGEBRA DUNGEON"
220    PRINT :
230    PRINT
240 MA = 0:CA = 0:G = 1000:M1 = 1:K = 0:TR = 0
250    PRINT "ENTER YOUR CHARACTER'S NAME?"
260    INPUT A$
270    GOSUB 440
280    PRINT : PRINT "YOU CARRY 1000 GOLD PIECES WITH YOU"
290    PRINT : GOSUB 440: PRINT A$;" . . . YOU ARE ON YOUR WAY"
300    GOSUB 440
310    GOSUB 480
320    HOME
330    PRINT "YOU HAVE ARRIVED AT . . . ."
340    PRINT
350    PRINT "THE ALGEBRA DUNGEON . . . LEVEL 2"
360    PRINT
370    PRINT "YOU WILL ENCOUNTER MONSTERS AND"
380    PRINT "THIEVES, AND GOLD . . . BUT WATCH"
390    PRINT "YOUR STEP . . . . . . . . . . ."
400    PRINT "TRAP DOORS CAN BE COSTLY . . . ."
410    FOR AB = 1 TO 4540
420    NEXT AB
430    GOTO 1010
440    REM  DELAY
450    FOR Z2 = 1 TO 908
460    NEXT Z2
470    RETURN
480    REM  SET UP 2 LEVEL DUNGEON
490    FOR X = 1 TO 8
500    FOR Y = 1 TO 8
510    FOR Z = 1 TO 2
520 A(X,Y,Z) =  INT ( RND (1) * 7 + 1)
530    NEXT Z
540    NEXT Y
550    NEXT X
560    REM  TRAP DOORS #8, MIN-1, MAX-3
570 H =  INT ( RND (1) * 3 + 1)
580    FOR A = 1 TO 2
590    FOR N = 1 TO H
600 X =  INT ( RND (1) * 8 + 1)
610 Y =  INT ( RND (1) * 8 + 1)
620 A(X,Y,A) = 8
```

```
630  NEXT N
640  NEXT A
650  REM  STAIRWAYS #9, MIN-3, MAX-6
660 S =  INT ( RND (1) * 4 + 1) + 2
670  FOR A = 1 TO 2
680  FOR N = 1 TO S
690 X =  INT ( RND (1) * 8 + 1)
700 Y =  INT ( RND (1) * 8 + 1)
710 A(X,Y,A) = 9
720  NEXT N
730  NEXT A
740  RETURN
750  REM  STAIRWAY
760 L1 = L1 - 1
770  PRINT "YOU WALK UP THE STAIRWAY"
780  GOSUB 440
790  PRINT "THE ENCHANTED KEY . . . OPENS THE LOCK"
800  GOSUB 440
810  IF L1 = 0 THEN 870
820 MA = 0:K = 0:K4 =  INT ( RND (1) * 4 + 1) + 4
830  PRINT :CB = CA + K4
840  PRINT "YOU ARE AT . . . . . LEVEL 1"
850  GOSUB 440: GOSUB 440: GOSUB 440: GOSUB 440
860  GOTO 1070
870  PRINT "YOU FOUND YOUR WAY . . ."
880  PRINT " . . . OUT OF THE ALGEBRA DUNGEON"
890  PRINT
900  PRINT "YOU HAVE ACQUIRED ";G;" GOLD PIECES"
910  GOSUB 930
920  GOTO 1910
930 GG = G + 100: REM  RATING
940 R =  INT ((GG * CA - 7000 + 1) / M1)
950  PRINT
960  PRINT "GAME RATING IS ";R
970  PRINT : IF G <  = 0 THEN 4280
980  PRINT "YOU TOOK ";M1;" TURNS TO FIND THE WAY OUT,"
990  PRINT "AND ANSWERED ";CA;" QUESTIONS CORRECTLY"
1000  PRINT "OUT OF ";TR;" QUESTIONS ASKED.": RETURN
1010  REM  SET UP 1ST MOVE
1020 C =  INT ( RND (1) * 8 + 1)
1030 D =  INT ( RND (1) * 8 + 1)
1040 A(C,D,2) = 1
1050 L1 = 2
1060 K4 =  INT ( RND (1) * 4 + 1) + 4
1070  REM  PLAYER MOVE ROUTINE
1080  HOME
1090 A = A(C,D,L1)
1100  GOSUB 440
1110  ON A GOSUB 2220,2280,2340,2340,2390,2700,2750,2790,3070
1120  PRINT
1130  IF G <  = 0 THEN 1820
1140  PRINT A$;",  WHAT IS YOUR ACTION OR MOVE?"
1150  PRINT
```

```
1160   PRINT "(N)ORTH, (E)AST, (S)OUTH, (W)EST"
1170   PRINT "(U)P, (M)AP, (G)OLD"
1180   INPUT M1$
1190 M1 = M1 + 1: IF K = 0 AND M1 > = 140 / L1 THEN 4190
1200   IF M1$ = "N" THEN 1290
1210   IF M1$ = "E" THEN 1340
1220   IF M1$ = "S" THEN 1390
1230   IF M1$ = "W" THEN 1440
1240   IF M1$ = "U" THEN 1490
1250   IF M1$ = "M" THEN 1610
1260   IF M1$ = "G" THEN 1670
1270   PRINT
1280   GOTO 1120
1290   REM  NORTH MOVEMENT
1300   IF A = 7 THEN 1710
1310   IF (D - 1) = 0 THEN 1980
1320 D = D - 1
1330   GOTO 1070
1340   REM  EAST MOVEMENT
1350   IF A = 6 THEN 1770
1360   IF (C + 1) = 9 THEN 2030
1370 C = C + 1
1380   GOTO 1070
1390   REM  SOUTH MOVEMENT
1400   IF A = 7 THEN 1710
1410   IF (D + 1) = 9 THEN 2050
1420 D = D + 1
1430   GOTO 1070
1440   REM  WEST MOVEMENT
1450   IF A = 6 THEN 1770
1460   IF (C - 1) = 0 THEN 2070
1470 C = C - 1
1480   GOTO 1070
1490   HOME : REM  STAIRWAY UP
1500   IF A < > 9 THEN 1580
1510   IF K = 1 THEN 750
1520   PRINT
1530   PRINT "YOU CANNOT GO UP THE STAIRWAY"
1540   PRINT "YOU DON'T HAVE THE KEY"
1550   GOSUB 440
1560   PRINT
1570   GOTO 1120
1580   PRINT "YOU ARE NOT AT A STAIRWAY"
1590   GOSUB 440
1600   GOTO 1120
1610   HOME : REM  MAP
1620   IF MA = 1 THEN 2090
1630   PRINT "YOU DON'T HAVE THE MAP"
1640   PRINT
1650   GOSUB 440
1660   GOTO 1120
1670   REM  GOLD PIECES
1680   HOME : PRINT "YOU HAVE ";G;" GOLD PIECES WITH YOU"
```

```
1690   PRINT
1700   GOTO 1120
1710   REM  EW CORRIDOR
1720   PRINT
1730   HOME : PRINT "YOU ARE IN AN EAST-WEST CORRIDOR"
1740   PRINT "YOU CAN ONLY GO EAST OR WEST"
1750   PRINT
1760   GOTO 1120
1770   REM  NS CORRIDOR
1780   PRINT
1790   HOME : PRINT "YOU ARE IN A NORTH-SOUTH CORRIDOR"
1800   PRINT "YOU CAN ONLY GO NORTH OR SOUTH"
1810   GOTO 1750
1820   REM  GOLD ZERO
1830   GOSUB 440: GOSUB 440
1840   PRINT
1850   PRINT "YOU LOST ALL YOUR GOLD AND YOU WERE"
1860   PRINT " . . . UNABLE TO MEET THE DEMANDS OF"
1870   PRINT " . . . THE ALGEBRA DUNGEON . . ."
1880   PRINT : PRINT
1890   PRINT "YOU CAN ONLY GO NORTH OR SOUTH"
1900   GOSUB 930
1910   PRINT
1920   PRINT "ANOTHER GAME?"
1930   PRINT "ENTER '1'-YES  '0'-NO"
1940   INPUT AA
1950   IF AA < > 1 THEN 1970
1960   HOME : GOTO 210
1970   END
1980   HOME : PRINT "YOU ARE AT THE EAST WALL"
1990   PRINT "YOU CANNOT PASS THROUGH"
2000   PRINT
2010   PRINT "TRY ANOTHER DIRECTION?"
2020   GOTO 1120
2030   HOME : PRINT "YOU ARE AT THE EAST WALL"
2040   GOTO 1990
2050   HOME : PRINT "YOU ARE AT THE SOUTH WALL"
2060   GOTO 1990
2070   HOME : PRINT "YOU ARE AT THE WEST WALL"
2080   GOTO 1990
2090   REM  DISPLAY MAP
2100   HOME
2120   PRINT
2130   FOR Q = 1 TO 8
2140   FOR N = 1 TO 8
2150   IF C = N AND D = Q THEN  PRINT "P1  ";: GOTO 2180
2160 S1 = A(N,Q,L1)
2170   ON S1 GOSUB 3110,3110,3130,3130,3150,3170,3190,3210,3220
2180   NEXT N
2190   PRINT
2200   NEXT Q
2210   GOTO 1120
2220   REM  EMPTY ROOM
```

```
2230   PRINT
2240   PRINT "YOU ARE IN A COLD AND DARK"
2250   PRINT " . . . . . . EMPTY CHAMBER"
2260   PRINT
2270   RETURN
2280   REM  EMPTY ROOM 2
2290   PRINT
2300   PRINT "YOU ARE IN A DAMP AND MISTY"
2310   PRINT ". . . . . . . EMPTY CHAMBER"
2320   PRINT
2330   RETURN
2340 TR = TR + 1: HOME : GOSUB 4140
2350 M4 =  INT ( RND (1) * 6 + 1)
2360   ON M4 GOSUB 3240,3370,3540,3670,4360,4420
2370   PRINT
2380   RETURN
2390   HOME : PRINT "THERE IS A THIEF IN THIS CHAMBER"
2400 A(C,D,L1) = 2
2410   GOSUB 440
2420 G4 =  INT ( RND (1) * 350 / L1 + 1)
2430 Y =  INT ( RND (1) * 8 + 1)
2440   IF Y <  = 3 THEN 2610
2450   PRINT
2460   PRINT " . . . . . . HE SURPRISES YOU": PRINT
2470   GOSUB 440
2480   PRINT "AS HE QUICKLY PASSES BY YOU HE"
2490   PRINT "SNATCHES . . . ";G4;" GOLD PIECES": PRINT
2500 G = G - G4
2510   REM  LOOK FOR MAP
2520   IF MA = 1 THEN  RETURN
2530 MA =  INT ( RND (1) * 4 + 1): IF MA <  = 2 THEN MA = 1
2540   IF MA = 1 THEN 2570
2550   RETURN
2560   GOSUB 440
2570   PRINT "YOU SEARCH THE CHAMBER AND"
2580   GOSUB 440
2590   PRINT "YOU . . . . . FIND A MAP"
2600   RETURN
2610   PRINT "YOU SURPRISED THE THIEF . . . ."
2620   PRINT : GOSUB 440
2630   PRINT "AS HE RUNS OUT HE DROPS . . . ."
2640   PRINT " . . . ";G4;" GOLD PIECES."
2650   PRINT "YOU PICK UP THE GOLD PIECES":G = G + G4
2660   PRINT : IF MA = 1 THEN  RETURN
2670 MA =  INT ( RND (1) * 4 + 1): IF MA <  = 2 THEN MA = 1
2680   IF MA = 1 THEN 2570
2690   RETURN
2700   HOME : REM  NORTH SOUTH CORRIDOR
2710   PRINT
2720   PRINT "YOU ENTER A NORTH-SOUTH CORRIDOR"
2730   PRINT "THRU A SECRET DOOR": PRINT : GOSUB 4310
2740   RETURN
2750   HOME : REM  EAST WEST CORRIDOR
```

```
2760   PRINT
2770   PRINT "YOU ENTER AN EAST-WEST CORRIDOR"
2780   GOTO 2730
2790   REM  TRAP DOOR
2800   PRINT "YOU ACTIVATED A . . . TRAP DOOR"
2810   GOSUB 440
2820 TD =  INT ( RND (1) * 4 + 1)
2830   IF TD >  = 3 THEN 2880
2840   PRINT
2850   PRINT "BUT . . . YOU CAUGHT YOURSELF"
2860   PRINT "FROM FALLING"
2870   RETURN
2880   IF L1 = 2 THEN 2990
2890 L1 = L1 + 1: PRINT :K = 1
2900   PRINT "YOU FELL THRU TO LEVEL 3 . . . AND"
2910 G = 100
2920   GOSUB 440
2930   PRINT
2940   PRINT "YOU . . . . . . . . LOST"
2950   PRINT "MOST OF YOUR GOLD PIECES": PRINT
2960   PRINT "YOU HAVE . . ";G;" GOLD PIECES LEFT"
2970   PRINT "BUT . . . YOU STILL HAVE YOUR KEY"
2980   RETURN
2990   PRINT "YOU FELL INTO A DEEP . . . PIT"
3000   GOSUB 440
3010   PRINT "YOU'RE LUCKY . . . . "
3020   PRINT "YOU DIDN'T GET HURT"
3030   PRINT
3040   GOSUB 440
3050   PRINT "BUT IN CLIMBING OUT . . ."
3060   GOTO 4230
3070   PRINT "YOU ARE AT A STAIRWAY"
3080   PRINT " . . . . . . GOING UP"
3090   PRINT
3100   RETURN
3110   PRINT "O    ";
3120   RETURN
3130   PRINT "M    ";
3140   RETURN
3150   PRINT "?    ";
3160   RETURN
3170   PRINT "NS   ";
3180   RETURN
3190   PRINT "EW   ";
3200   RETURN
3210   GOTO 3150
3220   PRINT "UP   ";
3230   RETURN
3240   REM  Y=PX
3250   GOSUB 4330
3260   GOSUB 3800
3270   GOSUB 3840:Y = P * X
3280   PRINT "Y = ";P;"X"
```

```
3290   PRINT : PRINT "IF Y= ";Y;" THEN SOLVE FOR X"
3300   PRINT : INPUT A1
3310   IF A1 = X THEN 3350
3320   REM  LOSE GOLD
3330   GOSUB 4000
3340   RETURN
3350   GOSUB 3900
3360   RETURN
3370   REM  Y=PX-Q
3380   GOSUB 4330
3390   GOSUB 3800
3400   GOSUB 3840:Y = P * X
3410   PRINT "Y = ";P;"X - ";Q
3420   PRINT : PRINT "IF Y = ";Y - Q;" THEN SOLVE FOR X"
3430   PRINT : INPUT A1
3440   IF A1 = X THEN 3470
3450   GOSUB 4000
3460   RETURN
3470   GOSUB 3900
3480   RETURN
3490   GOSUB 480
3500 H = 1:O = 9:W = 8
3510 B = O:E = 5:R = 14
3520 C = O:PR = 0
3530   GOTO 1010
3540   REM  Y=PX+Q
3550   GOSUB 4330
3560   GOSUB 3800
3570   GOSUB 3840:Y = P * X
3580   PRINT "Y = ";P;"X + ";Q
3590   PRINT : PRINT "IF Y = ";Y + Q;" THEN SOLVE FOR X"
3600   PRINT : INPUT A1
3610   IF A1 = X THEN 3650
3620   REM  LOSE GOLD
3630   GOSUB 4000
3640   RETURN
3650   GOSUB 3900
3660   RETURN
3670   REM  X=PY+Q
3680   GOSUB 4330
3690   GOSUB 3800
3700   GOSUB 3840:X = P * Y + Q
3710   PRINT "X = ";P;"Y + ";Q
3720   PRINT : PRINT "IF Y = ";Y;" THEN SOLVE FOR X"
3730   PRINT : INPUT A1
3740   IF A1 = X THEN 3780
3750   REM  LOSE GOLD
3760   GOSUB 4000
3770   RETURN
3780   GOSUB 3900
3790   RETURN
3800   PRINT "YOU MAY NOT PASS THRU UNTIL"
3810   PRINT "YOU SOLVE THIS EQUATION FOR X"
```

```
3820  PRINT
3830  RETURN
3840  REM  RANDOM ROUTINE
3850 X =  INT ( RND (1) * 50 / L1 + 1):P =  INT ( RND (1) * 50 / L1 + 1)
3860 Y =  INT ( RND (1) * 50 / L1 + 1):Q =  INT ( RND (1) * 50 / L1 + 1)
3870  GOSUB 440
3880  GOSUB 440
3890  RETURN
3900  PRINT "CORRECT"
3910 G4 =  INT ( RND (1) * 400 / L1 + 1) + 25
3920 G = G + G4
3930  GOSUB 440
3940  PRINT "YOU WIN ";G4;" GOLD PIECES"
3950 A(C,D,L1) = 1
3960 CA = CA + 1: IF K = 1 THEN  RETURN
3970  IF L1 = 1 THEN 4210
3980  IF CA = K4 THEN 4090
3990  RETURN
4000  PRINT
4010  PRINT "INCORRECT"
4020  PRINT "THE CORRECT ANSWER IS ";X
4030  PRINT
4040 G4 =  INT ( RND (1) * 350 / L1 + 1)
4050 G = G - G4
4060  GOSUB 440
4070  PRINT "YOU LOSE ";G4;" GOLD PIECES"
4080  RETURN
4090  GOSUB 440
4100 K = 1
4110  PRINT : PRINT "YOU HAVE FOUND THE ENCHANTED KEY . . ."
4120  GOSUB 440
4130  RETURN
4140  PRINT "YOU DISTURBED A MONSTER IN THIS CHAMBER"
4150  GOSUB 440
4160  PRINT "AND HE SPEAKS . . . . . . . . .": PRINT
4170  GOSUB 440
4180  RETURN
4190  GOSUB 4100
4200  GOTO 1200
4210  IF CA = CB THEN 4090
4220  RETURN
4230 G = 100: GOSUB 440: PRINT
4240  PRINT "YOU . . . . . . DROPPED"
4250  PRINT "MOST OF YOUR GOLD PIECES."
4260  PRINT "YOU HAVE . .";G;" GOLD PIECES LEFT"
4270  RETURN
4280  PRINT "YOU ANSWERED ";CA;" QUESTIONS CORRECTLY"
4290  PRINT "OUT OF ";TR;" QUESTIONS ASKED,": PRINT " . . . . . IN ";M1;" TURNS."
4300  RETURN
4310  PRINT "THE DOOR CLOSES AND LOCKS BEHIND YOU": GOSUB 440
4320  RETURN
4330  PRINT "HALT . . . I AM THE KEEPER"
4340  PRINT "OF . . . . . . . . ALGEBRA"
```

```
4350   PRINT : RETURN
4360   REM  X=PY
4370   GOSUB 4330
4380   GOSUB 3800
4390   GOSUB 3840:X = P * Y
4400   PRINT "X = ";P;"Y"
4410   GOTO 3720
4420   REM  X=PY-Q
4430   GOSUB 4330
4440   GOSUB 3800
4450   GOSUB 3840:X = P * Y - Q
4460   PRINT "X = ";P;"Y - ";Q
4470   GOTO 3720
```

CHAPTER 3

Word Association

The Word Association program is an educational exercise for children. It gives a twenty-question test, with each question displaying four words. The word that is "not like the others" must be chosen. The program is written in BASIC for your microcomputer. See Program 3-1 for the program listing.

THE PROGRAM

The program begins by accepting the student's name, then requesting the entry of a 1 to begin the test. Each question displays four words, three of which are on a related subject, and the fourth is not related. The student must enter the word that is not related to the others. CORRECT is displayed for a correct response, and INCORRECT is displayed for an incorrect entry. This is repeated for all twenty questions, then the student's score is calculated. Finally, the number of correct out of twenty is displayed, along with the percent score. See Fig. 3-1 for a sample run.

THE QUESTIONS

The words are stored in DATA statements beginning at line 690. The first three words in each statement are related, and the fourth is not related. Each time a question is displayed, the unrelated word will appear in one of four positions on the display. The word list may be changed for a different set of questions.

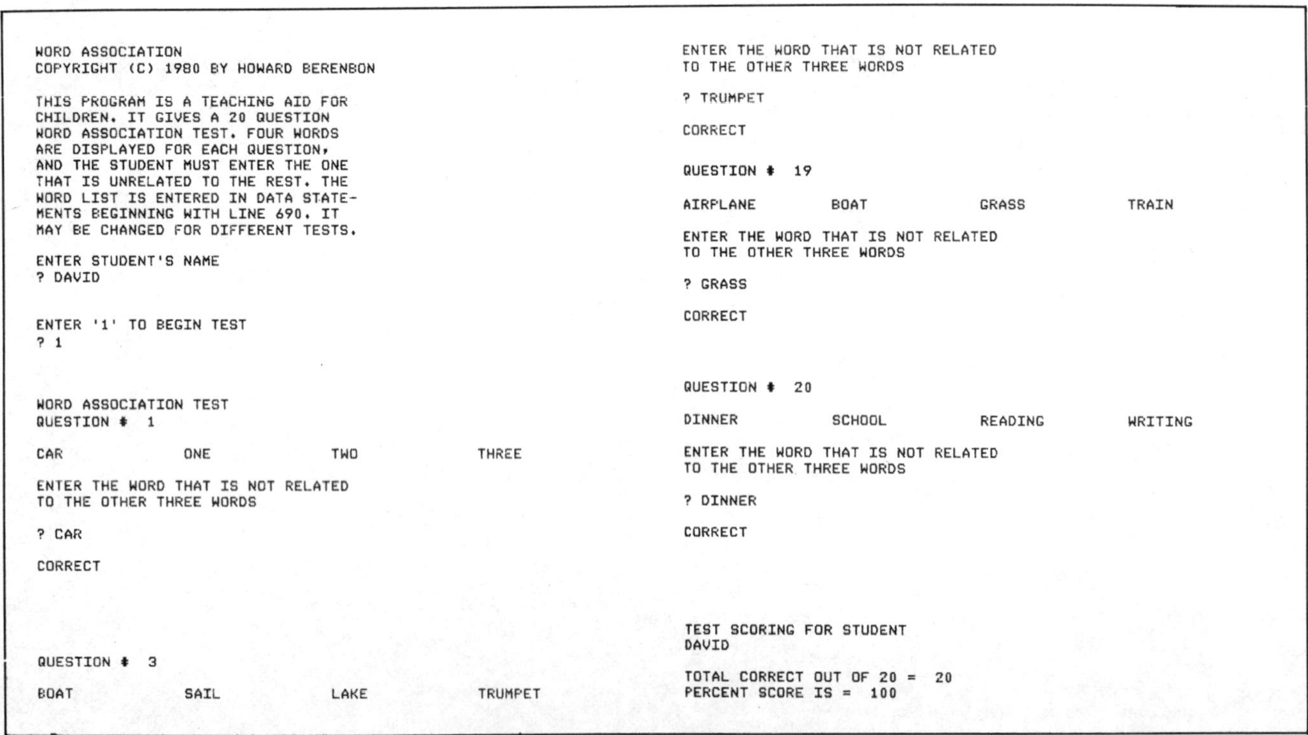

Fig. 3-1. Word Association sample run.

```
100   HOME : PRINT "WORD ASSOCIATION"
110   PRINT "COPYRIGHT (C) 1980 BY HOWARD BERENBON"
120   PRINT "APPLE II"
130   PRINT
140   PRINT "THIS PROGRAM IS A TEACHING AID FOR"
150   PRINT "CHILDREN. IT GIVES A 20 QUESTION"
160   PRINT "WORD ASSOCIATION TEST. FOUR WORDS"
170   PRINT "ARE DISPLAYED FOR EACH QUESTION,"
180   PRINT "AND THE STUDENT MUST ENTER THE ONE"
190   PRINT "THAT IS UNRELATED TO THE REST. THE"
200   PRINT "WORD LIST IS ENTERED IN DATA STATE-"
210   PRINT "MENTS BEGINNING WITH LINE 690. IT"
220   PRINT "MAY BE CHANGED FOR DIFFERENT TESTS."
230   PRINT
240   PRINT "ENTER STUDENT'S NAME"
250   INPUT A$:S = 0
260   PRINT
270   PRINT "ENTER '1' TO BEGIN TEST"
280   INPUT A: HOME
290   PRINT "WORD ASSOCIATION TEST"
300   FOR T = 1 TO 20: PRINT "QUESTION # ";T
310   PRINT : READ B$,C$,D$,E$
320 R =  INT ( RND (1) * 4 + 1)
330   ON R GOSUB 450,470,490,510
340   GOSUB 420
350   INPUT F$
360   IF F$ = E$ THEN 530
370   PRINT : PRINT "INCORRECT"
380   PRINT
390   PRINT "THE CORRECT WORD IS ";E$
400   GOSUB 660: HOME : NEXT T
410   GOTO 580
420   PRINT : PRINT "ENTER THE WORD THAT IS NOT RELATED"
430   PRINT "TO THE OTHER THREE WORDS"
440   PRINT : RETURN
450   PRINT B$;"   ";C$;"   ";D$;"   ";E$
460   RETURN
470   PRINT C$;"   ";D$;"   ";E$;"   ";B$
480   RETURN
490   PRINT D$;"   ";E$;"   ";B$;"   ";C$
500   RETURN
510   PRINT E$;"   ";B$;"   ";C$;"   ";D$
520   RETURN
530 S = S + 5
540   PRINT
550   PRINT "CORRECT"
560   PRINT
570   GOTO 400
580   HOME
590   PRINT "TEST SCORING FOR STUDENT"
600   PRINT A$
610   PRINT
620   PRINT "TOTAL CORRECT OUT OF 20 = ";S / 5
```

```
630   PRINT "PERCENT SCORE IS = ";S
640   PRINT
650   END
660   FOR A = 1 TO 2045
670   NEXT A
680   RETURN
690   DATA ONE,TWO,THREE,CAR
700   DATA TIRE,CAR,FENDER,SAIL
710   DATA BOAT,SAIL,LAKE,TRUMPET
720   DATA GUITAR,TRUMPET,VIOLIN,SISTER
730   DATA BROTHER,SISTER,FATHER,BOOK
740   DATA BINDING,BOOK,PAGES,DRILL
750   DATA SAW,CUT,DRILL,GYM
760   DATA FOOTBALL,BASKETBALL,BASEBALL,TRUCK
770   DATA ARM,HAND,EYES,TIME
780   DATA HOURS,MINUTES,SECONDS,PEOPLE
790   DATA PENCIL,PAPER,PEN,AIRPLANE
800   DATA FLYING,AIRPORT,AIRPLANE,SING
810   DATA TALK,SING,WHISPER,JUMP
820   DATA WALK,STAND,RUN,EAT
830   DATA SALT,PEPPER,GARLIC,GLUE
840   DATA LAKE,RIVER,STREAM,TRAIN
850   DATA COOKIES,CAKE,BROWNIES,STEAM
860   DATA ICE,WATER,STEAM,MOUNTAIN
870   DATA  TRAIN,AIRPLANE,BOAT,GRASS
880   DATA SCHOOL,READING,WRITING,DINNER
```

CHAPTER 4

Advanced Math: Algebra

Here's a program that gives a ten-question algebra test. Each question is randomly generated from six different algebra equations. The program is written in BASIC for your microcomputer. See Program 4-1 for the program listing.

THE PROGRAM

After you run the program, enter the difficulty level: 1 for moderate or 2 for difficult. Then the test will begin. An equation will be displayed, where you must solve for the value of X. You have two tries to enter the correct answer. CORRECT will be displayed for a correct response, and the program will go on to the next question; INCORRECT will be displayed for a wrong answer. After two incorrect entries, the correct answer will be displayed, and the program will advance to the next question. After all ten questions are answered, your score will be displayed, with the number correct out of ten and the percent score. Finally, another test may be taken, or you can end the program. See Fig. 4-1 for a sample run.

THE PROBLEMS

The problems are generated randomly using program lines 530 through 1020. A random-number generator subroutine is used to generate the X, Y, P, and Q components of the problems. The following equations are used to generate the problems. In all cases, X must be solved for:

$$Y = PX \qquad Y = PX - Q \qquad Y = PX + Q$$
$$X = PY \qquad X = PY - Q \qquad X = PY + Q$$

In any case where division is required to solve for X, the division will result in an integer.

```
ADVANCED MATH: ALGEBRA
COPYRIGHT (C) 1980 BY HOWARD BERENBON

THIS IS AN ALGEBRA TEST PROGRAM WHICH
RANDOMLY GENERATES A 10-QUESTION TEST.
YOU HAVE 2-TRIES PER QUESTION.

ENTER DIFFICULTY LEVEL

1) MODERATE
2) DIFFICULT
? 1


              ALGEBRA TEST
PROBLEM  1
TRIAL  1

X =  15 Y +  24

IF Y =  17   THEN SOLVE FOR X

? 279


CORRECT


              ALGEBRA TEST
PROBLEM  2
TRIAL  1

Y =  4 X +  19

IF Y =  115   THEN SOLVE FOR X

? 24


CORRECT
```

```
              ALGEBRA TEST
PROBLEM  9
TRIAL  1

Y =  6 X -  4

IF Y =  134   THEN SOLVE FOR X

? 23


CORRECT


              ALGEBRA TEST
PROBLEM  10
TRIAL  1

Y =  19 X -  23

IF Y =  376   THEN SOLVE FOR X

? 21


CORRECT




YOU HAVE  10  CORRECT OUT OF 10
THAT'S A SCORE OF  100  %

ANOTHER TEST? 1-YES  0-NO
? 1
```

Fig. 4-1. Advanced math: Algebra sample run.

```
100   HOME : PRINT "ADVANCED MATH: ALGEBRA"
110   PRINT "APPLE II"
120   PRINT "COPYRIGHT (C) 1980 BY HOWARD BERENBON": PRINT
130   PRINT "THIS IS AN ALGEBRA TEST PROGRAM WHICH"
140   PRINT "RANDOMLY GENERATES A 10-QUESTION TEST."
150   PRINT "YOU HAVE 2-TRIES PER QUESTION."
160   PRINT : GOSUB 380
170 S = 0
180   FOR A = 1 TO 10
190 R =   INT ( RND (1) * 6 + 1)
200 T = 1
210   GOSUB 470
220   HOME : PRINT  TAB( 10)"ALGEBRA TEST"
230   GOSUB 340
240   ON R GOTO 530,610,690,770,950,990
250   NEXT A
260   PRINT
270   PRINT "YOU HAVE ";S;" CORRECT OUT OF 10"
280   PRINT "THAT'S A SCORE OF ";S * 10;" %"
290   PRINT
300   PRINT "ANOTHER TEST? 1-YES  0-NO"
310   INPUT Z
320   HOME : IF Z = 1 THEN 160
330   END
340   PRINT "PROBLEM ";A
350   PRINT "TRIAL ";T
360   PRINT
370   RETURN
380   PRINT "ENTER DIFFICULTY LEVEL"
390   PRINT
400   PRINT "1) MODERATE"
410   PRINT "2) DIFFICULT"
420   INPUT E
430   ON E GOTO 450,460
440   GOTO 380
450 D = 25: RETURN
460 D = 50: RETURN
470 X =   INT ( RND (1) * D + 1):P =   INT ( RND (1) * D + 1)
480 Y =   INT ( RND (1) * D + 1):Q =   INT ( RND (1) * D + 1)
490   RETURN
500   FOR Z = 1 TO 1500
510   NEXT Z
520   RETURN
530   REM  Y=PX
540 Y = P * X
550   PRINT "Y = ";P;"X"
560   PRINT : PRINT "IF Y = ";Y;" THEN SOLVE FOR X"
570   PRINT : INPUT A1
580   IF A1 = X THEN 600
590   GOTO 880
600   GOTO 850
610   REM  Y=PX-Q
620 Y = P * X
```

```
630   PRINT "Y = ";P;"X - ";Q
640   PRINT : PRINT "IF Y = ";Y - Q;" THEN SOLVE FOR X"
650   PRINT : INPUT A1
660   IF A1 = X THEN 680
670   GOTO 880
680   GOTO 850
690   REM   Y=PX+Q
700   Y = P * X
710   PRINT "Y = ";P;"X + ";Q
720   PRINT : PRINT "IF Y = ";Y + Q;" THEN SOLVE FOR X"
730   PRINT : INPUT A1
740   IF A1 = X THEN 760
750   GOTO 880
760   GOTO 850
770   REM   X=PY+Q
780   X = P * Y + Q
790   PRINT "X = ";P;"Y + ";Q
800   PRINT : PRINT "IF Y = ";Y;" THEN SOLVE FOR X"
810   PRINT : INPUT A1
820   IF A1 = X THEN 840
830   GOTO 880
840   REM   CORRECT
850   PRINT "CORRECT": GOSUB 500
860 S = S + 1
870   GOTO 250
880   PRINT
890   PRINT "INCORRECT": GOSUB 500
900 T = T + 1: IF T = 3 THEN 920
910   GOTO 220
920   PRINT "THE CORRECT ANSWER IS ";X
930   GOSUB 500
940   GOTO 250
950   REM   X=PY
960   X = P * Y
970   PRINT "X = ";P;"Y"
980   GOTO 800
990   REM   X=PY-Q
1000  X = P * Y - Q
1010  PRINT "X = ";P"Y - ";Q
1020  GOTO 800
```

CHAPTER 5

Memory Challenger II: Random Letters

The Memory Challenger II is a game used to test your memory and concentration. It generates and displays random letters (A–Z) of different lengths. You must enter the letters that are flashed on the screen. The program is written in BASIC for your microcomputer. See Program 5-1 for the program listing.

THE PROGRAM

The program begins by accepting entry of the difficulty level. Enter a 1 for easy, 2 for medium difficulty, or 3 for most difficult. Letters will be displayed from slow to fast, depending on the difficulty level; 1 is the slowest and 3 is the quickest.

After entering a 1 to begin, GET READY will be printed at the top center of the display. Then a set of random letters will be displayed at a random location on the screen, for a short period. Enter the letters that were displayed. The correct answer is displayed, and CORRECT or INCORRECT is printed. Then the number of correct answers out of the number of tries is displayed. Finally, TRY AGAIN will be displayed; and you have a choice of playing again at the same difficulty level, playing again at another difficulty level, or ending the test. When you decide to end the test, your final percent score will be displayed. See Fig. 5-1 for a sample run.

```
MEMORY CHALLENGER II: RANDOM LETTERS
COPYRIGHT (C) 1981 BY HOWARD BERENBON

THE PROGRAM GENERATES & DISPLAYS RANDOM
LETTERS OF DIFFERENT LENGTHS. ENTER
THE LETTERS THAT ARE FLASHED AT RANDOM
LOCATIONS ON THE SCREEN.

ENTER DIFFICULTY LEVEL:
1=EASY
2=MEDIUM DIFFICULTY
3=MOST DIFFICULT
? 2


ENTER '1' TO BEGIN
? 1




                    GET READY




              PFOZ
                    DIFFICULTY LEVEL  2
ENTER LETTERS
? PFOZ
THE ANSWER IS 'PFOZ'


CORRECT
YOU HAVE  1  CORRECT OUT OF  1  TRIES
```

```
,RY AGAIN?
1 = YES & SAME DIFFICULTY-**GET READY**
2 = YES & CHANGE DIFFICULTY
0 = NO
? 1




                         GET READY




                                  PCDH


                    DIFFICULTY LEVEL  2
ENTER LETTERS
? PCDH
THE ANSWER IS 'PCDH'

CORRECT
YOU HAVE  2  CORRECT OUT OF  2  TRIES

TRY AGAIN?
1 = YES & SAME DIFFICULTY-**GET READY**
2 = YES & CHANGE DIFFICULTY
0 = NO
? 0


YOUR FINAL SCORE IS  100  PERCENT
```

Fig. 5-1. Memory Challenger II: Random Letters sample run.

```
100   HOME : PRINT "MEMORY CHALLENGER II: RANDOM LETTERS"
110   PRINT "APPLE II"
120   PRINT "COPYRIGHT  (C) 1981 BY HOWARD BERENBON"
130   PRINT : DIM F$(6)
140   PRINT "THE PROGRAM GENERATES & DISPLAYS RANDOM"
150   PRINT "LETTERS OF DIFFERENT LENGTHS. ENTER"
160   PRINT "THE LETTERS THAT ARE FLASHED AT RANDOM"
170   PRINT "LOCATIONS ON THE SCREEN."
180   PRINT
190 Z = 0
200 W = 0
210   PRINT "ENTER DIFFICULTY LEVEL:"
220   PRINT "1=EASY"
230   PRINT "2=MEDIUM DIFFICULTY"
240   PRINT "3=MOST DIFFICULT"
250   INPUT A
260   HOME
270   IF A = 1 THEN 600
280   IF A = 2 THEN 640
290   IF A = 3 THEN 680
300   GOTO 210
310   HOME
320   IF D = 1 THEN 340
330   PRINT "ENTER '1' TO BEGIN": INPUT B
340   FOR T = 1 TO 5
350 F$(T) = ""
360   NEXT T
370   HOME : VTAB 4
380   PRINT  TAB( 18)"GET READY"
390   FOR D = 1 TO 454
400   NEXT D
410   HOME
420   GOSUB 870
430 K =  INT ( RND (1) * 22 + 1):K1 =  INT ( RND (1) * 37 + 1)
440   VTAB K: PRINT  TAB( K1);G$
450   GOSUB 720
460   HOME
470   PRINT  TAB( 20)"DIFFICULTY LEVEL ";A
480   PRINT "ENTER LETTERS"
490 Z = Z + 1
500   INPUT C$
510   PRINT "THE ANSWER IS '";G$;"'"
520   PRINT
530   IF G$ = C$ THEN 570
540   PRINT "INCORRECT"
550   PRINT "YOU HAVE ";W;" CORRECT OUT OF ";Z;" TRIES"
560   GOTO 770
570   PRINT "CORRECT"
580 W = W + 1
590   GOTO 550
600 G = 79
610 F = 2
620 N =  INT ( RND (1) * 454 + 1)
```

```
630   GOTO 320
640 N =   INT ( RND (1) * 340 + 1)
650 G = 102
660 F = 4
670   GOTO 320
680 N =   INT ( RND (1) * 227 + 1)
690 G = 68
700 F = 5
710   GOTO 320
720   FOR E = 1 TO G + N
730   NEXT E
740   RETURN
750   PRINT "YOUR FINAL SCORE IS "; INT (W / Z * 100);" PERCENT"
760   END
770   PRINT
780   PRINT "TRY AGAIN?"
790   PRINT "1 = YES & SAME DIFFICULTY-**GET READY**"
800   PRINT "2 = YES & CHANGE DIFFICULTY"
810   PRINT "0 = NO"
820   INPUT D
830   IF D = 1 THEN 260
840   IF D = 2 THEN 210
850   IF D = 0 THEN 750
860   GOTO 770
870 F$(0) = ""
880   FOR T = 1 TO F
890 X =   INT ( RND (1) * 26 + 1)
900   FOR B = 1 TO X
910   READ F$(0)
920   NEXT B
930 F$(T) = F$(0)
940   RESTORE
950   NEXT T
960 G$ = F$(1) + F$(2) + F$(3) + F$(4) + F$(5)
970   RETURN
980   DATA A,B,C,D,E,F,G,H,I,J,K,L,M
990   DATA N,O,P,Q,R,S,T,U,V,W,X,Y,Z
```

CHAPTER 6

Memory Challenger III: Random Words

The Memory Challenger III is another game used to test your memory and concentration. It's similar to the Memory Challenger II of Chapter 5, except that it displays random words taken from DATA statements beginning at line 1000. You must enter the word that is flashed at a random location on the screen. The program is written in BASIC for your microcomputer. See Program 6-1 for the program listing.

THE PROGRAM

The program begins by accepting entry of the difficulty level. Enter a 1 for easy, 2 for medium difficulty, or 3 for most difficult. Words will be displayed from slow to fast, depending on the difficulty level; 1 is the slowest and 3 is the quickest.

After entering a 1 to begin, GET READY will be printed at the top center of the display. Then a word is displayed at a random location on the screen for a short period. Enter the word that was displayed. The correct answer is displayed, and CORRECT or INCORRECT is printed. Then the number of correct answers out of the number of tries is displayed. Finally, TRY AGAIN will be displayed; and you have a choice of playing again at the same difficulty level, playing again at another difficulty level, or ending the test. When you decide to end the test, your final percent score will be displayed. See Fig. 6-1 for a sample run.

THE WORD LIST

The word list begins at program line 1000. Its content is arbitrary, with no specific purpose in mind. It may be changed, but the choice of words is up to you. They can be just random words with no apparent connection, or they can be words relating to a specific subject.

To enter a new word list, type in a set of 50 words, in DATA statements, beginning at line 1000. Limit the word length to no longer than six characters, otherwise the word may be too difficult to catch when displayed at difficulty levels 2 and 3. Alternately, you may enter longer words, but limit the difficulty level to level 1.

```
MEMORY CHALLENGER III: RANDOM WORDS              TRY AGAIN?
COPYRIGHT (C) 1981 BY HOWARD BERENBON             1 = YES & SAME DIFFICULTY-**GET READY**
                                                  2 = YES & CHANGE DIFFICULTY
MEMORY CHALLENGER III IS USED TO TEST             0 = NO
YOUR MEMORY. IT DISPLAYS WORDS RANDOMLY           ? 1
FROM A LIST OF 50 WORDS, LOCATED IN DATA
STATEMENTS BEGINNING AT 1000. EACH WORD
WILL APPEAR AT A RANDOM LOCATION ON THE
SCREEN. ENTER THE WORD THAT WAS FLASHED
ON THE SCREEN.

ENTER DIFFICULTY LEVEL:
1=EASY
2=MEDIUM DIFFICULTY
3=MOST DIFFICULT                                                      GET READY
? 2


ENTER '1' TO BEGIN
? 1
                                                                                      KIND



                                                                DIFFICULTY LEVEL  2
                                                  ENTER THE WORD
                GET READY                         ? KIND
                                                  THE ANSWER IS 'KIND'

                                                  CORRECT
                                                  YOU HAVE  2  CORRECT OUT OF  2  TRIES
        SALUTE
                                                  TRY AGAIN?
                                                  1 = YES & SAME DIFFICULTY-**GET READY**
                                                  2 = YES & CHANGE DIFFICULTY
                    DIFFICULTY LEVEL  2            0 = NO
ENTER THE WORD                                    ? 0
? SALUTE
THE ANSWER IS 'SALUTE'

CORRECT
YOU HAVE  1  CORRECT OUT OF  1  TRIES             YOUR FINAL SCORE IS  100  PERCENT
```

Fig. 6-1. Memory Challenger III: Random Words sample run.

```
100   HOME : PRINT "MEMORY CHALLENGER III: RANDOM WORDS"
105   PRINT "APPLE II"
110   PRINT "COPYRIGHT (C) 1981 BY HOWARD BERENBON"
120   PRINT
125   PRINT "MEMORY CHALLENGER III IS USED TO TEST"
130   PRINT "FROM A LIST OF 59 WORDS, LOCATED IN DATA"
145   PRINT "STATEMENTS BEGINNING AT 1000. EACH WORD"
150   PRINT "WILL APPEAR AT A RANDOM LOCATION ON THE"
155   PRINT "SCREEN. ENTER THE WORD THAT WAS FLASHED"
160   PRINT "ON THE SCREEN.": PRINT
170 Z = 0
180 W = 0
190   PRINT "ENTER DIFFICULTY LEVEL:"
200   PRINT "1=EASY"
210   PRINT "2=MEDIUM DIFFICULTY"
220   PRINT "3=MOST DIFFICULT"
230   INPUT A
240   HOME
250   IF A = 1 THEN 550
260   IF A = 2 THEN 590
270   IF A = 3 THEN 630
280   GOTO 190
290   HOME
300   IF D = 1 THEN 330
310   PRINT "ENTER '1' TO BEGIN": INPUT B
330   HOME : VTAB 4
340   PRINT  TAB( 18)"GET READY"
350   FOR D = 1 TO 454
360   NEXT D
370   GOSUB 820
380   HOME
385 R =  INT ( RND (1) * 22 + 1):R1 =  INT ( RND (1) * 37 + 1)
390   VTAB R: PRINT  TAB( R1);G$
400   GOSUB 670
410   HOME
420   PRINT  TAB( 20)"DIFFICULTY LEVEL ";A
430   PRINT "ENTER THE WORD"
440 Z = Z + 1
450   INPUT C$
460   PRINT "THE ANSWER IS '";G$;"'"
470   PRINT
480   IF G$ = C$ THEN 520
490   PRINT "INCORRECT"
500   PRINT "YOU HAVE ";W;" CORRECT OUT OF ";Z;" TRIES"
510   GOTO 720
520   PRINT "CORRECT"
530 W = W + 1
540   GOTO 500
550   REM  DIFFICULTY LEVELS
560 G = 170
570 N =  INT ( RND (1) * 454 + 1)
580   GOTO 300
590 N =  INT ( RND (1) * 340 + 1)
```

```
600 G = 79
620  GOTO 300
630 N =  INT ( RND (1) * 227 + 1)
640 G = 68
660  GOTO 300
670  FOR E = 1 TO G + N
680  NEXT E
690  RETURN
700  PRINT "YOUR FINAL SCORE IS "; INT (W / Z * 100);" PERCENT"
710  END
720  PRINT
730  PRINT "TRY AGAIN?"
740  PRINT "1 = YES & SAME DIFFICULTY-**GET READY**"
750  PRINT "2 = YES & CHANGE DIFFICULTY"
760  PRINT "0 = NO"
770  INPUT D
780  IF D = 1 THEN 330
790  IF D = 2 THEN 190
800  IF D = 0 THEN 700
810  GOTO 720
820 X =  INT ( RND (1) * 50 + 1)
830  FOR T = 1 TO X
840  READ G$
845  NEXT T
850  RESTORE
860  RETURN
1000  DATA ABOVE,ACID,ADMIT,BARGE,BEAR
1010  DATA CAKE,CAR,COW,DODGE,DUST
1020  DATA EDIT,EGG,EVICT,FIRE,FLASH
1030  DATA GAME,GATE,GOLD,HEAT,HEAVY
1040  DATA INCISE,INFANT,INTO,JUST,JUDGE
1050  DATA KNOW,KIND,LADY,LAUGH,LEAVE
1060  DATA MAGIC,MARK,NICE,NEW,PANE
1070  DATA QUART,QUICK,RAFT,RADIO,SALUTE
1080  DATA TREE,THRUST,ULTRA,UNTIL,VEST
1090  DATA WELL,WHITE,YOUNG,ZOOM,ZINC
```

CHAPTER 7

Perception Testing: Eidetic Imagery

Here's a program that may be used in perception testing. It will test for the ability to form eidetic images. Eidetic imagery is the ability of the mind to form an almost photographic image of an object. A recalled eidetic image is a visual sensation and should be perfect. (A very accurate description is not necessarily eidetic.) The program is written in BASIC for your microcomputer. See Program 7-1 for the program listing.

THE PROGRAM

The program will generate two pictures, each made up of asterisks (*). When one is superimposed on the other, a recognizable pattern will result.

Enter a 1 to display the first picture. Study the picture and try to remember it. When you think you have memorized it, enter a 1 to display the second picture. This will erase the first picture and display the second. Now, try to recall the first picture and superimpose its pattern on the second. If you think you can identify what you have seen, then enter the answer at the keyboard. Otherwise enter NO. See Fig. 7-1 for a sample run.

A person that has the ability to form eidetic images will immediately recognize what he or she sees, and the answer will become apparent.

```
PERCEPTION TESTING
EIDETIC IMAGERY
COPYRIGHT (C) 1980 BY HOWARD BERENBON

THIS PROGRAM WILL TEST YOU FOR
THE ABILITY TO FORM EIDETIC IMAGES.
IT WILL GENERATE TWO PICTURES, WHICH
YOU MUST TRY TO MEMORIZE. IF YOU
CAN IDENTIFY THE IMAGE FORMED BY
SUPERIMPOSING THE 1ST ON THE 2ND
THEN ENTER THE ANSWER.

ENTER '1' TO DISPLAY 1ST
PICTURE
? 1


  XXXX
  X
  X
  X
  X   XX
  X

  X
  X     X
   XX X

TRY TO MEMORIZE THIS PICTURE
```

```
ENTER '1' TO DISPLAY 2ND
PICTURE
? 1


  X
        X
        X
        X
    XX
        X
  X     X
        X

  X   X

NOW TRY TO RECALL THE 1ST PICTURE AND
SUPERIMPOSE ITS PATTERN ON THE 2ND.

ENTER '1' TO CONTINUE
? 1


IF YOU CAN IDENTIFY WHAT YOU
HAVE SEEN, THEN ENTER YOUR
ANSWER AT THE KEYBOARD.

OTHERWISE ENTER 'NO'.
?
```

Fig. 7-1. Perception Testing: Eidetic Imagery sample run.

```
100    HOME : PRINT "PERCEPTION TESTING"
110    PRINT "EIDETIC IMAGERY"
120    PRINT "COPYRIGHT (C) 1980 BY HOWARD BERENBON"
130    PRINT "APPLE II"
140    PRINT
150    PRINT "THIS PROGRAM WILL TEST YOU FOR"
160    PRINT "THE ABILITY TO FORM EIDETIC IMAGES."
170    PRINT "IT WILL GENERATE TWO PICTURES, WHICH"
180    PRINT "YOU MUST TRY TO MEMORIZE. IF YOU"
190    PRINT "CAN IDENTIFY THE IMAGE FORMED BY"
200    PRINT "SUPERIMPOSING THE 1ST ON THE 2ND"
210    PRINT "THEN ENTER THE ANSWER."
220    PRINT
230    PRINT "ENTER '1' TO DISPLAY 1ST"
240    PRINT "PICTURE"
250    INPUT A: HOME
260    GOSUB 760
270    PRINT
280    PRINT "TRY TO MEMORIZE THIS PICTURE"
290    PRINT
300    PRINT "ENTER '1' TO DISPLAY 2ND"
310    PRINT "PICTURE"
320    INPUT A: HOME
330    GOSUB 870
340    PRINT
350    PRINT "NOW TRY TO RECALL THE 1ST PICTURE AND"
360    PRINT "SUPERIMPOSE ITS PATTERN ON THE 2ND."
370    PRINT
380    PRINT "ENTER '1' TO CONTINUE"
390    INPUT A: HOME
400    PRINT
410    PRINT "IF YOU CAN IDENTIFY WHAT YOU"
420    PRINT "HAVE SEEN, THEN ENTER YOUR"
430    PRINT "ANSWER AT THE KEYBOARD."
440    PRINT
450    PRINT "OTHERWISE ENTER 'NO'."
460    INPUT A$
470    IF A$ = "B" THEN 640
480    IF A$ = "NO" THEN 520
490    PRINT
500    HOME : PRINT "YOUR ENTRY IS INCORRECT . ."
510    PRINT
520    PRINT "FROM THE ABOVE TEST, THERE IS"
530    PRINT "NO INDICATION THAT YOU HAVE THE"
540    PRINT "ABILITY TO FORM EIDETIC IMAGES."
550    GOSUB 570
560    GOTO 630
570    PRINT
580    PRINT "THE PATTERN SEEN WHEN THE TWO"
590    PRINT "PICTURES ARE SUPERIMPOSED"
600    PRINT "FORMS THE LETTER 'B'."
610    PRINT
620    RETURN
```

```
630  END
640  PRINT
650  HOME : PRINT "CORRECT"
660  GOSUB 570
670  PRINT
680  PRINT "THERE IS AN INDICATION"
690  PRINT "THAT YOU HAVE THE ABILITY"
700  PRINT "TO FORM EIDETIC IMAGES."
710  PRINT
720  PRINT "FURTHER TESTING IS RECOMMENDED,"
730  PRINT "TO VERIFY THIS CONCLUSION."
740  PRINT
750  GOTO 630
760  PRINT " ****"
770  PRINT "*"
780  PRINT "*"
790  PRINT "*"
800  PRINT "*  **"
810  PRINT "*"
820  PRINT
830  PRINT "*"
840  PRINT "*     *"
850  PRINT " ** *"
860  RETURN
870  PRINT "*"
880  PRINT "      *"
890  PRINT "      *"
900  PRINT "      *"
910  PRINT " **"
920  PRINT "      *"
930  PRINT "*     *"
940  PRINT "      *"
950  PRINT
960  PRINT "*  *"
970  RETURN
```

CHAPTER 8

Presidents of the United States

This program tests your knowledge of the Presidents of the United States. It displays a list of Presidents giving their number, name, party, and first year of term. Then, a ten-question test may be taken. The problems are randomly generated from the list of forty Presidents. The program is written in BASIC for your microcomputer. See Program 8-1 for the program listing.

THE PROGRAM

You may review the list of Presidents by entering a 1. Entering a 2 will generate the ten-question test. Each question will display the President's number, his name, and his political party (abbreviated using initials). It requires entry of the first year of the term of office. CORRECT will be displayed if your entry is correct. If your entry is incorrect, then INCORRECT will be displayed along with the correct answer.

After all ten questions are answered, your final score will be displayed, with the number correct out of ten and your percent score. You may now review the list and take another test, or end the program. Four ten-question tests can be taken before any of the questions will be repeated. See Fig. 8-1 for a sample run.

```
PRESIDENTS OF THE UNITED STATES              1ST YEAR OF TERM?
COPYRIGHT (C) 1980 BY HOWARD BERENBON         (ENTER YEAR)
                                              ? 1933
HERE'S AN EDUCATIONAL PROGRAM THAT TESTS      CORRECT
YOUR KNOWLEDGE OF THE PRESIDENTS. IT
DISPLAYS A LIST OF THE PRESIDENTS GIVING
THEIR #, NAME, PARTY, AND FIRST YEAR OF       QUESTION #  3   PRESIDENTS QUIZ
TERM. THEN, A 10 QUESTION QUIZ  MAY BE
TAKEN. RANDOMLY, A NAME OF A PRESIDENT        PRESIDENT OF THE UNITED STATES
IS DISPLAYED. YOU MUST ENTER THE FIRST
YEAR OF THAT TERM.                            PRESIDENT #  4
                                              JAMES MADISON (DR)
ENTER A  '1' TO REVIEW THE LIST
ENTER A  '2' TO TAKE THE TEST                 1ST YEAR OF TERM?
? 2                                           (ENTER YEAR)
                                              ? 1809
                                              CORRECT
10 QUESTION PRESIDENT QUIZ

ENTER '1' TO BEGIN THE TEST
? 1


                                              QUESTION #  10   PRESIDENTS QUIZ

QUESTION #  1   PRESIDENTS QUIZ               PRESIDENT OF THE UNITED STATES

PRESIDENT OF THE UNITED STATES               PRESIDENT #  39
                                              JAMES E. CARTER, JR. (D)
PRESIDENT #  31
HERBERT C. HOOVER (R)                         1ST YEAR OF TERM?
                                              (ENTER YEAR)
1ST YEAR OF TERM?                             ? 1977
(ENTER YEAR)                                  CORRECT
? 1929
CORRECT


                                              FINAL SCORE
QUESTION #  2   PRESIDENTS QUIZ                10 QUESTIONS CORRECT OUT OF 10
                                              THAT'S 100 % CORRECT
PRESIDENT OF THE UNITED STATES
                                              ANOTHER QUIZ  AND REVIEW THE LIST?
PRESIDENT #  32                               ENTER 1-YES 2-NO
FRANKLIN D. ROOSEVELT (D)                     ? 1
```

Fig. 8-1. Presidents of The United States sample run.

```
100   HOME : PRINT "PRESIDENTS OF THE UNITED STATES"
110   PRINT "APPLE II"
120   PRINT "COPYRIGHT (C) 1980 BY HOWARD BERENBON"
130   PRINT : DIM B(50): GOSUB 1150
140   PRINT "HERE'S AN EDUCATIONAL PROGRAM THAT TESTS"
150   PRINT "YOUR KNOWLEGE OF THE PRESIDENTS. IT"
160   PRINT "DISPLAYS A LIST OF THE PRESIDENTS GIVING"
170   PRINT "THEIR #, NAME, PARTY, AND FIRST YEAR OF"
180   PRINT "TERM. THEN, A 10 QUESTION QUIZ MAY BE"
190   PRINT "TAKEN. RANDOMLY, A NAME OF A PRESIDENT"
200   PRINT "IS DISPLAYED. YOU MUST ENTER THE FIRST"
210   PRINT "YEAR OF TERM."
220   PRINT :Q3 = 0
230   PRINT "ENTER A  '1' TO REVIEW THE LIST"
240   PRINT "ENTER A  '2' TO TAKE THE TEST"
250   INPUT A
260   IF A = 1 THEN 290
270   IF A = 2 THEN 410
280   GOTO 230
290   HOME : REM  REVIEW THE LIST
300   FOR B = 1 TO 40
310   HOME
320   PRINT "PRES #    NAME & PARTY           1ST YR-TERM"
330   PRINT
340   READ A$,E
350   PRINT B;"         ";A$;"       ";E
360   GOSUB 920
370   NEXT B
380   RESTORE
390   PRINT
400   GOTO 230
410   HOME : REM  10 QUESTION QUIZ
420   PRINT "10 QUESTION QUIZ"
430   PRINT
440   PRINT "ENTER '1' TO BEGIN THE TEST"
450   INPUT A
460   HOME
470   IF A = 1 THEN 490
480   GOTO 440
490   REM  DISPLAY NAME
500 CA = 0
510   FOR A = 1 TO 10
520   HOME
530   PRINT "QUESTION # ";A,"PRESIDENTS QUIZ"
540   PRINT : GOSUB 1190
550 Q =  INT ( RND (1) * 40 + 1)
560   IF B(Q) = 1 THEN 550
570 B(Q) = 1
580   FOR A1 = 1 TO Q
590   READ A$,E
600   NEXT A1
610   RESTORE
620   PRINT "PRESIDENT OF THE UNITED STATES"
```

```
630   PRINT
640   PRINT "PRESIDENT # ";Q
650   PRINT A$
660   PRINT
670   PRINT "1ST YEAR OF TERM?"
680   PRINT "(ENTER YEAR)"
690   INPUT F
700   IF F = E THEN 760
710   GOSUB 900
720   PRINT "THE CORRECT YEAR IS ";E
730   GOSUB 920
740   NEXT A
750   GOTO 800
760   PRINT "CORRECT"
770 CA = CA + 1
780   GOSUB 920
790   NEXT A
800   HOME
810   PRINT "FINAL SCORE"
820   PRINT CA;" QUESTIONS CORRECT OUT OF 10"
830   PRINT "THAT'S ";10 * CA;" % CORRECT"
840   PRINT
850   PRINT "ANOTHER QUIZ AND REVIEW THE LIST?"
860   PRINT "ENTER  1-YES  2-NO"
870   INPUT Y
880   IF Y = 1 THEN 230
890   END
900   PRINT "INCORRECT"
910   RETURN
920   FOR T = 1 TO 2270
930   NEXT T
940   RETURN
950   DATA "GEORGE WASHINGTON (F)",1789,"JOHN ADAMS (F)       ",1797
960   DATA "THOMAS JEFFERSON (DR)",1801,"JAMES MADISON (DR)",1809
970   DATA "JAMES MONROE (DR)",1817,"JOHN Q. ADAMS (DR)",1825
980   DATA "ANDREW JACKSON (D)",1829,"MARTIN VAN BUREN (D)",1837
990   DATA "WILLIAM H. HARRISON (W)",1841,"JOHN TYLER (W)       ",1841
1000  DATA "JAMES KNOX POLK (D)",1845,"ZACHARY TAYLOR (W)",1849
1010  DATA "MILLARD FILLMORE (W)",1850,"FRANKLIN PIERCE (D)",1853
1020  DATA "JAMES BUCHANAN (D)",1857,"ABRAHAM LINCOLN (R)",1861
1030  DATA "ANDREW JOHNSON (R)",1865,"ULYSSES S. GRANT (R)",1869
1040  DATA "RUTHERFORD B. HAYES (R)",1877,"JAMES A. GARFIELD (R)",1881
1050  DATA "CHESTER A. ARTHUR (R)",1881,"GROVER CLEVELAND (D)",1885
1060  DATA "BENJAMIN HARRISON (R)",1889,"GROVER CLEVELAND (D)",1893
1070  DATA "WILLIAM MCKINLEY (R)",1897,"THEODORE ROOSEVELT (R)",1901
1080  DATA "WILLIAM H. TAFT (R)",1909,"WOODROW WILSON (D)",1913
1090  DATA "WARREN G. HARDING (R)",1921,"CALVIN COOLIDGE (R)",1923
1100  DATA "HERBERT C. HOOVER (R)",1929,"FRANKLIN D. ROOSEVELT (D)",1933
1110  DATA "HARRY S. TRUMAN (D)",1945,"DWIGHT D. EISENHOWER (R)",1953
1120  DATA "JOHN F. KENNEDY (D)",1961,"LYNDON B. JOHNSON (D)",1963
1130  DATA "RICHARD M. NIXON (R)",1969,"GERALD R. FORD (R)",1974
1140  DATA "JAMES E. CARTER, JR. (D)",1977,"RONALD REAGAN (R)",1981
1150  FOR I = 1 TO 40
```

```
1160 B(I) = 0
1170  NEXT I
1180  RETURN
1190 Q3 = Q3 + 1
1200  IF Q3 > 40 THEN Q3 = 0: GOSUB 1150
1210  RETURN
```

CHAPTER 9

State Capitals

This program tests your knowledge of the state capitals of the United States. For a review it displays a list of all fifty states and their capitals. Then a ten-question test may be taken. The program is written in BASIC for your microcomputer. See Program 9-1 for the program listing.

THE PROGRAM

After you run the program, you may enter a 1 to review the state capitals, enter a 2 to take the ten-question test, or enter a 3 to end the program.

After you enter a 2 to take the test, enter a 1 to begin. You are required to enter the name of the state capital for the state that is displayed. CORRECT will be displayed for a correct entry. If your answer is incorrect, then INCORRECT will be displayed, along with the correct answer. When all ten questions are answered, your final score will be displayed, with the number correct out of ten and the percent score. You may now review the states, take another test, or end the program. Five tests may be taken without any of the questions being repeated.

See Fig 9-1 for a sample run.

```
STATE CAPITALS
COPYRIGHT (C) 1980 BY HOWARD BERENBON

THIS PROGRAM TESTS YOUR KNOWLEDGE
OF STATE CAPITALS. IT GIVES A TEN
QUESTION QUIZ , RANDOMLY CHOOSING
THE QUESTIONS. THE LIST OF STATES AND
CAPITALS MAY BE REVIEWED BEFORE TAKING
THE TEST.

ENTER 1-REVIEW STATE CAPITALS
      2-FOR TEST
      3-END PROGRAM
? 2


10 QUESTION STATE CAPITAL TEST

ENTER '1' TO BEGIN
? 1


QUESTION #  1  STATE CAPITALS

THE STATE IS: MASSACHUSETTS

ENTER ITS CAPITAL
? BOSTON

CORRECT




QUESTION #  2  STATE CAPITALS

THE STATE IS: WASHINGTON

ENTER ITS CAPITAL
? OLYMPIA

CORRECT


QUESTION #  3  STATE CAPITALS

THE STATE IS: DELAWARE

ENTER ITS CAPITAL
? DOVER

CORRECT




QUESTION #  10  STATE CAPITALS

THE STATE IS: CONNECTICUT

ENTER ITS CAPITAL
? HARTFORD

CORRECT




FINAL SCORE:
  10  QUESTIONS CORRECT OUT OF 10
THAT'S  100  % CORRECT




ENTER 1-REVIEW STATE CAPITALS
      2-FOR TEST
      3-END PROGRAM
? 1
```

Fig. 9-1. State Capitals sample run.

```
100   HOME : PRINT "STATE CAPITALS"
110   PRINT "COPYRIGHT (C) 1980 BY HOWARD BERENBON"
120   PRINT "APPLE II":Q3 = 0
130   PRINT : DIM B(50): GOSUB 1100
140   PRINT "THIS PROGRAM TESTS YOUR KNOWLEDGE"
150   PRINT "OF STATE CAPITALS. IT GIVES A TEN"
160   PRINT "QUESTION QUIZ, RANDOMLY CHOOSING"
170   PRINT "THE QUESTIONS. THE LIST OF STATES AND"
180   PRINT "CAPITALS MAY BE REVIEWED BEFORE TAKING"
190   PRINT "THE TEST."
200   PRINT
210   PRINT "ENTER 1-REVIEW STATE CAPITALS"
220   PRINT  TAB( 7)"2-FOR TEST"
230   PRINT  TAB( 7)"3-END PROGRAM"
240   INPUT A
250   ON A GOTO 270,420,800
260   GOTO 200
270   HOME : PRINT "REVIEWING THE STATES"
280 GT = 2: GOSUB 380
290   FOR A = 1 TO 50
300   READ S$,C$
310   PRINT "STATE","CAPITAL"
320   PRINT
330   PRINT S$,C$
340 GT = 2: GOSUB 380
350   NEXT A
360   RESTORE
370   GOTO 200
380   FOR T = 1 TO 750 * GT
390   NEXT T
400   HOME
410   RETURN
420   HOME : PRINT "TEN QUESTION STATE CAPITAL TEST"
430   PRINT
440   PRINT "ENTER '1' TO BEGIN"
450   INPUT D
460   HOME
470   IF D = 1 THEN 490
480   GOTO 430
490 CA = 0
500   FOR Q = 1 TO 10
510   HOME : PRINT "QUESTION # ";Q;" STATE CAPITALS"
520   PRINT : GOSUB 810
530 R =  INT ( RND (1) * 50 + 1)
540   IF B(R) = 1 THEN 530
550 B(R) = 1
560   FOR H = 1 TO R
570   READ S$,C$
580   NEXT H
590   RESTORE
600   PRINT "THE STATE IS: ";S$
610   PRINT
620   PRINT "ENTER ITS CAPITAL"
```

```
630  INPUT C1$
640  IF C1$ = C$ THEN 710
650  PRINT
660  PRINT "INCORRECT"
670  PRINT "THE CAPITAL OF ";S$;" IS '";C$;"'"
680 GT = 3: GOSUB 380
690  NEXT Q
700  GOTO 750
710  PRINT
720  PRINT "CORRECT"
730 CA = CA + 1
740  GOTO 680
750  HOME : PRINT "FINAL SCORE:"
760  PRINT CA;" QUESTIONS CORRECT OUT OF 10"
770  PRINT "THAT'S ";10 * CA;" % CORRECT"
780 GT = 3: GOSUB 380
790  GOTO 200
800  END
810 Q3 = Q3 + 1
820  IF Q3 > 50 THEN Q3 = 0: GOTO 840
830  RETURN
840  GOSUB 1100: RETURN
850  DATA ALABAMA,MONTGOMERY,ALASKA,JUNEAU
860  DATA ARIZONA,PHOENIX,ARKANSAS,LITTLE ROCK
870  DATA CALIFORNIA,SACRAMENTO,COLORADO,DENVER
880  DATA CONNECTICUT,HARTFORD,DELAWARE,DOVER
890  DATA FLORIDA,TALLAHASSEE,GEORGIA,ATLANTA
900  DATA HAWAII,HONOLULU,IDAHO,BOISE
910  DATA ILLINOIS,SPRINGFIELD,INDIANA,INDIANAPOLIS
920  DATA IOWA,DES MOINES,KANSAS,TOPEKA
930  DATA KENTUCKY,FRANKFORT,LOUISIANA,BATON ROUGE
940  DATA MAINE,AUGUSTA,MARYLAND,ANNAPOLIS
950  DATA MASSACHUSETTS,BOSTON,MICHIGAN,LANSING
960  DATA MINNESOTA,ST. PAUL,MISSISSIPPI,JACKSON
970  DATA MISSOURI,JEFFERSON CITY,MONTANA,HELENA
980  DATA NEBRASKA,LINCOLN,NEVADA,CARSON CITY
990  DATA NEW HAMPSHIRE,CONCORD,NEW JERSEY,TRENTON
1000  DATA NEW MEXICO,SANTA FE,NEW YORK,ALBANY
1010  DATA NORTH CAROLINA,RALEIGH,NORTH DAKOTA,BISMARCK
1020  DATA OHIO,COLUMBUS,OKLAHOMA,OKLAHOMA CITY
1030  DATA OREGON,SALEM,PENNSYLVANIA,HARRISBURG
1040  DATA RHODE ISLAND,PROVIDENCE,SOUTH CAROLINA,COLUMBIA
1050  DATA SOUTH DAKOTA,PIERRE,TENNESSEE,NASHVILLE
1060  DATA TEXAS,AUSTIN,UTAH,SALT LAKE CITY
1070  DATA  VERMONT,MONTPELIER,VIRGINIA,RICHMOND
1080  DATA WASHINGTON,OLYMPIA,WEST VIRGINIA,CHARLESTON
1090  DATA WISCONSIN,MADISON,WYOMING,CHEYENNE
1100  FOR I = 1 TO 50
1110 B(I) = 0
1120  NEXT I
1130  RETURN
```

CHAPTER 10

The Student Grader

The Student Grader is a program designed to aid the teacher. It will accept entry of each student's individual grades, and it will display each set of grades with their average. It will also display the class average for any number of students in the list. The program is written in BASIC for your microcomputer. See Program 10-1 for the program listing.

THE PROGRAM

The program accepts entry of the student's grades, in DATA statements, beginning at line 500. Enter each student's name, each grade in percent (separated by commas), and the number 999, which is used to detect the end of each student's grades. After the whole list of students' grades is entered, DATA "END" must be entered as the last DATA statement in the list. The following are examples of DATA statement entries:

```
550 DATA TOM SMITH,86,78,79,88,80,999
560 DATA MIKE ROSS,78,88,90,90,85,83,999
```

Each of the students' grade lists may have a different number of percent scores. The program calculates the average score on the number of grades in each student's DATA statement.

After you run the program, enter a 1 to begin.

The program will display each of the student's grades, and the average grade, for all of the students in the list. The program will also display the class average, calculated by adding each average grade of each student and dividing by the total number of students.

See Fig. 10-1 for a sample run.

```
THE STUDENT GRADER
COPYRIGHT (C) 1980 BY HOWARD BERENBON


THIS PROGRAM WILL AID THE TEACHER
IN RECORDING AND GRADING TEST SCORES.

ENTER EACH STUDENT'S NAME AND GRADES
IN DATA STATEMENTS BEGINNING AT LINE
500. ENTER AS FOLLOWS:
DATA NAME,60,70,80,78,79,67,999
999 MUST BE THE LAST NUMBER, WHICH
DETECTS THE END OF THE GRADES. ALSO,
DATA 'END' MUST BE THE LAST DATA
STATEMENT IN THE DATA LIST.

ENTER A '1' TO BEGIN
? 1


THE STUDENT GRADER

NAME       GRADE(%)

RICK   86   78   85   79   88   80   AVE= 83
BRUCE  78   80   78   90   91   78   AVE= 83
DAVE   89   88   87   67   68   90   AVE= 82
MIKE   56   60   67   56   80   70   AVE= 65

CLASS AVERAGE WITH  4  STUDENTS
IS  78  PERCENT
```

Fig. 10-1. The Student Grader sample run.

```
100   HOME : PRINT "THE STUDENT GRADER"
110   PRINT "COPYRIGHT (C) 1980 BY HOWARD BERENBON"
120   PRINT "APPLE II"
130   PRINT : PRINT : GOSUB 480
140   PRINT "THIS PROGRAM WILL AID THE TEACHER"
150   PRINT "IN RECORDING AND GRADING TEST SCORES."
160   PRINT
170   PRINT "ENTER EACH STUDENT'S NAME AND GRADES"
180   PRINT "IN DATA STATEMENTS BEGINNING AT LINE"
190   PRINT "500. ENTER AS FOLLOWS:"
200   PRINT "DATA NAME,60,70,80,78,79,67,999"
210   PRINT "999 MUST BE THE LAST NUMBER, WHICH"
220   PRINT "DETECTS THE END OF THE GRADES. ALSO,"
230   PRINT "DATA 'END' MUST BE THE LAST DATA"
240   PRINT "STATEMENT IN THE DATA LIST."
250   PRINT
260   PRINT "ENTER A '1' TO BEGIN"
270   INPUT S
280   HOME :N = 0:C = 0
290 N1 = 0:C1 = 0
300   PRINT "THE STUDENT GRADER"
310   PRINT
320   PRINT "NAME"; TAB( 10)"GRADE(%)"
330   PRINT
340   READ A$: IF A$ = "END" THEN 440
350   PRINT A$;" ";
360   READ B: IF B = 999 THEN 410
370   PRINT B;" ";
380 N = N + 1
390 C = B + C
400   GOTO 360
410 S1 =  INT ((C / N) + .5): PRINT " AVE=";S1: GOSUB 480
420 C1 = S1 + C1:N = 0:C = 0:N1 = N1 + 1
430   GOTO 340
440   RESTORE : PRINT
450 A1 =  INT ((C1 / N1) + .5): PRINT "CLASS AVERAGE WITH ";N1;" STUDENTS"
460   PRINT "IS ";A1;" PERCENT"
470   END
480   FOR T = 1 TO 2043
490   NEXT T: RETURN
500   DATA "RICK",86,78,85,79,88,80,999
510   DATA "BRUCE",78,80,78,90,91,78,999
520   DATA "DAVE",89,88,87,67,68,90,999
530   DATA "MIKE",56,60,67,56,80,70,999
540   DATA "END"
```

CHAPTER 11

Relativistic Mass Simulation

Here's a scientific program using Einstein's theory of relativity. It takes the formula for the mass of a body in motion as it relates to the speed of light, and allows an interesting simulation. The program will display the change in mass for an object traveling at a given velocity, having a rest mass of m_o. It is written in BASIC for your microcomputer. See Program 11-1 for the program listing.

THE PROGRAM

The program creates the relativistic mass simulation using Einstein's equation:

$$m = \frac{m_o}{\sqrt{1 - v^2/c^2}}$$

where
    m is the mass of the moving object,
    m_o is the mass of the object at rest,
    v is the velocity of the object,
    c is the speed of light (2.997925×10^8 meters/
    second).

It allows the entry of the rest mass, m_o, of a given object, and its velocity, v. Enter the mass of the object in kilograms, and its velocity in meters per second. The program displays the mass of the object at rest, the mass at the velocity entered, the change in mass, and the percent change in mass.

Entering a small velocity will display no apparent change in mass. But as you increase the velocity, the change will become noticeable. When your test velocity approaches the speed of light, the mass change will become more apparent. The program will accept entry of any initial mass value, but it will limit the velocity entry to less than the speed of light, following Einstein's Special Theory of Relativity.

After the simulation is complete, enter a 1 to continue with the same mass and different velocity, enter a 2 to continue the simulation with a different mass, enter a 3 for a new simulation, or enter a 4 to end the program.

See Fig. 11-1 for a sample run.

Fig. 11-1. Relativisitc Mass Simulation sample run.

```
RELATIVISTIC MASS SIMULATION
COPYRIGHT (C) 1980 BY HOWARD BERENBON

THIS PROGRAM  WILL DISPLAY THE
CHANGE IN MASS FOR AN OBJECT
TRAVELING AT A GIVEN VELOCITY,
HAVING A REST MASS OF M0.
IT USES EINSTEIN'S RELATIONSHIP
THAT THE MASS OF AN OBJECT
INCREASES AS ITS VELOCITY INCREASES

ENTER THE NAME OF THE OBJECT
IN THE SIMULATION
? SPACE CAPSULE


ENTER THE MASS AT REST (KG)
FOR THE OBJECT 'SPACE CAPSULE'
? 2724

ENTER SIMULATED VELOCITY (M/S)
FOR THE OBJECT 'SPACE CAPSULE'
? 20000

GIVEN THE OBJECT: SPACE CAPSULE
WITH A REST MASS OF  2724  KG

THE MASS OF THE OBJECT:
SPACE CAPSULE-AT  20000  M/S IS
 2724  KG

THE INCREASE IN MASS IS
 0  KG, OR  0  %

ENTER 1-CONT. SIMULATION-SAME MASS
      2-CONT. SIMULATION-DIFF. MASS
      3-NEW SIMULATION
      4-END PROGRAM
? 1

ENTER THE SIMULATED VELOCITY (M/S)
FOR THE OBJECT 'SPACE CAPSULE'
? 2200000

GIVEN THE OBJECT: SPACE CAPSULE
WITH A REST MASS OF  2724  KG

THE MASS OF THE OBJECT:
SPACE CAPSULE-AT  2.2E+06  M/S IS
 2724.07  KG

THE INCREASE IN MASS IS
 .0732422  KG, OR  2.68877E-03  %

ENTER 1-CONT. SIMULATION-SAME MASS
      2-CONT. SIMULATION-DIFF. MASS
      3-NEW SIMULATION
      4-END PROGRAM
? 1


ENTER THE SIMULATED VELOCITY (M/S)
FOR THE OBJECT 'SPACE CAPSULE'
? 2.24E+08


GIVEN THE OBJECT: SPACE CAPSULE
WITH A REST MASS OF  2724  KG

THE MASS OF THE OBJECT:
SPACE CAPSULE-AT  2.24E+08  M/S IS
 4098.6  KG

THE INCREASE IN MASS IS
 1374.6  KG, OR  50.4624  %

ENTER 1-CONT. SIMULATION-SAME MASS
      2-CONT. SIMULATION-DIFF. MASS
      3-NEW SIMULATION
      4-END PROGRAM
? 4
```

```
100   HOME
110   PRINT "RELATIVISTIC MASS SIMULATION"
120   PRINT "COPYRIGHT (C) 1980 BY HOWARD BERENBON"
130   PRINT "APPLE II"
140   PRINT :C = 2.997925E + 8
150   PRINT "THIS PROGRAM WILL DISPLAY THE"
160   PRINT "CHANGE IN MASS FOR AN OBJECT"
170   PRINT "TRAVELING AT A GIVEN VELOCITY,"
180   PRINT "HAVING A REST MASS OF MO."
190   PRINT "IT USES EINSTEIN'S RELATIONSHIP"
200   PRINT "THAT THE MASS OF AN OBJECT"
210   PRINT "INCREASES AS ITS VELOCITY INCREASES"
220   PRINT
230   PRINT "ENTER THE NAME OF THE OBJECT"
240   PRINT "IN THE SIMULATION"
250   INPUT A$
260   PRINT
270   PRINT "ENTER THE MASS AT REST (KG)"
280   PRINT "FOR THE OBJECT '";A$;"'"
290   INPUT M
300   PRINT
310   PRINT "ENTER THE SIMULATED VELOCITY (M/S)"
320   PRINT "FOR THE OBJECT '";A$;"'"
330   INPUT V
340   IF V >  = C THEN 570
350  V2 = V * V
360   HOME :C2 = C * C
370   PRINT "GIVEN THE OBJECT: ";A$
380   PRINT "WITH A  REST MASS OF ";M;" KG"
390  Q =  SQR (1 - (V2 / C2))
400  MR = M / Q:T = MR - M
410   PRINT
420   PRINT "THE MASS OF THE OBJECT:"
430   PRINT A$;"-AT ";V;" M/S IS"
440   PRINT MR;" KG"
450   PRINT
460   PRINT "THE INCREASE IN MASS IS"
470   PRINT T;" KG";: GOSUB 650
480   PRINT
490   PRINT "ENTER 1-CONT. SIMULATION-SAME MASS"
500   PRINT  TAB( 7)"2-CONT. SIMULATION-DIFF. MASS"
510   PRINT  TAB( 7)"3-NEW SIMULATION"
520   PRINT  TAB( 7)"4-END PROGRAM"
530   INPUT T
540   ON T GOTO 300,260,110,560
550   GOTO 480
560   END
570   PRINT
580   PRINT "EINSTEIN SAID THAT NO OBJECT CAN"
590   PRINT "TRAVEL EQUAL TO OR GREATER THAN"
600   PRINT "SPEED OF LIGHT."
610   PRINT
620   PRINT "ENTER A VELOCITY LESS THAN THE"
```

```
630  PRINT "SPEED OF LIGHT."
640  GOTO 300
650 P = (T / M) * 100
660  PRINT ", OR ";P;" %"
670  RETURN
```

SECTION II

Home Applications

This section describes some useful home application programs including a monthly budget program, a valuables inventory, a telephone number directory, a special date calendar, a weekly calendar, gas and water usage analysis, electrical appliance operating cost analysis, family dental expenses, weekly jogging record, and, finally, a cost of food analysis.

Monthly Budget

Here's a program that will help you budget your household expenses. It accepts entry of your monthly net wage and individual expenses to calculate the amount available to save. The program is written in BASIC for your microcomputer. See Program 12-1 for the program listing.

THE PROGRAM

The program begins by requesting the month number (1–12) for analysis. Then it requests your monthly net wage. Next, you are required to enter all monthly expenses, under the following categories:

1. Rent, or house payment
2. Utility expenses
   a. Telephone bill
   b. Electric bill
   c. Gas or oil costs
   d. Water bill
3. Garbage pickup
4. Monthly food bills
5. Clothing, shoes, linen
6. Drugstore purchases
7. Medical expenses
8. Bank charges
9. House expenses
10. Automobile expenses
11. Entertainment expenses
12. Miscellaneous expenses

The monthly food bill category allows entry of individual food bills, for that month. Entering a 999 allows you to advance to the next category. All other categories accept only one expense entry per month.

After all your monthly expenses are entered, the program calculates the total expense for that month. It then displays the month number, monthly wage (allowed budget amount), and your total monthly expense.

The difference between your total monthly expense and your monthly budget amount is calculated and displayed. If you spent less during the month than your budget allows, then it is recommended that the amount left over be saved. If you are over your monthly budget, then this will be noted.

See Fig. 12-1 for a sample run.

```
MONTHLY BUDGET
COPYRIGHT '(C) 1980 BY HOWARD BERENBON

THE MONTHLY BUDGET PROGRAM WILL
HELP YOU BUDGET YOUR HOUSEHOLD
EXPENSES. ENTER YOUR MONTHLY NET
WAGE, OR AMOUNT ALLOWED, AND TOTAL
MONTHLY EXPENSES. THE AMOUNT LEFT
OVER AFTER ALL BILLS ARE PAID WILL
BE THE AMOUNT AVAILABLE TO SAVE.

ENTER MONTH # (1-12)
? 4


ENTER MONTHLY NET WAGE (BUDGET AMT)
? 816


ENTER MONTHLY STATISTICS

RENT OR HOUSE PAYMENT
? 300

UTILITY EXPENSES

TELEPHONE
? 10
ELECTRIC
? 15
GAS OR OIL
? 15
WATER
? 4

GARBAGE PICKUP
? 10


MONTHLY FOOD BILLS
1 BILL PER ENTRY
(ENTER 999 TO STOP)
# 1
? 75

MONTHLY FOOD BILLS
1 BILL PER ENTRY
(ENTER 999 TO STOP)
# 2
? 999




ENTER MONTHLY STATISTICS

CLOTHING, SHOES, LINEN
? 24
DRUG STORE PURCHASES
? 15
MEDICAL EXPENSES
(DOCTOR, DENTIST, ETC.)
? 25
BANK CHARGES
? 0
HOUSE EXPENSES (INSURANCE, REPAIRS, ETC)
? 10


AUTOMOBILE EXPENSES
(REPAIRS, GAS, ETC.)
? 50
ENTERTAINMENT (MOVIES, PLAYS, DINNERS
BOOKS, MAGAZINES, ETC.)
? 85
MISCELLANEOUS EXPENSES
? 25




MONTHLY BUDGET STATISTICS FOR
MONTH # 4

MONTHLY WAGE OR ALLOWED AMT=$ 816

YOUR TOTAL MONTHLY EXPENSE
IS $ 663

YOU SPENT LESS IN MONTH # 4 , AND
HAVE $ 153  LEFT OVER TO SAVE.
```

Fig. 12-1. Monthly Budget sample run.

```
100    HOME : PRINT "MONTHLY BUDGET"
110    PRINT "COPYRIGHT (C) 1980 BY HOWARD BERENBON"
120    PRINT "APPLE II"
130    PRINT
140    PRINT "THE MONTHLY BUDGET PROGRAM WILL"
150    PRINT "HELP YOU BUDGET YOUR HOUSEHOLD"
160    PRINT "EXPENSES. ENTER YOUR MONTHLY NET"
170    PRINT "WAGE, OR AMOUNT ALLOWED, AND TOTAL"
180    PRINT "MONTHLY EXPENSES. THE AMOUNT LEFT"
190    PRINT "OVER AFTER ALL BILLS ARE PAID WILL"
200    PRINT "BE THE AMOUNT AVAILABLE TO SAVE."
210    PRINT
220    PRINT "ENTER MONTH # (1-12)"
230    INPUT N: IF N < 1 OR N > 12 THEN 210
240    PRINT
250    PRINT "ENTER MONTHLY NET WAGE (BUDGET AMT)"
260    INPUT W
270    GOSUB 890
280    PRINT "RENT OR HOUSE PAYMENT"
290    INPUT R: PRINT
300    PRINT "UTILITY EXPENSES"
310    PRINT
320    PRINT "TELEPHONE"
330    INPUT T
340    PRINT "ELECTRIC"
350    INPUT E
360    PRINT "GAS OR OIL"
370    INPUT G
380    PRINT "WATER"
390    INPUT WA
400    PRINT "GARBAGE PICKUP"
410    INPUT GA
420    HOME :F = O:FC = 1
430    PRINT "MONTHLY FOOD BILLS"
440    PRINT "1 BILL PER ENTRY"
450    PRINT "(ENTER 999 TO STOP)"
460    PRINT "#";FC
470 FC = FC + 1
480    INPUT FD: IF FD = 999 THEN 510
490    PRINT :F = FD + F
500    GOTO 430
510    GOSUB 890
520    PRINT "CLOTHING, SHOES, LINEN"
530    INPUT CL
540    PRINT "DRUG STORE PURCHASES"
550    INPUT DR
560    PRINT "MEDICAL EXPENSES"
570    PRINT "(DOCTOR, DENTIST, ETC.)"
580    INPUT M
590    PRINT "BANK CHARGES"
600    INPUT BC
610    PRINT "HOUSE EXPENSES (INSURANCE, REPAIRS, ETC)"
620    INPUT HR
```

```
630   PRINT "AUTOMOBILE EXPENSES"
640   PRINT "(REPAIRS, GAS, ETC.)"
650   INPUT AU
660   PRINT "ENTERTAINMENT (MOVIES, PLAYS, DINNERS"
670   PRINT "BOOKS, MAGAZINES, ETC.)"
680   INPUT EN
690   PRINT "MISCELLANEOUS EXPENSES"
700   INPUT MS
710   REM  CALCULATE EXPENSES
720 TL = R + T + E + G + WA + GA + F + CL + DR + M + BC + HR + AU + EN + MS
730   HOME
740 BU = W - TL
750   PRINT "MONTHLY BUDGET STATISTICS FOR"
760   PRINT "MONTH #";N
770   PRINT
780   PRINT "MONTHLY WAGE OR ALLOWED AMT=$";W
790   PRINT
800   PRINT "YOUR TOTAL MONTHLY EXPENSE"
810   PRINT "IS $";TL
820   PRINT : IF TL > W THEN 860
830   PRINT "YOU SPENT LESS IN MONTH #";N;", AND"
840   PRINT "HAVE $";BU;" LEFT OVER TO SAVE."
850   GOTO 880
860 ET = TL - W
870   PRINT "YOU SPENT $";ET;" OVER YOUR BUDGET"
880   END
890   HOME : PRINT "ENTER MONTHLY STATISTICS"
900   PRINT
910   RETURN
```

CHAPTER 13

Valuables Inventory

The Valuables Inventory program keeps a list of your valuables, including the name of each item and its price. It is useful for keeping a record of your valuables for insurance purposes. The program is written in BASIC for your microcomputer. See Program 13-1 for the program listing.

THE PROGRAM

The valuables data must be entered into DATA statements, beginning at line 850. Enter the items in the following format:

DATA CATEGORY #,NAME,PRICE

or

850 DATA 1,BRACELET,225

The category number is a number from 1 to 6. It represents the following types of items:

1—Gold, silver, jewelry
2—Appliances
3—Furniture
4—Clothing
5—Collectables (art, antiques, etc.)
6—Miscellaneous

Each item should have its own data statement with the category number, its name, and its value entered. After all items are entered, then DATA 9999,0,0 must be the last DATA statement in the list.

After running the program, enter a 1 to begin. The program calculates and displays the cumulative total worth of your valuables. Then you have the option of listing the items, prices, and cumulative total for each category separately (1–6), display the total list, or end the program. Enter a 7 to display the total list, or an 8 to end the program. See Fig. 13-1 for a sample run.

IDENTIFICATION NUMBER

Use the DATA statement line number as an identification number (ID) for each item in your valuables list. Engrave the statement number, if possible, to the corresponding item. In case of a fire or theft, you have a record of each item, with its separate ID number. Keep a cassette copy of the program, with the inventory data list, in a safety deposit box for insurance purposes.

```
VALUABLES INVENTORY
COPYRIGHT (C) 1980 BY HOWARD BERENSON

THIS PROGRAM WILL KEEP A LIST
OF YOUR VALUABLES, AND ALLOW YOU
TO DISPLAY A PARTIAL OR FULL LIST
WITH EACH ITEM NAME, VALUE, AND
CUMULATIVE VALUE. ENTER THE ITEMS
IN DATA STATEMENTS BEGINNING AT
LINE 850, IN THE FOLLOWING FORMAT:
DATA CATEGORY,NAME,PRICE
DATA 1,BRACELET,225
DATA 9999,0,0 IS THE LAST STATEMENT
ENTER '1' TO BEGIN
? 1


ENTER CATEGORY #
1-GOLD, SILVER, JEWELRY
2-APPLIANCES
3-FURNITURE
4-CLOTHING
5-COLLECTABLES
6-MISCELLANEOUS
7-TOTAL LIST
8-END PROGRAM

? 5


5
COLLECTABLES

ITEM            PRICE           CUM. TOTAL
OIL PAINTING    1700            1700
WATER COLOR     190             1890



6
MISCELLANEOUS

ITEM            PRICE           CUM. TOTAL
BICYCLE         175             175
CHESS SET       200             375
```

Fig. 13-1. Valuables Inventory sample run.

```
100   HOME : PRINT "VALUABLES INVENTORY"
110   PRINT "COPYRIGHT (C) 1980 BY HOWARD BERENBON"
120   PRINT "APPLE II"
130   PRINT
140   PRINT "THIS PROGRAM WILL KEEP A LIST"
150   PRINT "OF YOUR VALUABLES, AND ALLOW YOU"
160   PRINT "TO DISPLAY A PARTIAL OR FULL LIST"
170   PRINT "WITH EACH ITEM NAME, VALUE, AND"
180   PRINT "CUMULATIVE VALUE. ENTER THE ITEMS"
190   PRINT "IN DATA STATEMENTS BEGINNING AT"
200   PRINT "LINE 850, IN THE FOLLOWING FORMAT:"
210   PRINT "DATA CATEGORY,NAME,PRICE"
220   PRINT "DATA 1,BRACELET,225"
230   PRINT "DATA 9999,0,0 IS THE LAST STATEMENT"
240   PRINT "ENTER '1' TO BEGIN"
250   INPUT A: HOME
260   RESTORE : IF B = 7 THEN A = A + 1: PRINT : GOTO 400
270   IF T > 0 THEN  PRINT "CUM. TOTAL =$";T
280   PRINT : PRINT "ENTER CATEGORY #"
290 T = 0:C = 0:E = 0
300   PRINT "1-GOLD, SILVER, JEWELRY"
310   PRINT "2-APPLIANCES"
320   PRINT "3-FURNITURE"
330   PRINT "4-CLOTHING"
340   PRINT "5-COLLECTABLES"
350   PRINT "6-MISCELLANEOUS"
360   PRINT "7-TOTAL LIST"
370   PRINT "8-END PROGRAM"
380   PRINT
390   INPUT A: IF A = 7 THEN B = 7
400   IF B = 7 THEN E = E + 1: IF E = 7 THEN 730
410   ON A GOTO 460,500,540,580,620,660,700,730
420   GOTO 280
430   FOR G = 1 TO 2043
440   NEXT G
450   RETURN
460   PRINT : PRINT "GOLD, SILVER, JEWELRY"
470   GOSUB 750
480   GOSUB 780
490   GOTO 260
500   PRINT "APPLIANCES"
510   GOSUB 750
520   GOSUB 780
530   GOTO 260
540   PRINT "FURNITURE"
550   GOSUB 750
560   GOSUB 780
570   GOTO 260
580   PRINT "CLOTHING"
590   GOSUB 750
600   GOSUB 780
610   GOTO 260
620   PRINT "COLLECTABLES"
```

```
630   GOSUB 750
640   GOSUB 780
650   GOTO 260
660   PRINT "MISCELLANEOUS"
670   GOSUB 750
680   GOSUB 780
690   GOTO 260
700   PRINT "TOTAL LIST"
710 A = 1:E = 1
720   GOTO 410
730   END
740   REM   TABLE
750   PRINT
760   PRINT "ITEM                  PRICE   CUM. TOTAL"
770   RETURN
780   READ C,D$,P
790   IF C = 9999 THEN   RETURN
800   IF C < > (A) THEN 780
810 T = P + T
820   PRINT D$; TAB( 22);P; TAB( 30);T
830   GOSUB 430
840   GOTO 780
850   DATA 1,"SILVERWARE",1500
860   DATA 1,"GOLD BRACELET",500
870   DATA 5,"OIL PAINTING",1700
880   DATA 4,"MINK COAT",1200
890   DATA 2,"COLOR TV",540
900   DATA 3,"COUCH",1195
910   DATA 3,"CHAIR",875
920   DATA 3,"DINING TABLE",880
930   DATA 2,"STEREO",695
940   DATA 1,"WATCH",295
950   DATA 6,"BICYCLE",175
960   DATA 5,"WATER COLOR",190
970   DATA 2,"COMPUTER",3500
980   DATA 2,"WASHER/DRYER",700
990   DATA 2,"BW TV",95
1000   DATA 6,"CHESS SET",200
1010   DATA 4,"COATS",450
1020   DATA 4,"SHOES",275
1030   DATA 3,"DESK",250
1040   DATA 9999,0,0
```

CHAPTER 14

Telephone Number Directory

The Telephone Number Directory will list names and telephone numbers from your list of names and numbers in DATA statements. The program is written in BASIC for your microcomputer. See Program 14-1 for the program listing.

THE PROGRAM

The program requires that your name and phone number list is stored in DATA statements beginning at line 660. Enter as follows:

DATA NAME,PHONE #

or

660 DATA SMITH,555-1212

The statement DATA END,0 must be the last DATA statement in your list. The size of your phone number list is limited only by your computer's RAM size.

After you run the program, you may display individual numbers by entering an N, display your whole list by entering an L, or end the program by entering an E. If you wish to display individual names and numbers, the computer will request your desired name entry. Enter the name as it appears in the list. The computer will search the list, comparing the name entered with the names in your list. When the name is found, the computer will display that name with its corresponding telephone number. You may now access another number or discontinue this function. If the name entered is not in the list, the computer will display ENTRY NOT FOUND. Entering an N will return the program to the main input routine, allowing access to individual numbers or the whole list. See Fig. 14-1 for a sample run.

```
TELEPHONE NUMBER DIRECTORY
COPYRIGHT (C) 1980 BY HOWARD BERENSON

THIS PROGRAM WILL LIST NAMES &
TELEPHONE NUMBERS FROM YOUR LIST
LOCATED IN DATA STATEMENTS
BEGINNING AT PROGRAM LINE 660.
ENTER THE DATA AS FOLLOWS:
DATA NAME,NUMBER
DATA SMITH,555-1212
THE LAST DATA STATEMENT IN THE
LIST MUST BE: DATA END,0



TELEPHONE # DIRECTORY

ENTER 'N' DISPLAY INDIVIDUAL #'S
      'L' DISPLAY FULL LIST
      'E' END PROGRAM
? N



TELEPHONE # DIRECTORY

ENTER NAME
? DAVE
SEARCHING LIST FOR 'DAVE'

NAME            PHONE NUMBER

DAVE            555-1963

ANOTHER ENTRY?
ENTER 'Y'-YES
      'N'-NO
?
```

Fig. 14-1. Telephone Number Directory sample run.

```
100    HOME : PRINT "TELEPHONE NUMBER DIRECTORY"
110    PRINT "COPYRIGHT (C) 1980 BY HOWARD BERENBON"
120    PRINT "APPLE II"
130    PRINT
140    PRINT "THIS PROGRAM WILL LIST NAMES &"
150    PRINT "TELEPHONE NUMBERS FROM YOUR LIST"
160    PRINT "LOCATED IN DATA STATEMENTS"
170    PRINT "BEGINNING AT PROGRAM LINE 660."
180    PRINT "ENTER THE DATA AS FOLLOWS:"
190    PRINT "DATA NAME,NUMBER"
200    PRINT "DATA SMITH,555-1212"
210    PRINT "THE LAST DATA STATEMENT IN THE"
220    PRINT "LIST MUST BE: DATA END,0"
230    FOR T = 1 TO 7491
240    NEXT T: GOSUB 330
250    PRINT : RESTORE
260    PRINT "ENTER 'N' DISPLAY INDIVIDUAL #'S"
270    PRINT  TAB( 7)"'L' DISPLAY FULL LIST"
280    PRINT  TAB( 7)"'E' END PROGRAM"
290    INPUT B$
300    IF B$ = "N" THEN 370
310    IF B$ = "L" THEN 570
320    END
330    HOME
340    PRINT "TELEPHONE # DIRECTORY"
350    PRINT
360    RETURN
370    GOSUB 330
380    PRINT "ENTER NAME"
390    INPUT A$
400    PRINT "SEARCHING LIST FOR '";A$;"'": PRINT
410    READ C$,D$
420    IF C$ = "END" THEN 450
430    IF C$ = A$ THEN 480
440    GOTO 410
450    PRINT "ENTRY NOT FOUND"
460    RESTORE
470    GOTO 500
480    PRINT "NAME","PHONE NUMBER": PRINT
490    PRINT C$,D$
500    PRINT
510    PRINT "ANOTHER ENTRY?"
520    PRINT "ENTER 'Y'-YES"
530    PRINT  TAB( 7)"'N'-NO"
540    INPUT B$
550    IF B$ = "Y" THEN 370
560    GOTO 250
570    GOSUB 330: PRINT "NAME","PHONE NUMBER": PRINT
580    READ C$,D$
590    IF C$ = "END" THEN 250
600    PRINT C$,D$
610    GOSUB 630
620    GOTO 580
```

```
630   FOR T = 1 TO 2270
640   NEXT T
650   RETURN
660   DATA RICK,555-5219
670   DATA BRUCE,555-1694
680   DATA DAVE,555-1963
690   DATA HARRY,555-1282
700   DATA END,0
```

CHAPTER 15

Special Date Calendar

The Special Date Calendar is a program that displays monthly dates and names, which are taken from DATA statements. It's useful in keeping track of your special dates and occasions. The program is written in BASIC for your microcomputer. See Program 15-1 for the program listing.

THE PROGRAM

Enter important dates and their occasion in DATA statements beginning at line 1000. Enter in the following format:

DATA MONTH,DAY,YEAR,OCCASION

or

1000 DATA 1,6,51,RICK'S BIRTHDAY

The statement DATA 999,0,0,0 must be the last DATA statement in the list.

After you run the program, enter the month number (1–12) to be displayed. The program will display each date and occasion in the month entered. After all the data for that month is displayed, you may display another month or end the program. See Fig. 15-1 for a sample run.

```
SPECIAL DATE CALENDAR
COPYRIGHT (C) 1980 BY HOWARD BERENBON

THIS PROGRAM WILL DISPLAY MONTHLY
DATES AND NAMES, SO YOU CAN KEEP
TRACK OF SPECIAL DATES AND OCCASIONS

ENTER IMPORTANT DATES IN DATA
STATEMENTS BEGINNING AT LINE
1000, AS IN THE FOLLOWING FORMAT:
DATA MO,DAY,YR,OCCASION
DATA 1,6,51,RICK'S BIRTHDAY
DATA 999,0,0,0 MUST BE THE LAST
DATA STATEMENT IN YOUR LIST


ENTER MONTH # (1-12)
TO BE DISPLAYED
? 1


SPECIAL DATE CALENDAR: MONTH  1

DATE            OCCASION

 1 / 6 / 51     RICK'S BIRTHDAY
 1 / 11 / 50    HARRY'S BIRTHDAY

ANOTHER MONTH FOR DISPLAY?
1-YES  0-NO
?
```

Fig. 15-1. Special Date Calendar sample run.

```
100    HOME
110    PRINT "SPECIAL DATE CALENDAR"
120    PRINT "APPLE II"
130    PRINT "COPYRIGHT (C) 1980 BY HOWARD BERENBON"
140    PRINT
150    PRINT "THIS PROGRAM WILL DISPLAY MONTHLY"
160    PRINT "DATES AND NAMES, SO YOU CAN KEEP"
170    PRINT "TRACK OF SPECIAL DATES AND OCCASIONS"
180    PRINT
190    PRINT "ENTER IMPORTANT DATES IN DATA"
200    PRINT "STATEMENTS BEGINNING AT LINE"
210    PRINT "1000, AS IN THE FOLLOWING FORMAT:"
220    PRINT "DATA MO,DAY,YR,OCCASION"
230    PRINT "DATA 1,6,51,RICK'S BIRTHDAY"
240    PRINT "DATA 999,0,0,0 MUST BE THE LAST"
250    PRINT "DATA STATEMENT IN YOUR LIST"
260    GOSUB 520
270    PRINT
280    PRINT "ENTER MONTH # (1-12)"
290    PRINT "TO BE DISPLAYED"
300    INPUT M
310    IF M < 1 THEN 270
320    IF M > 12 THEN 270
330 M =  INT (M): HOME
340    PRINT "SPECIAL DATE CALENDAR: MONTH ";M
350    PRINT
360    PRINT "DATE"; TAB( 16)"OCCASION"
370    PRINT
380    READ A,B,C,A$
390    IF A = 999 THEN 450
400    IF A = M THEN 420
410    GOTO 380
420    PRINT A;"/";B;"/";C;"    ";A$
430    GOSUB 520
440    GOTO 380
450    RESTORE : PRINT
460    PRINT "ANOTHER MONTH FOR DISPLAY?"
470    PRINT "1-YES  0-NO"
480    INPUT P
490    IF P = 1 THEN 270
500    END
510    PRINT
520    REM  DELAY
530    FOR T1 = 1 TO 2043
540    NEXT T1
550    RETURN
1000   DATA 12,21,52,"BRUCE'S BIRTHDAY"
1010   DATA 8,31,49,"DAVID'S BIRTHDAY"
1020   DATA 1,6,51,"RICK'S BIRTHDAY"
1030   DATA 1,11,50,"HARRY'S BIRTHDAY"
1040   DATA 999,0,0,0
```

CHAPTER 16

Weekly Calendar

The Weekly Calendar program allows you to display a weekly calendar of events. It's useful in keeping track of your daily activities. The program is written in BASIC for your microcomputer. See Program 16-1 for the program listing.

THE PROGRAM

Enter your daily activity data in DATA statements beginning at line 670. Enter in the following format:

DATA DAY #,TIME,ACTIVITY

or

670 1,7-30AM,BREAKFAST

The first element is the day number, where 1 through 7 is Sunday through Saturday. The second element is the time, where a dash (–) is used in place of a colon (:) ; and the last element is the activity. Enter as many DATA statements, per day, as you have activities, and continue until all your weekly activities are entered. Finally, the statement DATA 99,0,0 must be the last DATA statement in your list.

After you run the program, enter the week date as MM/DD/YY, and the day number to be displayed. The program will display each activity for that day, and the time of the activity. After the data for that day is displayed, you may display another day or end the program. See Fig. 16-1 for a sample run.

```
WEEKLY CALENDAR
COPYRIGHT (C) 1980 BY HOWARD BERENBON

THIS PROGRAM ALLOWS YOU TO
DISPLAY A WEEKLY CALENDAR.
DAILY DATA IS ENTERED INTO DATA
STATEMENTS BEGINNING AT LINE
670. ENTER DAILY ACTIVITIES
AS FOLLOWS:
DATA  DAY #,TIME,ACTIVITY
DATA 1,7-30 AM,BREAKFAST
THE LAST DATA STATEMENT IN
THE LIST MUST BE: DATA 99,0,0


ENTER WEEK DATE
(MM/DD/YY)
? 5/3/81


5/3/81

ENTER DAY # FOR DISPLAY
1-SUN  2-MON  3-TUES  4-WED
5-THUR 6-FRI  7-SAT
? 1


WEEKLY CALENDAR: WEEK DATE 5/3/81

SUNDAY

TIME            ACTIVITY

7-30            BREAKFAST
12              LUNCH
8-00            MOVIE

DISPLAY ANOTHER DAY?
1-YES  0-NO
? 0
```

Fig. 16-1. Weekly Calendar sample run.

```
100    HOME : PRINT "WEEKLY CALENDAR"
110    PRINT "COPYRIGHT (C) 1980 BY HOWARD BERENBON"
120    PRINT "APPLE II"
130    PRINT
140    PRINT "THIS PROGRAM ALLOWS YOU TO"
150    PRINT "DISPLAY A WEEKLY CALENDAR."
160    PRINT "DAILY DATA IS ENTERED INTO DATA"
170    PRINT "STATEMENTS BEGINNING AT LINE"
180    PRINT "670. ENTER DAILY ACTIVITIES"
190    PRINT "AS FOLLOWS:"
200    PRINT "DATA   DAY #,TIME,ACTIVITY"
210    PRINT "DATA 1,7-30 AM,BREAKFAST"
220    PRINT "THE LAST DATA STATEMENT IN"
230    PRINT "THE LIST MUST BE: DATA 99,0,0"
240    PRINT : GOSUB 440: GOSUB 470
250    PRINT : PRINT "ENTER DAY # FOR DISPLAY"
260    PRINT "1-SUN  2-MON  3-TUES  4-WED"
270    PRINT "5-THUR 6-FRI  7-SAT"
280    INPUT D
290    IF D < 1 THEN 250
300    IF D > 7 THEN 250
310    HOME : PRINT "WEEKLY CALENDAR: WEEK DATE ";W$
320    PRINT
330    READ D1,T$,A$
340    IF D1 = D THEN 610
350    IF D1 = 99 THEN 370
360    GOTO 330
370    PRINT : PRINT "NO ACTIVITY DATA FOR DAY ";D;": ";
380    GOSUB 510
390    RESTORE : PRINT
400    PRINT "DISPLAY ANOTHER DAY?"
410    PRINT "1-YES  0-NO": INPUT AA
420    IF AA = 1 THEN 250
430    END
440    FOR A = 1 TO 2043
450    NEXT A
460    RETURN
470    PRINT "ENTER WEEK DATE"
480    PRINT "(MM/DD/YY)"
490    INPUT W$
500    RETURN
510    IF D = 1 THEN  PRINT "SUNDAY"
520    IF D = 2 THEN  PRINT "MONDAY"
530    IF D = 3 THEN  PRINT "TUESDAY"
540    IF D = 4 THEN  PRINT "WEDNESDAY"
550    IF D = 5 THEN  PRINT "THURSDAY"
560    IF D = 6 THEN  PRINT "FRIDAY"
570    IF D = 7 THEN  PRINT "SATURDAY"
580    PRINT : RETURN
590    PRINT "TIME","ACTIVITY"
600    RETURN
610    GOSUB 510: GOSUB 590: PRINT
620    PRINT T$,A$
```

```
630    GOSUB 440
640    READ D1,T$,A$
650    IF D1 = D THEN 620
660    GOTO 390
670    DATA 1,7-30,BREAKFAST
680    DATA 1,12,LUNCH
690    DATA 1,8-00,MOVIE
700    DATA 2,7-30,BREAKFAST
710    DATA 2,9-00,BUSINESS MEET
720    DATA 2,12,BUS. LUNCH
730    DATA 2,9-00,DINNER
740    DATA 99,0,0
```

CHAPTER 17

Gas Usage Analysis

Conservation is the key to reducing our energy consumption and costs, with the rising prices and pending shortages of all types of energy. You can help out by using the Gas Usage Analysis program. It will indicate differences in natural gas usage from one year to another, so that you can see possible imbalances in usage and correct them. The program is written in BASIC for your microcomputer. See Program 17-1 for the program listing.

THE PROGRAM

The program requires that your yearly natural gas usage data is stored in DATA statements at program lines 1000 and 1010. The first data element in line 1000 must be the comparison year (base year), followed by twelve months of gas usage units, beginning with January of that year. Program line 1010 holds the data for the "recent" year. Example:

    1000 DATA 1977,310,268,225,110,76,60,25,28,29,100,
         260,290

    1010 DATA 1981,296,282,207,141,58,63,29,27,51,123,
         233,270

The "base" year can be any past year, possibly the year that you moved into your house or apartment, or even the previous year. The "recent" year would be a full year's data for a recent energy consumption.

The program prints the "base" year data, including average units used per month, total units used, units used per month, and the percent of total units used per month. Then it prints the "recent" year's data, with a comparison with the "base" year. It gives the difference between the two years, with the monthly increase (+) or decrease (−) from the "base" year. See Fig. 17-1 for a sample run.

ANALYSIS

If there is a significant monthly increase in natural gas usage, pay close attention to those months. You may be using more energy than necessary. Check your insulation for possible air leaks. This leakage can cause your furnace to work overtime and use more gas than necessary. Other increases may be due to natural gas leaks. Have your natural gas appliances periodically checked for leaks; escaping gas can cause explosions and death.

```
GAS USAGE ANALYSIS
COPYRIGHT (C) 1981 BY HOWARD BERENBON

THIS PROGRAM WILL COMPARE AND DISPLAY
A 'BASE' YEAR AND 'RECENT' YEAR GAS
USAGE, IN UNITS.

ENTER THE 'BASE' YEAR DATA AT LINE 1000,
AND THE 'RECENT' YEAR DATA AT LINE 1010.

ENTER A '1' TO DISPLAY
THE 'BASE' YEAR DATA
? 1


BASE YEAR  1977                AV/MO=  148.417
TOTAL UNITS=  1781
MONTH              UNITS       % TOTAL
  1                 310         17.4
  2                 268         15.04
  3                 225         12.63
  4                 110         6.17
  5                 76          4.26
  6                 60          3.36
  7                 25          1.4
  8                 28          1.57
  9                 29          1.62
 10                 100         5.61
 11                 260         14.59
 12                 290         16.28
ENTER '1' FOR COMPARISON? 1


RECENT YEAR  1981                  AV/MO=  148.333
TOTAL UNITS=  1780      RECENT-BASE= -1
MO.    UNITS   % TOTAL   + OR - FROM BASE
  1     296     16.62       -14
  2     282     15.84        14
  3     207     11.62       -18
  4     141     7.92         31
  5     58      3.25        -18
  6     63      3.53         3
  7     29      1.62         4
  8     27      1.51        -1
  9     51      2.86         22
 10     123     6.91         23
 11     233     13.08       -27
 12     270     15.16       -20
```

Fig. 17-1. Gas Usage Analysis sample run.

```
100    HOME : DIM A(50)
110    PRINT "GAS USAGE ANALYSIS: APPLE II"
120    PRINT "COPYRIGHT (C) 1981 BY HOWARD BERENBON"
130    PRINT
140    PRINT "THIS PROGRAM WILL COMPARE AND DISPLAY"
150    PRINT "A 'BASE' YEAR AND 'RECENT' YEAR GAS"
160    PRINT "USAGE, IN UNITS."
170    PRINT
180    PRINT "ENTER THE 'BASE' YEAR DATA AT LINE 1000,"
190    PRINT "AND THE 'RECENT' YEAR DATA AT LINE 1010."
200    PRINT
210    PRINT "ENTER A '1' TO DISPLAY"
220    PRINT "THE 'BASE' YEAR DATA"
230    INPUT A
240 B = 0:R = 0
250    READ P
260    FOR E = 1 TO 12
270    READ C
280 A(E) = C
290 B = A(E) + B
300    NEXT E
310    READ T
320    FOR E = 13 TO 24
330    READ C
340 A(E) = C
350 R = A(E) + R
360    NEXT E
370    PRINT "BASE YEAR ";P,"AV/MO= ";B / 12
380    PRINT "TOTAL UNITS= ";B
390    PRINT "MONTH","UNITS","% TOTAL"
400    FOR A = 1 TO 12
410    PRINT A,A(A), INT (A(A) / B * 10000) / 100
420    NEXT A
430    PRINT "ENTER '1' FOR COMPARISON";
440    INPUT A
450    PRINT
460    PRINT
470    PRINT "REC. YEAR ";T,"AV/MO= ";R / 12
480    PRINT "TOTAL UNITS= ";R;"  RECENT-BASE= ";R - B
490    PRINT "MO.   UNITS   % TOTAL   + OR - FROM BASE"
500    FOR A = 13 TO 24
510    PRINT A - 12; TAB( 6);A(A); TAB( 15); INT (A(A) / R * 10000) / 100; TAB( 26);
       A(A) - A(A - 12)
520    NEXT A
530    GOTO 530
980    REM  ENTER 'BASE' YEAR GAS DATA IN LINE 1000
990    REM  ENTER 'RECENT' YEAR GAS DATA IN LINE 1010
1000   DATA 1977,310,268,225,110,76,60,25,28,29,100,260,290
1010   DATA 1981,296,282,207,141,58,63,29,27,51,123,233,270
```

CHAPTER 18

Water Usage Analysis

Here is a program that can help you reduce your water usage. (It's similar to the Gas Usage Analysis program in Chapter 17.) It will indicate differences in water usage from one year to another, so that you can see possible imbalances in usage and correct them. The program is written in BASIC for your microcomputer. See Program 18-1 for the program listing.

THE PROGRAM

The program requires that your yearly water usage data is stored in DATA statements at program lines 1000 and 1010. The first data element in line 1000 must be the comparison year (base year), followed by the four quarters of water usage units, beginning with January or February of that year. Program line 1010 holds the data for the "recent" year. Example:

1000 DATA 1977,15,19,19,18

1010 DATA 1981,14,17,14,17

The "base" year can be any past year, possibly the year that you moved into your house, or even the previous year. The "recent" year would be a full year's data for a recent water consumption.

The program prints the "base" year data, including average units used per quarter, total units used, units used per quarter, and the percent of total units used per quarter. Then it prints the "recent" year's data, with a comparison with the "base" year. It gives the difference between the two years, with the quarterly increase (+) or decrease (−) from the "base" year. See Fig. 18-1 for a sample run.

ANALYSIS

If there is a significant quarterly increase in water usage, pay close attention to those quarters. You may be using more water than necessary. Check your faucets and pipes for leaks. Replace worn washers or faucets and pipes if necessary.

```
WATER USAGE ANALYSIS
COPYRIGHT (C) 1981 BY HOWARD BERENBON

THIS PROGRAM WILL COMPARE AND DISPLAY
A 'BASE' YEAR AND 'RECENT' YEAR WATER
USAGE, IN UNITS.

ENTER THE 'BASE' YEAR DATA AT LINE 1000,
AND THE 'RECENT' YEAR DATA AT LINE 1010.

ENTER A '1' TO DISPLAY
THE 'BASE' YEAR DATA
? 1


BASE YEAR  1977                 AV/QU=  17.75
TOTAL UNITS=  71
QUART            UNITS            % TOTAL
  1               15              21.12
  2               19              26.76
  3               19              26.76
  4               18              25.35
ENTER '1' FOR COMPARISON? 1




RECENT YEAR  1981                 AV/QU=  15.5
TOTAL UNITS=  62    RECENT-BASE= -9
QU.    UNITS    % TOTAL    + OR - FROM BASE
  1      14      22.58       -1
  2      17      27.41       -2
  3      14      22.58       -5
  4      17      27.41       -1
```

Fig. 18-1. Water Usage Analysis sample run.

```
100   HOME : DIM A(10)
110   PRINT "WATER USAGE ANALYSIS: APPLE II"
120   PRINT "COPYRIGHT (C) 1981 BY HOWARD BERENBON"
130   PRINT
140   PRINT "THIS PROGRAM WILL COMPARE AND DISPLAY"
150   PRINT "A 'BASE' YEAR AND 'RECENT' YEAR WATER"
160   PRINT "USAGE, IN UNITS."
170   PRINT
180   PRINT "ENTER THE 'BASE' YEAR DATA AT LINE 1000,"
190   PRINT "AND THE 'RECENT' YEAR DATA AT LINE 1010."
200   PRINT
210   PRINT "ENTER A '1' TO DISPLAY"
220   PRINT "THE 'BASE' YEAR DATA"
230   INPUT A
240 B = 0:R = 0
250   READ P
260   FOR E = 1 TO 4
270   READ C
280 A(E) = C
290 B = A(E) + B
300   NEXT E
310   READ T
320   FOR E = 5 TO 8
330   READ C
340 A(E) = C
350 R = A(E) + R
360   NEXT E
370   PRINT "BASE YEAR ";P,"AV/QU= ";B / 4
380   PRINT "TOTAL UNITS= ";B
390   PRINT "QUART","UNITS","% TOTAL"
400   FOR A = 1 TO 4
410   PRINT A,A(A), INT (A(A) / B * 10000) / 100
420   NEXT A
430   PRINT "ENTER '1' FOR COMPARISON";
440   INPUT A
450   PRINT
460   PRINT
470   PRINT "REC. YEAR ";T,"AV/QU= ";R / 4
480   PRINT "TOTAL UNITS= ";R;"  RECENT-BASE= ";R - B
490   PRINT "QU.   UNITS   % TOTAL   + OR - FROM BASE"
500   FOR A = 5 TO 8
510   PRINT A - 4; TAB( 6);A(A); TAB( 15); INT (A(A) / R * 10000) / 100; TAB( 26);
      A(A) - A(A - 4)
520   NEXT A
530   GOTO 530
980   REM  ENTER 'BASE' YEAR WATER USAGE DATA IN LINE 1000
990   REM  ENTER 'RECENT' YEAR WATER USAGE DATA IN LINE 1010
1000   DATA 1977,15,19,19,18
1010   DATA 1981,14,17,14,17
```

Appliance Operating Cost Analysis

An interesting and useful application program for the home computer is the Appliance Operating Cost Analysis program. It's written in BASIC for your microcomputer. See Program 19-1 for the program listing.

THE PROGRAM

The program will calculate the cost of operating electrical appliances, given the number of watts they consume, the average number of hours of daily use, and the cost per kilowatt hour, for each appliance under analysis.

After you run the program, enter the number of appliances for analysis. Then enter the cost of electrical use per kilowatt-hour, in dollars. (Example: typically $0.065. Call your local power company for the exact amount. This will vary for different areas of the country.) The program will print APPLIANCE #1 and request the name of the first appliance (limit entry to eight characters). Enter the power consumed in watts and the average number of hours (or minutes) in daily use. The program is set to accept hours, but will accept minutes if 9999 is entered first. Then it will advance to accept data on the next appliance. After the last appliance data is entered, the analysis will begin.

The program then displays a table with the appliance name, watts consumed, operating cost per day, estimated cost per month, and the estimated kilowatt-hour use per month. This is repeated for each appliance. Finally, the program displays the total kilowatt-hours used and the total monthly cost for all appliances.

See Fig. 19-1 for a sample run.

ANALYSIS

The program will show you what operating each appliance costs. It may help you decide to use less of one or more appliances that require a lot of power to run, to save on energy costs.

Probably the most expensive electrical appliance to operate is the air conditioner. Proper home insulation will allow it to operate more efficiently. Also, raising the thermostat will reduce the amount of energy required to cool your home, thus reducing electricity costs.

The proper use of lighting can greatly reduce your electric bills. Make sure that all unnecessary lights are turned off. Also, the wattage of some of the light bulbs you use could be higher than necessary. Changing these bulbs to a lower wattage will reduce energy costs.

```
APPLIANCE OPERATING COST ANALYSIS              ENTER POWER CONSUMED IN WATTS
COPYRIGHT (C) 1980 BY HOWARD BERENBON           ? 200

THIS PROGRAM WILL CALCULATE                     ENTER AVERAGE # OF HOURS IN
THE COST OF OPERATING ELECTRICAL                DAILY USE (MAY ENTER FRACTIONS).
APPLIANCES, GIVEN THE NUMBER OF                 IF YOU DESIRE TO ENTER MINUTES
WATTS THEY CONSUME, THE AVERAGE                 THEN ENTER 9999
NUMBER OF HOURS OF DAILY USE,                   ? 3
AND THE COST PER KILOWATT HOUR
FOR EACH APPLIANCE UNDER ANALYSIS               APPLIANCE # 3
                                                ENTER TYPE (NAME)
ENTER THE # OF APPLIANCES                        LIMIT TO 8 CHARACTERS
UNDER ANALYSIS                                   ? LIGHTS
? 3
                                                ENTER POWER CONSUMED IN WATTS
ENTER THE COST PER KILOWATT HOUR                 ? 500
(TYPICAL - $.065)
? .07                                           ENTER AVERAGE # OF HOURS IN
                                                DAILY USE (MAY ENTER FRACTIONS).
APPLIANCE # 1                                    IF YOU DESIRE TO ENTER MINUTES
ENTER TYPE (NAME)                                THEN ENTER 9999
LIMIT TO 8 CHARACTERS                            ? 8
? COLOR TV

ENTER POWER CONSUMED IN WATTS
? 110                                           APPLIANCE OPERATING COST ANALYSIS

ENTER AVERAGE # OF HOURS IN                      APPL.     WATTS    COST/DAY   COST/MO   KWHS/MO
DAILY USE (MAY ENTER FRACTIONS).                COLOR TV    110      .0385      1.155     16.5
IF YOU DESIRE TO ENTER MINUTES                  STEREO      200      .042       1.26      18
THEN ENTER 9999                                 LIGHTS      500      .28        8.4       120
? 5
                                                TOTAL KILOWATT HOURS USED PER MONTH
                                                FOR  3  APPLIANCES IS  154.5   KWHOURS

APPLIANCE # 2                                   TOTAL MONTHLY COST FOR  3
ENTER TYPE (NAME)                               APPLIANCE(S) IS $ 10.82
LIMIT TO 8 CHARACTERS
? STEREO
```

Fig. 19-1. Appliance Operating Cost Analysis sample run.

Program 19-1. Appliance Operating Cost Analysis Program Listing

```
100   HOME
110   PRINT "APPLIANCE OPERATING COST ANALYSIS"
120   PRINT "APPLE II"
130   PRINT "COPYRIGHT (C) 1980 BY HOWARD BERENBON"
140   PRINT
150   PRINT "THIS PROGRAM WILL CALCULATE"
160   PRINT "THE COST OF OPERATING ELECTRICAL"
170   PRINT "APPLIANCES, GIVEN THE NUMBER OF"
180   PRINT "WATTS THEY CONSUME, THE AVERAGE"
190   PRINT "NUMBER OF HOURS OF DAILY USE,"
200   PRINT "AND THE COST PER KILOWATT HOUR"
210   PRINT "FOR EACH APPLIANCE UNDER ANALYSIS"
220   PRINT
230   PRINT "ENTER THE # OF APPLIANCES"
240   PRINT "UNDER ANALYSIS"
250   INPUT I
260   DIM B$(I),W(I),U(I),R(I),S(I)
270   PRINT
280   PRINT "ENTER THE COST PER KILOWATT HOUR"
290   PRINT "(TYPICAL - $.065)"
300   INPUT K
310   FOR Q = 1 TO I
320   HOME
330   PRINT "APPLIANCE #";Q
340   PRINT "ENTER TYPE (NAME)"
350   PRINT "LIMIT TO 8 CHARACTERS"
360   INPUT A$:B$(Q) = A$
370   PRINT
380   PRINT "ENTER POWER CONSUMED IN WATTS"
390   INPUT W:W(Q) = W
400   PRINT
410   PRINT "ENTER AVERAGE # OF HOURS IN"
420   PRINT "DAILY USE (MAY ENTER FRACTIONS)."
430   PRINT "IF YOU DESIRE TO ENTER MINUTES"
440   PRINT "THEN ENTER 9999"
450   INPUT H
460   IF H = 9999 THEN 700
470 C = (W / 1000) * H
480 U(Q) = C * K
490 R(Q) = U(Q) * 30
500 S(Q) = C * 30
510   NEXT Q
520   HOME :S = 0:V = 0
530   PRINT "APPLIANCE OPERATING COST ANALYSIS"
540   PRINT
550   PRINT "APPL.     WATTS  COST/DY  CST/MO  KWH/MO"
560   FOR Q = 1 TO I
570   PRINT B$(Q); TAB( 11);W(Q); TAB( 18);U(Q); TAB( 27);R(Q); TAB( 35);S(Q)
580 S = S + R(Q)
590 V = V + S(Q)
600   FOR A = 1 TO 1498
610   NEXT A
620   NEXT Q
```

```
630   PRINT
640   PRINT "TOTAL KILOWATT HOURS USED PER MONTH"
650   PRINT "FOR ";I;" APPLIANCES IS ";V;" KWHOURS"
660   PRINT :S =  INT (100 * S + .5) / 100
670   PRINT "TOTAL MONTHLY COST FOR ";I
680   PRINT "APPLIANCE(S) IS $";S
690   END
700   PRINT "ENTER AVERAGE # OF MINUTES"
710   PRINT "IN DAILY USE"
720   INPUT M
730 H = M / 60
740   GOTO 470
```

CHAPTER 20

Family Dental Expenses

A useful way to keep track of your dental expenses is with the Family Dental Expense program. It's written in BASIC for your microcomputer. See Program 20-1 for the program listing.

THE PROGRAM

The program requires that you enter dental expenses in DATA statements beginning with program line 500. Limit the type of expense to a 14-character description. Enter each dental expense as follows:

DATA DATE,TYPE OF EXPENSE,COST

or

DATA 1/17/80,CLEANING,25

DATA END,0,0 must be the last DATA statement in the list.

After you run the program, enter the year of the report. Then enter a 1 to begin. The program will display each dental expense with the date, the type (description), the cost, and the cumulative total. After all the data is displayed, then the total yearly expense is given. See Fig. 20-1 for a sample run.

```
FAMILY DENTAL EXPENSES
COPYRIGHT (C) 1980 BY HOWARD BERENBON


THIS PROGRAM WILL KEEP TRACK OF
YOUR FAMILY DENTAL EXPENSES.
ENTER EACH DENTAL EXPENSE RECEIPT
IN DATA STATEMENTS BEGINNING AT
LINE 500, AS FOLLOWS:
DATA DATE,TYPE,COST
DATA 1/17/80,CLEANING,25-LIMIT TYPE
TO A 14 CHARACTER DESCRIPTION.
DATA END,0,0 MUST BE THE LAST
STATEMENT IN YOUR LIST.

ENTER THE YEAR OF THE REPORT
? 1980


ENTER '1' TO BEGIN
? 1


FAMILY DENTAL EXPENSE REPORT
FOR THE YEAR:  1980

DATE            TYPE            COST        CUM. TOT.

1/17/80         CLEANING        25          25
1/25/80         FILLING         35          60
2/20/80         FILLING         30          90
2/27/80         CROWN WORK      75          165
3/10/80         CROWN WORK      100         265
3/17/80         CROWN WORK      15          280
3/25/80         CROWN DONE      100         380
6/14/80         CLEAN-XRAY      35          415


FAMILY DENTAL EXPENSE REPORT
FOR THE YEAR:  1980

THE TOTAL YEARLY EXPENSE =$ 415
```

Fig. 20-1. Family Dental Expenses sample run.

```
100   HOME : PRINT "FAMILY DENTAL EXPENSES"
110   PRINT "COPYRIGHT (C) 1980 BY HOWARD BERENBON"
120   PRINT "APPLE II"
130   GOSUB 470: GOSUB 470
140   HOME : PRINT :C = 0
150   PRINT "THIS PROGRAM WILL KEEP TRACK OF"
160   PRINT "YOUR FAMILY DENTAL EXPENSES."
170   PRINT "ENTER EACH DENTAL EXPENSE RECEIPT"
180   PRINT "IN DATA STATEMENTS BEGINNING AT"
190   PRINT "LINE 500, AS FOLLOWS:"
200   PRINT "DATA DATE,TYPE,COST"
210   PRINT "DATA 1/17/80,CLEANING,25-LIMIT TYPE"
220   PRINT "TO A 14 CHARACTER DESCRIPTION."
230   PRINT "DATA END,0,0 MUST BE THE LAST"
240   PRINT "STATEMENT IN YOUR LIST."
250   PRINT
260   PRINT "ENTER THE YEAR OF THE REPORT"
270   INPUT Y
280   PRINT
290   PRINT "ENTER '1' TO BEGIN"
300   INPUT A
310   HOME : PRINT "FAMILY DENTAL EXPENSE REPORT"
320   PRINT "FOR THE YEAR: ";Y
330   PRINT
340   PRINT "DATE         TYPE             COST    CUM TOT"
350   PRINT
360   READ A$,B$,B
370   IF A$ = "END" THEN 420
380 C = C + B
390   PRINT A$; TAB( 11);B$; TAB( 26);B; TAB( 34);C
400   GOSUB 470
410   GOTO 360
420   PRINT : PRINT "FAMILY DENTAL EXPENSE REPORT"
430   PRINT "FOR THE YEAR: ";Y
440   PRINT
450   PRINT "THE TOTAL YEARLY EXPENSE =$";C
460   END
470   FOR A = 1 TO 2270
480   NEXT A
490   RETURN
500   DATA 1/17/80,CLEANING,25
510   DATA 1/25/80,FILLING,35
520   DATA 2/20/80,FILLING,30
530   DATA 2/27/80,CROWN WORK,75
540   DATA 3/10/80,CROWN WORK,100
550   DATA 3/17/80,CROWN WORK,15
560   DATA 3/25/80,CROWN DONE,100
570   DATA 6/14/80,CLEAN-XRAY,35
580   DATA END,0,0
```

CHAPTER 21

Weekly Jogging Record

Jogging has been a popular pastime for many people. It's a good form of exercise that requires very little cost to do. If you're a jogger, then this program can help you. It keeps a record of your weekly jogging data and displays a graph of your performance. It's written in BASIC for your microcomputer. See Program 21-1 for the program listing.

THE PROGRAM

The program requires that you enter your weekly jogging distance data in DATA statements beginning at line 960. Enter the maximum distance you ran (in miles or fraction of miles) for each day of week 1 through week W. Only enter the data for the days that you ran. If you ran three days out of seven, only enter three numbers, or all seven if you ran every day of that week. Also, 99 must be the last number in each DATA statement, and DATA 555 must be the last DATA statement in your list. Enter the data as in the following example:

Week 1	960	DATA 2,2,4,1,3,99
Week 2	970	DATA 2,2,2,3,4,2,99
Week 3	980	DATA 3,3,4,4,5,4,5,99
Week 4	990	DATA 4,3,4,5,99
	1000	DATA 555

After you run the program, it calculates the number of weeks in your data list. It then calculates the number of miles you ran for each week and the average daily miles per week. Then a table is displayed with the week number, the average miles per day, the total miles per week, and the approximate calories expended per week.

ANALYSIS

The data is analyzed using your first week of data as the "base" week. The average jog during a "base" week day is displayed. Then the average jog during the last week day is displayed. Next, the (+) increase or (−) decrease in the average daily jogging distance, from a "base" week to the last (final) week W, is displayed. Finally, you can have a plot of your weekly progress. Enter a 1 for yes or 0 for no. The plot will display the average daily miles per week, for each week in your data list. It is a horizontal plot, using the TAB function to display a plus (+) sign on the horizontal line, for the average daily miles per week. The maximum distance that can be plotted is 40 miles per week.

See Fig. 21-1 for a sample run.

```
WEEKLY JOGGING RECORD
COPYRIGHT (C) 1980 BY HOWARD BERENBON

HERE'S A PROGRAM THAT KEEPS A RECORD
OF YOUR WEEKLY JOGGING DATA, AND
GIVES A PLOT OF YOUR PERFORMANCE.
ENTER THE MAXIMUM DISTANCE YOU RAN
(IN MILES OR FRACTIONS) FOR EACH DAY
OF WEEK 1 THRU WEEK W, IN DATA STATE-
MENTS BEGINNING AT LINE 960. ENTER
ONLY THE DATA FOR DAYS THAT YOU RAN.
IF YOU RAN 3 DAYS OUT OF 7, THEN ONLY
ENTER 3 NUMBERS; OR ALL 7 IF YOU RAN
EACH DAY. ENTER AS FOLLOWS:
ENTER '1' TO CONTINUE? 1


DATA DAY1,DAY2,DAY3,DAY4,DAY5,DAY6,DAY7,99
DATA 2.5,2,3.5,5,4.5,4,5,99-99 MUST BE
LAST ENTRY IN EACH DATA STATEMENT; DATA 555
MUST BE THE LAST STATEMENT IN THE LIST.
ENTER '1' TO CONTINUE? 1


WEEK#           AV-MIL/D        MILES/WK        CALORIES/WK

1               2.375           9.5             902.5
2               2.7             13.5            1282.5
3               3.2             16              1520
4               2.7             13.5            1282.5
5               3.75            15              1425
6               4               16              1520

AVERAGE JOG  DURING A BASE WEEK (#1)
DAY =  2.38  MILES

AVERAGE JOG  DURING A LAST (FINAL)
WEEK DAY =  4  MILES

ENTER '1' TO CONTINUE? 1
```

Fig. 21-1. Weekly Jogging Record sample run.

```
100   HOME : PRINT "WEEKLY JOGGING RECORD"
110   PRINT "COPYRIGHT (C) 1980 BY HOWARD BERENBON"
120   PRINT "APPLE II"
130   GOSUB 900
140   PRINT "HERE'S A PROGRAM THAT KEEPS A RECORD"
150   PRINT "OF YOUR WEEKLY JOGGING DATA, AND"
160   PRINT "GIVES A PLOT OF YOUR PERFORMANCE."
170   PRINT "ENTER THE MAXIMUM DISTANCE YOU RAN"
180   PRINT "(IN MILES OR FRACTIONS) FOR EACH DAY"
190   PRINT "OF WEEK 1 THRU WEEK W, IN DATA STATE-"
200   PRINT "MENTS BEGINNING AT LINE 960. ENTER"
210   PRINT "ONLY THE DATA FOR DAYS THAT YOU RAN."
220   PRINT "IF YOU RAN 3 DAYS OUT OF 7, THEN ONLY"
230   PRINT "ENTER 3 NUMBERS; OR ALL 7 IF YOU RAN"
240   PRINT "EACH DAY. ENTER AS FOLLOWS:": GOSUB 930
250   PRINT "DATA DAY1,DAY2,DAY3,DAY4,DAY5,DAY6,DAY7,99"
260   PRINT "DATA 2.5,2,3.5,5,4.5,4,5,99-99 MUST BE"
270   PRINT "LAST ENTRY IN EACH DATA STATEMENT; DATA 555"
280   PRINT "MUST BE THE LAST STATEMENT IN THE LIST."
290   GOSUB 930
300   HOME :W = 0:R1 = 0:Q = 0
310   READ R
320   IF R = 99 THEN W = W + 1
330   IF R = 555 THEN 350
340   GOTO 310
350   RESTORE
360   READ R
370   IF R = 99 THEN 400
380 Q = Q + 1:R1 = R + R1
390   GOTO 360
400 R1 = R1 / Q: RESTORE
410   DIM A(W + 1),B(W + 1)
420   FOR G = 1 TO W
430 Q = 0:S = 0
440   READ R
450   IF R = 99 THEN 480
460 Q = Q + 1:S = R + S: GOTO 440
470   NEXT G: GOTO 500
480 S1 = S / Q:A(G) = S1
490 B(G) = S: GOTO 470
500 R1 =  INT (R1 * 100 + .5) / 100
510 S1 =  INT (S1 * 100 + .5) / 100
520   HOME
530   PRINT "WEEK#  AV-MIL/D  MILES/WK  CALORIES/WK"
540   PRINT
550   FOR G = 1 TO W
560   PRINT G; TAB( 8);A(G); TAB( 18);B(G); TAB( 28);95 * B(G)
570   GOSUB 900
580   NEXT G
590   PRINT
600   PRINT "AVERAGE JOG DURING A BASE WEEK (#1)"
610   PRINT "DAY = ";R1;" MILES"
620   PRINT
```

```
630   PRINT "AVERAGE JOG DURING A LAST (FINAL)"
640   PRINT "WEEK DAY = ";S1;" MILES"
650   PRINT
660   GOSUB 930: GOSUB 820
670   PRINT
680   PRINT "DO YOU WISH A PLOT?"
690   PRINT "1-YES  0-NO"
700   INPUT A
710   IF A = 1 THEN 730
720   END
730   HOME : PRINT "PLOT OF WEEKLY PROGRESS"
740   PRINT
750   PRINT "AVERAGE MILES/DAY (TOTAL DAYS)"
760   PRINT "0+++++++5+++++++++++10+++++++15+++++++20"
770   FOR G = 1 TO W:Z =  INT (A(G) + .5)
780   PRINT  TAB( Z * 2)"+   WEEK #";G
790   GOSUB 900
800   NEXT G
810   GOTO 720
820   PRINT "THE (+) INCREASE OR (-) DECREASE IN THE"
830   PRINT "AVERAGE DAILY JOGGING DISTANCE, FROM THE"
840   PRINT "BASE-1ST-WEEK TO THE LAST-FINAL-WEEK ";W;","
850 D = S1 - R1:PC = (D / R1) * 100
860   PRINT "IS ";D;" MILES"
870   PRINT :PC =  INT (PC * 100) / 100
880   PRINT "THAT'S A ";PC;" PERCENT CHANGE"
890   RETURN
900   FOR A = 1 TO 2270
910   NEXT A
920   RETURN
930   PRINT "ENTER '1' TO CONTINUE";
940   INPUT A: PRINT
950   RETURN
960   DATA 2,2.5,2,3,99
970   DATA 2.5,2.5,3,3.5,2,99
980   DATA 3,3,3.5,3,3.5,99
990   DATA 2.5,2,2.5,3,3.5,99
1000   DATA 3,4,4,4,99
1010   DATA 4,4,4.5,3.5,99
1020   DATA 555
```

CHAPTER 22

Cost of Food Analysis

The cost of living has been on a constant increase over the years. Due to inflation, each year it takes more and more money to buy the same goods, compared with previous years' prices. This program is used to calculate the change in cost of food, by comparing the weekly price of six "basic" foods to previous weeks' price data. It will indicate the weekly changes in these prices, to help you budget your allotted food money more efficiently. The program is written in BASIC for your microcomputer. See Program 22-1 for the program listing.

THE PROGRAM

Enter the week's food price data in DATA statements beginning at line 850, as follows:

    DATA P1,P2,P3,P4,P5,P6

where P1 through P6 are the prices of one gallon of milk, one pound of butter, one dozen eggs, one pound of hamburger, one loaf of bread (20 oz), and five pounds of sugar, respectively.

Enter any number of weeks of data, beginning with a "base" week's pricing. The "base" week's data should be taken from some weeks past. The final week in your data list should be the most recent week's food costs. The last DATA statement in your list must be DATA 0,0,0,0,0,0.

	Example of Data List
BASE WEEK	DATA 1.95,.75,.85,1.79,.61,1.59
	DATA 2.00,.85,.95,1.85,.72,1.78
	DATA 2.09,.89,.95,1.85,.75,1.75
FINAL WEEK	DATA 2.05,.79,.87,2.20,.65,1.79
	DATA 0,0,0,0,0,0

After you run the program, it will display the "base" week's total "basic" food cost. Then for each week, it prints the total "basic" food cost and the difference between the previous week's $(N-1)$ total "basic" food cost and the current week's (N) total, and the percent change. Also displayed is the total change/increase from week No. 1 (the "base" week) to the previous week $(N-1)$, and the percent change. Finally, a cost of food plot may be displayed, by entering a 1 for yes. The plot will display the total "basic" food cost for each week in your data list. It is a horizontal plot, using the TAB function to display a plus (+) sign on the horizontal line, for the weekly food costs. Then the program will display the total change/increase from week No. 1 (the "base" week) to the final (most recent) week in your data list, along with the percent change.

See Fig. 22-1 for a sample run.

```
COST OF FOOD ANALYSIS
COPYRIGHT (C) 1980 BY HOWARD BERENBON

THIS PROGRAM IS USED TO CALCULATE THE
CHANGE IN COST OF FOOD, BY COMPARING
THE WEEKLY PRICE OF MILK, BUTTER, EGGS,
HAMBURGER, BREAD, AND SUGAR TO PREVIOUS
WEEKS DATA. IT ALSO PLOTS THE COMBINED
PRICE OF THESE ITEMS FROM WEEK TO WEEK,
TO SHOW THE RISE OR FALL OF PRICES FOR
A GIVEN NUMBER OF WEEKS.

ENTER A '1' TO CONTINUE
? 1


ENTER THE WEEKS FOOD PRICE DATA IN
DATA STATEMENTS BEGINNING AT LINE 850,
AS FOLLOWS:
DATA P1,P2,P3,P4,P5,P6   WHERE
P1 THRU P6 ARE THE PRICES OF 1 GALLON
OF MILK, 1 LB OF BUTTER, 1 DOZ EGGS,
1 LB HAMBURGER, 1 LOAF OF BREAD, AND
5 LBS OF SUGAR, RESPECTIVELY.
ENTER ANY # OF WEEKS OF DATA BEGINNING
WITH A BASE WEEK PRICING, TAKEN SOME
WEEKS PAST. THE LAST DATA STATEMENT IN
THE LIST MUST BE: DATA 0,0,0,0,0,0

ENTER A '1' TO CONTINUE
? 1

BASE WEEK  1  : FOOD PRICE=$ 7.54
WEEK #  2  : FOOD PRICE=$ 8.15

DIFFERENCE FROM WEEK #  1 TO
 2  IS $ .61
A CHANGE OF  7.48466  PERCENT

ENTER A '1' TO CONTINUE
? 1


WEEK #  3  : FOOD PRICE=$ 8.28

DIFFERENCE FROM WEEK #  2 TO
 3  IS $ .13
A CHANGE OF  1.57005  PERCENT

ENTER A '1' TO CONTINUE
? 1


WEEK #  4  : FOOD PRICE=$ 8.35

DIFFERENCE FROM WEEK #  3 TO
 4  IS $ .0700007
A CHANGE OF  .838331  PERCENT

ENTER A '1' TO CONTINUE
? 1

TOTAL CHANGE/INCREASE FROM WEEK
1 TO  4  IS $ .810001
A CHANGE OF  10.7427  PERCENT

DO YOU WISH A PLOT?
1-YES  0-NO
? 1


COST OF FOOD PLOT

FOOD COST
0.........5.........10........15........20
WEEK #  1        +
WEEK #  2         +
WEEK #  3         +
WEEK #  4         +

TOTAL CHANGE/INCREASE FROM WEEK
1 TO  4  IS $ .810001
A CHANGE OF  10.7427  PERCENT
```

Fig. 22-1. Cost of Food Analysis sample run.

```
100   HOME : PRINT "COST OF FOOD ANALYSIS"
110   PRINT "COPYRIGHT (C) 1980 BY HOWARD BERENBON"
120   PRINT "APPLE II"
130   PRINT :Z = 0
140   PRINT "THIS PROGRAM IS USED TO CALCULATE THE"
150   PRINT "CHANGE IN COST OF FOOD, BY COMPARING"
160   PRINT "THE WEEKLY PRICE OF MILK, BUTTER, EGGS,"
170   PRINT "HAMBURGER, BREAD, AND SUGAR TO PREVIOUS"
180   PRINT "WEEKS DATA. IT ALSO PLOTS THE COMBINED"
190   PRINT "PRICE OF THESE ITEMS FROM WEEK TO WEEK,"
200   PRINT "TO SHOW THE RISE OR FALL OF PRICES FOR"
210   PRINT "A GIVEN NUMBER OF WEEKS."
220   PRINT
230   GOSUB 780
240   PRINT "ENTER THE WEEKS FOOD PRICE DATA IN"
250   PRINT "DATA STATEMENTS BEGINNING AT LINE 850,"
260   PRINT "AS FOLLOWS:"
270   PRINT "DATA P1,P2,P3,P4,P5,P6  WHERE"
280   PRINT "P1 THRU P6 ARE THE PRICES OF 1 GALLON"
290   PRINT "OF MILK, 1 LB OF BUTTER, 1 DOZ EGGS,"
300   PRINT "1 LB HAMBURGER, 1 LOAF OF BREAD, AND"
310   PRINT "5 LBS OF SUGAR, RESPECTIVELY."
320   PRINT "ENTER ANY # OF WEEKS OF DATA BEGINNING"
330   PRINT "WITH A BASE WEEK PRICING, TAKEN SOME"
340   PRINT "WEEKS PAST. THE LAST DATA STATEMENT IN"
350   PRINT "THE LIST MUST BE: DATA 0,0,0,0,0,0
360   PRINT :N = 1
370   GOSUB 780
380   GOSUB 710:FA = BA
390   PRINT "BASE WEEK ";N;" : FOOD PRICE=$";BA
400 N = N + 1: GOSUB 710: IF B = O THEN 440
410   PRINT "WEEK # ";N;" : FOOD PRICE=$";BA
420   GOSUB 660
430   GOSUB 780: GOTO 400
440   PRINT : GOSUB 580
450   PRINT "DO YOU WISH A PLOT?"
460   PRINT "1-YES  0-NO"
470   INPUT A
480   IF A = 1 THEN 500
490   END
500   HOME : PRINT "COST OF FOOD PLOT": PRINT
510   PRINT "FOOD COST"
520   PRINT "0.........5.........10.......15.......20"
530 N = 1: RESTORE
540   GOSUB 710
550   IF B = O THEN 640
560   PRINT "WEEK # ";N; TAB( Z * 2)"+"
570 N = N + 1: GOSUB 820: GOTO 540
580   PRINT :HA = Z - FA
590   PRINT "TOTAL CHANGE/INCREASE FROM WEEK"
600   PRINT "1 TO ";N - 1;" IS $";HA
610   PRINT "A CHANGE OF ";HA / FA * 100;" PERCENT"
620   PRINT
```

```
630   RETURN
640   GOSUB 580
650   GOTO 490
660   PRINT
670   PRINT "DIFFERENCE FROM WEEK # ";N - 1;" TO"
680   PRINT N;" IS $";GA
690   PRINT "A CHANGE OF ";GA / Z * 100;" PERCENT"
700   PRINT : RETURN
710   READ B,C,D,E,F,G
720   H = B + C + D + E + F + G
730   AV = H
740   BA =   INT (AV * 100 + 5) / 100
750   GA = BA - Z: IF B = 0 THEN 770
760   Z = BA
770   RETURN
780   PRINT "ENTER A '1' TO CONTINUE"
790   INPUT A
800   HOME
810   RETURN
820   FOR A = 1 TO 2043
830   NEXT A
840   RETURN
850   DATA 1.95,.75,.85,1.79,.61,1.59
860   DATA 2.00,.85,.95,1.85,.72,1.78
870   DATA 2.09,.89,.95,1.85,.75,1.75
880   DATA 2.05,.79,.87,2.20,.65,1.79
890   DATA 0,0,0,0,0,0
```

Money and Investment

This section describes some useful application programs dealing with money and investment, including a checkbook balancing program, a monthly savings plan, compound interest program, money market interest, a stock buying guide, a stock record keeper, and, finally, a stock plotter.

CHAPTER 23

Double Check

Double Check is a program that will help you keep a record of your personal checks and keep your checking account in balance. It's written in BASIC for your microcomputer. See Program 23-1 for the program listing.

THE PROGRAM

The program accepts your check and deposit data in DATA statements beginning at line 570. Enter each check, bank charge, and deposit in the following format:

DATA CHECK #,DATE (MM/DD/YY),NAME PAYABLE TO,AMOUNT

or

DATA 702,12/10/80,EDISON,14.75

DATA CHARGE CODE,DATE (MM/DD/YY),CHARGE, AMOUNT

or

DATA C,12/19/80,BANK CHARGE,4.00

DATA DEPOSIT CODE,DATE (MM/DD/YY),DEPOSIT, AMOUNT

or

DATA D,12/22/80,DEPOSIT,350

The first entry into your data list must be a past balance or a deposit. Then enter the checks, bank charges, and deposits, as they appear in your checking account deposit record.

Enter the check number, the date (as MM/DD/YY—do not use commas), the name payable to, and the amount for each check written. Enter your bank charges with a C for the charge code, the date, the words BANK CHARGE, and the charge amount. Enter the deposit with a D for the deposit code, the date, the word DEPOSIT, and the deposit

amount. Finally, the last statement in your data list must be DATA END,0,0,0.

After you run the program, it will list each check, bank charge, and deposit, as entered in the data list, plus the balance after each transaction. Then it will display the total number of transactions and the balance in your account. See Fig. 23-1 for a sample run.

SAVING THE PROGRAM AND DATA LIST

Each time there is a transaction in your checking account, enter it into the data list in the program. Then save the program on cassette or disk, to keep an ongoing record of your transactions.

```
DOUBLE CHECK
COPYRIGHT (C) 1980 BY HOWARD BERENBON


THIS PROGRAM WILL HELP YOU KEEP A
RECORD OF YOUR PERSONAL CHECKS, &
KEEP YOUR ACCOUNT IN BALANCE. IT'S
USED TO DOUBLE CHECK YOUR PERSONAL
CHECKING ACCOUNT RECORDS.
ENTER THE DATA IN DATA STATEMENTS
BEGINNING AT LINE 570, AS FOLLOWS:
DATA CHECK#,DATE,NAME PAYABLE TO,AMT.
YOUR DEPOST OR LAST BALANCE MUST BE
THE FIRST ENTRY IN YOUR DATA LIST.
THE LAST STATEMENT IN THE DATA LIST
MUST BE: DATA END,0,0,0



          DOUBLE CHECK

#    DATE      NAME        AMT       BAL

D    12/19/80  BALANCE     545.15    545.15
702  12/19/80  ELECTRIC    14.75     530.4
703  12/20/80  TELEPHONE   10.55     519.85
704  12/22/80  VISA        145.12    374.73
705  12/23/80  DR. SIMONS  5         369.73
706  12/23/80  RADIO SHACK 70        299.73
707  12/28/80  BOOK CLUB   9.95      289.78
D    12/28/80  DEPOSIT     200.35    490.13



THE TOTAL # OF TRANSACTIONS
IS  8 . YOUR BALANCE IS $ 490.13 .

CHECK THIS BALANCE WITH THE BALANCE
IN YOUR CHECKING ACCOUNT DEPOSIT
RECORD, AND COMPARE WITH YOUR BANK
STATEMENT FOR ACCURACY.
```

Fig. 23-1. Double Check sample run.

```
100   HOME : PRINT "DOUBLE CHECK"
110   PRINT "COPYRIGHT (C) 1980 BY HOWARD BERENBON"
120   PRINT "APPLE II"
130 GT = 2: GOSUB 540: HOME
140 B = 0:N = 0
150   PRINT "THIS PROGRAM WILL HELP YOU KEEP A"
160   PRINT "RECORD OF YOUR PERSONAL CHECKS, &"
170   PRINT "KEEP YOUR ACCOUNT IN BALANCE. IT'S"
180   PRINT "USED TO DOUBLE CHECK YOUR PERSONAL"
190   PRINT "CHECKING ACCOUNT RECORDS."
200   PRINT "ENTER THE DATA IN DATA STATEMENTS"
210   PRINT "BEGINNING AT LINE 570, AS FOLLOWS:"
220   PRINT "DATA CHECK#,DATE,NAME PAYABLE TO,AMT."
230   PRINT "YOUR DEPOSIT OR LAST BALANCE MUST BE"
240   PRINT "THE FIRST ENTRY IN YOUR DATA LIST."
250   PRINT "THE LAST STATEMENT IN THE DATA LIST"
260   PRINT "MUST BE: DATA END,0,0,0"
270 GT = 12: GOSUB 540
280   HOME
290   PRINT  TAB( 10)"DOUBLE CHECK"
300   PRINT
310   READ N$,D$,NA$,AM
320   IF N$ = "END" THEN 350
330 N = N + 1
340   GOTO 310
350   RESTORE
360   PRINT "#      DATE      NAME          AMT        BAL"
370   PRINT
380   READ N$,D$,NA$,AM
390   IF N$ = "END" THEN 450
400   IF N$ = "D" THEN B = B + AM: GOTO 420
410 B = B - AM
420   PRINT N$; TAB( 5);D$; TAB( 14);NA$; TAB( 26);AM; TAB( 34);B
430 GT = 2: GOSUB 540
440   GOTO 380
450 FT = 2: GOSUB 540: PRINT
460   PRINT "THE TOTAL # OF TRANSACTIONS"
470   PRINT "IS ";N;". YOUR BALANCE IS $";B;"."
480   PRINT
490   PRINT "CHECK THIS BALANCE WITH THE BALANCE"
500   PRINT "IN YOUR CHECKING ACCOUNT DEPOSIT"
510   PRINT "RECORD, AND COMPARE WITH YOUR BANK"
520   PRINT "STATEMENT FOR ACCURACY."
530   END
540   FOR A = 1 TO 750 * GT
550   NEXT A
560   RETURN
570   DATA D,12/19/80,BALANCE,545.15
580   DATA 702,12/19/80,ELECTRIC,14.75
590   DATA 703,12/20/80,TELEPHONE,10.55
600   DATA 704,12/22/80,VISA,145.12
610   DATA 705,12/23/80,DR. SIMONS,5.00
620   DATA 706,12/23/80,RADIO SHACK,70.00
```

```
630   DATA 707,12/28/80,BOOK CLUB,9.95
640   DATA D,12/28/80,DEPOSIT,200.35
650   DATA END,0,0,0
```

CHAPTER 24

Monthly Savings Plan

A savings plan is a good way to force yourself to save money for some future purchase. Here is a program that will calculate and display a monthly savings plan, given the initial amount, the monthly savings amount, the yearly interest rate, and the number of months to be displayed. The interest is calculated on a monthly basis. The program is written in BASIC for your microcomputer. See Program 24-1 for the program listing.

THE PROGRAM

After you run the program, enter the initial amount of your savings plan, the monthly savings amount, the yearly interest rate (in percent), and the number of months to be displayed. The program will display the initial amount, the interest rate, and the starting amount (initial amount plus monthly savings amount). Then it will display a table including the month number, the balance, the interest, and the cumulative interest for each month in your savings plan. Finally, it will display the balance in your savings account and the total cumulative interest for the number of months in your plan.

You can use this program to project the number of months to a savings goal. By adjusting the amount entered into your account each month, or the number of months in your plan, you can reach your savings goal in a specific period.

See Fig. 24-1 for a sample run.

```
MONTHLY SAVINGS PLAN
COPYRIGHT (C) 1980 BY HOWARD BERENBON

THIS PROGRAM CALCULATES AND DISPLAYS
A MONTHLY SAVINGS PLAN, GIVEN THE
INITIAL AMOUNT, MONTHLY SAVINGS
AMOUNT, THE YEARLY INTEREST RATE,
AND THE # OF MONTHS TO BE DISPLAYED.

ENTER THE INITIAL AMOUNT OF THE PLAN
? 200

ENTER THE MONTHLY SAVINGS AMOUNT
? 100

ENTER THE YEARLY INTEREST RATE (%)
? 5.25

ENTER THE # OF MONTHS TO BE DISPLAYED
? 12


MONTHLY SAVINGS PLAN
INITIAL AMOUNT = $ 200          INTEREST RATE =  5.25
MONTHLY SAVINGS AMT = $ 100     STARTING AMT = $ 300
MONTH        BALANCE            INTEREST       CUM. INT.
1            301.31             1.31           1.31
2            403.07             1.76           3.07
3            505.27             2.2            5.27
4            607.92             2.65           7.92
5            711.02             3.1            11.02
6            814.57             3.55           14.57
7            918.57             4              18.57
8            1023.03            4.46           23.03
9            1127.94            4.91           27.94
10           1233.31            5.37           33.31
11           1339.14            5.83           39.14
12           1445.44            6.3            45.44


BALANCE AFTER  12  MONTHS = $ 1445.44
TOTAL CUMULATIVE INTEREST = $ 45.44
ANOTHER DISPLAY?
1 = YES   0 = NO
? 0
```

Fig. 24-1. Monthly Savings Plan sample run.

```
100    HOME : PRINT "MONTHLY SAVINGS PLAN"
110    PRINT "APPLE II"
120    PRINT "COPYRIGHT (C) 1980 BY HOWARD BERENBON"
130    PRINT :CI = 0
140    PRINT "THIS PROGRAM CALCULATES AND DISPLAYS"
150    PRINT "A MONTHLY SAVINGS PLAN, GIVEN THE"
160    PRINT "INITIAL AMOUNT, MONTHLY SAVINGS"
170    PRINT "AMOUNT, THE YEARLY INTEREST RATE,"
180    PRINT "AND THE # OF MONTHS TO BE DISPLAYED."
190    PRINT
200    PRINT "ENTER THE INITIAL AMOUNT OF THE PLAN"
210    INPUT J
220    PRINT
230    PRINT "ENTER THE MONTHLY SAVINGS AMOUNT"
240    INPUT P
250 K = P
260 B = J
270    PRINT
280    PRINT "ENTER THE YEARLY INTEREST RATE (%)"
290    INPUT I
300    PRINT
310    PRINT "ENTER THE # OF MONTHS TO BE DISPLAYED"
320    INPUT M
330 MI = (I / 12) / 100
340    HOME
350    PRINT "MONTHLY SAVINGS PLAN"
360    PRINT "INITIAL AMOUNT=$";J;"  INTEREST RATE=";I
370    PRINT "MONTHLY SAV AMT=$";K;"  START AMT=$";J + K
380    PRINT "MONTH  BALANCE  INTEREST  CUM. INT."
390    FOR A = 1 TO M
400    GOSUB 520
410    PRINT A; TAB( 8);B; TAB( 17);IN; TAB( 27);CI
420    FOR T = 1 TO 908
430    NEXT T
440    NEXT A
450    PRINT "BALANCE AFTER ";M;" MONTHS = $";B
460    PRINT "TOTAL CUMULATIVE INTEREST = $";CI
470    PRINT "ANOTHER DISPLAY?"
480    PRINT "1 = YES   0 = NO"
490    INPUT A
500    IF A = 1 THEN 100
510    END
520    REM  CALCULATE MONTHLY DATA
530 B = B + P
540 IN = B * MI
550 IN =  INT (IN * 100 + .5) / 100
560 B = B + IN
570 B =  INT (B * 100 + .5)
580 B = B / 100
590 CI = CI + IN
600    RETURN
```

CHAPTER 25

Compound Interest Table

This program calculates and displays the compound interest for a savings account, given the type of compounding, the principal, and the yearly interest rate. It's written in BASIC for your microcomputer. See Program 25-1 for the program listing.

THE PROGRAM

After you run the program, it requests your entry of the type of compounding. Enter 1 for daily, 2 for monthly, or 3 for quarterly interest compounding. Then it requests entry of the principal amount of your account and the yearly interest rate of your savings and loan or bank. Now enter the number of days, months, or quarters to be displayed. A table will be printed for the type of compounding requested. It displays the principal, the yearly interest rate, the day, month, or quarter number, the balance, the interest, and the cumulative interest for the desired number of days, months, or quarters. Finally, the balance is displayed with the total cumulative interest. You may now enter a 1 for another display, or a 0 to end the program. See Fig. 25-1 for a sample run.

```
COMPOUND INTEREST TABLE
COPYRIGHT (C) 1980 BY HOWARD BERENBON

THIS PROGRAM CALCULATES AND DISPLAYS
THE COMPOUND INTEREST FOR A SAVINGS
ACCOUNT, GIVEN THE TYPE OF COMPOUNDING,
THE PRINCIPAL, & YEARLY INTEREST RATE.

ENTER THE TYPE OF COMPOUNDING:
1 = DAILY
2 = MONTHLY
3 = QUARTERLY
? 1




ENTER THE PRINCIPAL AMOUNT
? 2500

ENTER THE YEARLY INTEREST RATE (%)
? 5.25


DAILY INTEREST TABLE

ENTER THE # OF DAYS TO BE DISPLAYED
? 12


DAILY COMPOUND INTEREST TABLE
PRINCIPAL = $ 2500          INTEREST RATE =  5.25
DAY          BALANCE        INTEREST       CUM. INT.
 1           2500.36        .36            .36
 2           2500.72        .36            .72
 3           2501.08        .36            1.08
 4           2501.44        .36            1.44
 5           2501.8         .36            1.8
 6           2502.16        .36            2.16
 7           2502.52        .36            2.52
 8           2502.88        .36            2.88
 9           2503.25        .37            3.25
10           2503.62        .37            3.62
11           2503.99        .37            3.99
12           2504.36        .37            4.36
```

```
BALANCE AFTER  12  DAYS = $ 2504.36
TOTAL CUM. INTEREST = $ 4.36
ANOTHER DISPLAY?
1 = YES   0 = NO
? 1


ENTER THE TYPE OF COMPOUNDING:
1 = DAILY
2 = MONTHLY
3 = QUARTERLY
? 2

ENTER THE PRINCIPAL AMOUNT
? 2500

ENTER THE YEARLY INTEREST RATE (%)
? 5.25


MONTHLY INTEREST TABLE

ENTER THE # OF MONTHS TO BE DISPLAYED
? 12


MONTHLY COMPOUND INTEREST TABLE
PRINCIPAL = $ 2500          INTEREST RATE =  5.25
MONTH         BALANCE       INTEREST       CUM. INT.
 1           2510.94        10.94          10.94
 2           2521.93        10.99          21.93
 3           2532.96        11.03          32.96
 4           2544.04        11.08          44.04
 5           2555.17        11.13          55.17
 6           2566.35        11.18          66.35
 7           2577.58        11.23          77.58
 8           2588.86        11.28          88.86
 9           2600.19        11.33          100.19
10           2611.57        11.38          111.57
11           2623          11.43          123
12           2634.48        11.48          134.48


BALANCE AFTER 12 MONTHS = $ 2634.48
TOTAL CUM. INTEREST = $ 134.48
ANOTHER DISPLAY?
1 = YES   0 = NO
? 0
```

Fig. 25-1. Compound Interest Table sample run.

```
100   HOME : PRINT "COMPOUND INTEREST TABLE"
110   PRINT "APPLE II"
120   PRINT "COPYRIGHT (C) 1980 BY HOWARD BERENBON"
130   PRINT :CI = 0
140   PRINT "THIS PROGRAM CALCULATES AND DISPLAYS#
150   PRINT "THE COMPOUND INTEREST FOR A SAVINGS"
160   PRINT "ACCOUNT, GIVEN THE TYPE OF COMPOUNDING,"
170   PRINT "THE PRINCIPAL, & YEARLY INTEREST RATE."
180   PRINT
190   PRINT "ENTER THE TYPE OF COMPOUNDING:"
200   PRINT "1 = DAILY"
210   PRINT "2 = MONTHLY"
220   PRINT "3 = QUARTERLY"
230   INPUT CP
240   IF CP = 1 THEN CM = 360
250   IF CP = 2 THEN CM = 12
260   IF CP = 3 THEN CM = 4
270   IF CP < 1 OR CP > 3 THEN 190
280   PRINT
290   PRINT "ENTER THE PRINCIPAL AMOUNT"
300   INPUT P
310   PRINT
320   PRINT "ENTER THE YEARLY INTEREST RATE (%)"
330   INPUT I
340   PRINT
350   ON CP GOTO 390,620,800
360   FOR T = 1 TO 908
370   NEXT T
380   RETURN
390   REM  DAILY INTEREST
400   HOME
410   PRINT "DAILY INTEREST TABLE"
420   PRINT
430   PRINT "ENTER THE # OF DAYS TO BE DISPLAYED"
440   INPUT D
450 DI = (I / CM) / 100
460   HOME
470   PRINT "DAILY COMPOUND INTEREST TABLE"
480   PRINT "PRINCIPAL=$";P;"  INTEREST RATE=";I
490   PRINT "DAY  BALANCE  INTEREST  CUM. INT."
500   FOR A = 1 TO D
510   GOSUB 980
520   PRINT A; TAB( 6);B; TAB( 15);IN; TAB( 24);CI
530   GOSUB 360
540   NEXT A
550   PRINT "BALANCE AFTER ";D;" DAYS = $";B
560   PRINT "TOTAL CUM. INTEREST = $";CI
570   PRINT "ANOTHER DISPLAY?"
580   PRINT "1 = YES   0 = NO"
590   INPUT G
600   IF G = 1 THEN 100
610   END
620   REM  MONTHLY INTEREST
```

```
630   HOME
640   PRINT "MONTHLY INTEREST TABLE"
650   PRINT
660   PRINT "ENTER THE # OF MONTHS TO BE DISPLAYED"
670   INPUT M
680 MI = (I / CM) / 100
690   HOME
700   PRINT "MONTHLY COMPOUND INTEREST TABLE"
710   PRINT "PRINCIPAL=$";P;"  INTEREST RATE=";I
720   PRINT "MONTH  BALANCE  INTEREST  CUM. INT."
730   FOR A = 1 TO M
740   GOSUB 1060
750   PRINT A; TAB( 8);B; TAB( 17);IN; TAB( 27);CI
760   GOSUB 360
770   NEXT A
780   PRINT "BALANCE AFTER ";M;" MONTHS = $";B
790   GOTO 560
800   REM  QUARTERLY INTEREST
810   HOME
820   PRINT "QUARTERLY INTEREST TABLE"
830   PRINT
840   PRINT "ENTER THE # OF QUARTERS TO BE DISPLAYED"
850   INPUT Q
860 QI = (I / CM) / 100
870   HOME
880   PRINT "QUARTERLY COMPOUND INTEREST TABLE"
890   PRINT "PRINCIPAL=$";P;"  INTEREST RATE=";I
900   PRINT "QUARTER  BALANCE  INTEREST  CUM. INT."
910   FOR A = 1 TO Q
920   GOSUB 1140
930   PRINT A; TAB( 10);B; TAB( 19);IN; TAB( 29);CI
940   GOSUB 360
950   NEXT A
960   PRINT "BALANCE AFTER ";Q;" QUARTERS = $";B
970   GOTO 560
980   REM  CALCULATE DAILY DATA
990 B = P
1000 IN = P * DI
1010 IN =  INT (IN * 100 + .5) / 100
1020 B = P + IN
1030 P = B
1040 CI = CI + IN
1050  RETURN
1060  REM  CALCULATE MONTHLY DATA
1070 B = P
1080 IN = P * MI
1090 IN =  INT (IN * 100 + .5) / 100
1100 B = P + IN
1110 P = B
1120 CI = CI + IN
1130  RETURN
1140  REM  CALCULATE QUARTERLY DATA
1150 B = P
```

```
1160 IN = P * QI
1170 IN =  INT (IN * 100 + .5) / 100
1180 B = P + IN
1190 P = B
1200 CI = CI + IN
1210  RETURN
```

CHAPTER 26

Money Market Interest Table

Here's another program for calculating interest on your savings. It's a Money Market interest calculator that calculates the simple interest for Money Market type accounts. The program is written in BASIC for your microcomputer. See Program 26-1 for the program listing.

THE PROGRAM

The program will display a table, given the type of interest calculation (daily, monthly, or quarterly), the principal, the yearly interest rate, and the number of days, months, or quarters for display.

After you run the program, enter the type of interest calculation desired. Enter a 1 for daily, 2 for monthly, or 3 for quarterly interest. Then the program requests entry of the principal amount of your Money Market Certificate and the yearly interest rate. Now enter the number of days, months, or quarters to be displayed. A table will be printed for the type of interest calculation requested. It displays the yearly interest rate, the day, month, or quarter number, the principal, the interest, and the cumulative interest for the desired number of days, months, or quarters. Finally, the total cumulative interest is displayed for the requested number of days, months, or quarters. You may now enter a 1 for another display, or a 0 to end the program. See Fig. 26-1 for a sample run.

```
MONEY MARKET INTEREST TABLE
COPYRIGHT (C) 1980 BY HOWARD BERENBON

THIS PROGRAM CALCULATES AND DISPLAYS
THE SIMPLE INTEREST FOR A MONEY MARKET
CERTIFICATE, GIVEN THE TYPE OF INTEREST
CALCULATION, THE PRINCIPAL, AND YEARLY
INTEREST RATE.

ENTER THE TYPE OF INTEREST
CALCULATION:
1 = DAILY
2 = MONTHLY
3 = QUARTERLY
? 1


ENTER THE PRINCIPAL AMOUNT
? 10000

ENTER THE YEARLY INTEREST RATE (%)
? 15.43



DAILY INTEREST TABLE

ENTER THE # OF DAYS TO BE DISPLAYED
? 12




DAILY INTEREST TABLE
INTEREST RATE =  15.43
DAY          PRINCIPAL      INTEREST      CUM. INT.
1            10000          4.29          4.29
2            10000          4.29          8.58
3            10000          4.29          12.87
4            10000          4.29          17.16
5            10000          4.29          21.45
6            10000          4.29          25.74
7            10000          4.29          30.03
8            10000          4.29          34.32
9            10000          4.29          38.61
10           10000          4.29          42.9
11           10000          4.29          47.19
12           10000          4.29          51.48
```

```
TOTAL CUM. INT. AFTER  12  DAYS
. . . IS $ 51.48
ANOTHER DISPLAY?
1 = YES   0 = NO
? 1


ENTER THE TYPE OF INTEREST
CALCULATION:
1 = DAILY
2 = MONTHLY
3 = QUARTERLY
? 2

ENTER THE PRINCIPAL AMOUNT
? 10000

ENTER THE YEARLY INTEREST RATE (%)
? 15.43


MONTHLY INTEREST TABLE

ENTER THE # OF MONTHS TO BE DISPLAYED
? 12


MONTHLY INTEREST TABLE
INTEREST RATE =  15.43
MONTH        PRINCIPAL      INTEREST      CUM. INT.
1            10000          128.58        128.58
2            10000          128.58        257.16
3            10000          128.58        385.74
4            10000          128.58        514.32
5            10000          128.58        642.9
6            10000          128.58        771.48
7            10000          128.58        900.06
8            10000          128.58        1028.64
9            10000          128.58        1157.22
10           10000          128.58        1285.8
11           10000          128.58        1414.38
12           10000          128.58        1542.96


TOTAL CUM. INT. AFTER  12  MONTHS
. . . IS $ 1542.96
ANOTHER DISPLAY?
1 = YES   0 = NO
? 0
```

Fig. 26-1. Money Market Interest Table sample run.

```
100   HOME : PRINT "MONEY MARKET INTEREST TABLE"
110   PRINT "APPLE II"
120   PRINT "COPYRIGHT (C) 1980 BY HOWARD BERENBON"
130   PRINT :CI = 0
140   PRINT "THIS PROGRAM CALCULATES AND DISPLAYS"
150   PRINT "THE SIMPLE INTEREST FOR A MONEY MARET"
160   PRINT "CERTIFICATE, GIVEN THE TYPE OF INTEREST"
170   PRINT "CALCULATION, THE PRINCIPAL, AND YEARLY"
180   PRINT "INTEREST RATE."
190   PRINT
200   PRINT "ENTER THE TYPE OF INTEREST"
210   PRINT "CALCULATION:"
220   PRINT "1 = DAILY"
230   PRINT "2 = MONTHLY"
240   PRINT "3 = QUARTERLY"
250   INPUT CP
260   IF CP = 1 THEN CM = 360
270   IF CP = 2 THEN CM = 12
280   IF CP = 3 THEN CM = 4
290   IF CP < 1 OR CP > 3 THEN 200
300   PRINT
310   PRINT "ENTER THE PRINCIPAL AMOUNT"
320   INPUT P
330   PRINT
340   PRINT "ENTER THE YEARLY INTEREST RATE (%)"
350   INPUT I
360   PRINT
370   ON CP GOTO 410,640,820
380   FOR T = 1 TO 908
390   NEXT T
400   RETURN
410   REM  DAILY INTEREST
420   HOME
430   PRINT "DAILY INTEREST TABLE"
440   PRINT
450   PRINT "ENTER THE # OF DAYS TO BE DISPLAYED"
460   INPUT D
470 DI = (I / CM) / 100
480   HOME
490   PRINT "DAILY INTEREST TABLE"
500   PRINT "INTEREST RATE = ";I
510   PRINT "DAY  PRINCIPAL  INTEREST  CUM. INT."
520   FOR A = 1 TO D
530   GOSUB 1000
540   PRINT A; TAB( 6);P; TAB( 17);IN; TAB( 27);CI
550   GOSUB 380
560   NEXT A
570   PRINT "TOTAL CUM. INT. AFTER ";D;" DAYS"
580   PRINT ". . . IS $";CI
590   PRINT "ANOTHER DISPLAY?"
600   PRINT "1 = YES   0 = NO"
610   INPUT G
620   IF G = 1 THEN 100
```

```
630   END
640   REM  MONTHLY INTEREST
650   HOME
660   PRINT "MONTHLY INTEREST TABLE"
670   PRINT
680   PRINT "ENTER THE # OF MONTHS TO BE DISPLAYED"
690   INPUT M
700 MI = (I / CM) / 100
710   HOME
720   PRINT "MONTHLY INTEREST TABLE"
730   PRINT "INTEREST RATE = ";I
740   PRINT "MONTH  PRINCIPAL  INTEREST  CUM. INT."
750   FOR A = 1 TO M
760   GOSUB 1060
770   PRINT A; TAB( 8);P; TAB( 19);IN; TAB( 29);CI
780   GOSUB 380
790   NEXT A
800   PRINT "TOTAL CUM. INT. AFTER ";M;" MONTHS"
810   GOTO 580
820   REM  QUARTERLY INTEREST
830   HOME
840   PRINT "QUARTERLY INTEREST TABLE"
850   PRINT
860   PRINT "ENTER THE # OF QUARTERS TO BE DISPLAYED"
870   INPUT Q
880 QI = (I / CM) / 100
890   HOME
900   PRINT "QUARTERLY INTEREST TABLE"
910   PRINT "INTEREST RATE = ";I
920   PRINT "QUARTER  PRINCIPAL  INTEREST  CUM. INT."
930   FOR A = 1 TO Q
940   GOSUB 1110
950   PRINT A; TAB( 10);P; TAB( 21);IN; TAB( 31);CI
960   GOSUB 380
970   NEXT A
980   PRINT "TOTAL CUM. INT. AFTER ";Q;" QUARTERS"
990   GOTO 580
1000  REM  CALCULATE DAILY DATA
1010 B = P
1020 IN = P * DI
1030 IN =  INT (IN * 100 + .5) / 100
1040 CI = CI + IN
1050  RETURN
1060  REM  CALCULATE MONTHLY DATA
1070 IN = P * MI
1080 IN =  INT (IN * 100 + .5) / 100
1090 CI = CI + IN
1100  RETURN
1110  REM  CALCULATE QUARTERLY DATA
1120 IN = P * QI
1130 IN =  INT (IN * 100 + .5) / 100
1140 CI = CI + IN
1150  RETURN
```

CHAPTER 27

Stock Buying Guide

Here's an investment program for the small investor. It's a stock market buying guide questionnaire to help you determine if a particular stock is a right choice for investment. The program is written in BASIC for your microcomputer. See Program 27-1 for the program listing.

THE PROGRAM

The program consists of a fifteen-question questionnaire, requiring entry of different point values per question. A total score of 27 or better is a recommendation to invest in the stock. A preliminary question must be answered with a "no" response, to allow entry into the questionnaire.

After you run the program, the following preliminary question will be displayed:

IS THE COMPANY IN A DEFICIT?
1—Yes 0—No

The entry of a 1 indicates a "yes" and 0 indicates a "no." If the answer is "yes" (the company is in a deficit), then the program will display:

THE STOCK IS NOT ACCEPTABLE
IT IS NOT RECOMMENDED FOR PURCHASE

You will not be allowed entry into the questionnaire, since the stock is a bad risk.

Answering the question with a "no" (0 entry) allows entry into the questionnaire, and question No. 1 will be displayed. Enter the number of points that is indicated for your stock. If zero is indicated, then enter 0. The program will print the "point value so far" and advance to the next question. After all fifteen questions are answered, it displays the final point score and whether the stock is acceptable, and recommended, or not acceptable, and not recommended for purchase. See Fig. 27-1 for a sample run.

ANALYSIS

A total score of 27 or greater is an indication that your stock choice will be a safe investment. But before investing, since the market is so unpredictable, consult your stockbroker for recent information on the company, and use this program along with your judgment, as a guide for investing.

```
STOCK BUYING GUIDE                        ENTER POINT VALUE
COPYRIGHT (C) 1980 BY HOWARD BERENBON      ? 2


USE THE FOLLOWING QUESTIONNAIRE TO
HELP DETERMINE IF A PARTICULAR STOCK
WILL BE A GOOD INVESTMENT. THERE ARE       POINTS SO FAR =  2
15 QUESTIONS WITH DIFFERENT POINT
VALUES FOR EACH ANSWER. A TOTAL SCORE
OF 27 OR BETTER IS A RECOMMENDATION        #2-PRICE FLUCTUATION
TO INVEST IN THE STOCK. THE PRELIMINARY    (LAST 6 MONTHS)
QUESTION MUST BE ANSWERED WITH A 'NO'
TO ALLOW ENTRY INTO THE QUESTIONNAIRE.     UP=2 POINTS
                                           DOWN = 0
PRELIMINARY QUESTION                       NO CHANGE = 1

IS THE COMPANY IN A DEFICIT?               ENTER POINT VALUE
1-YES  0-NO                                ? 2
? 0

STOCK BUYING GUIDE

#1-STOCK PRICE                             POINTS SO FAR =  4

$6 TO $30 = 4 POINTS
GREATER THAN $30 = 2 POINTS                #3-PE RATIO
LESS THAN $6 = 0
                                           4/1 TO 8/1 = 4 POINTS
                                           9/1 TO 13/1 = 3
```

Fig. 27-1. Stock Buying Guide sample run.

```
14/1 TO 17/1 = 2
18/1 TO 24/1 = 1
25/1 AND ABOVE = 0

ENTER POINT VALUE
? 1


POINTS SO FAR =  5


#4-VOLUME SOLD, LAST (HUNDREDS)

0 TO 300 = 0 POINTS
301 TO 600 = 1
601 TO 1000 = 2
1001 AND GREATER = 3

ENTER POINT VALUE
? 3


POINTS SO FAR =  8


#5-DIVIDENDS

NONE = 0 POINTS
1 TO 2% = 1
2.1 TO 3% = 2
3.1 TO 6% = 3
6.1 TO 12% = 4
12.1% AND ABOVE =2

ENTER POINT VALUE
? 0


POINTS SO FAR =  8


#6-EARNINGS

UP = 2 POINTS
DOWN = 0
NO CHANGE = 1

ENTER POINT VALUE
? 2



POINTS SO FAR =  10


#7-RECENT NEWS ABOUT COMPANY

NO NEWS = 1
GOOD NEWS = 2
BAD NEWS = 0

ENTER POINT VALUE
? 2



POINTS SO FAR =  12


#8-INVESTMENT TYPE

SHORT TERM INVESTMENT = 2
LONG TERM INVESTMENT = 1

ENTER POINT VALUE
? 2



POINTS SO FAR =  14


#9-RECENT SPLITS

YES = 4
NO = 0

ENTER POINT VALUE
? 4



POINTS SO FAR =  18
```

```
#10-BROKER COMMISSION

3% OR LESS = 2 POINTS
3.1 TO 4% = 1
4.1% OR GREATER = 0

ENTER POINT VALUE
? 2



POINTS SO FAR =  20


#11-EXCHANGE TRADED ON

NEW YORK = 4 POINTS
AMERICAN = 2
OTHERS = 0

ENTER POINT VALUE
? 4



POINTS SO FAR =  24


#12-NUMBER OF YEARS IN BUSINESS

0 TO 6 = 0
7 TO 20 = 1
21 TO 30 = 2
31 TO 40 = 3
41 AND ABOVE = 4

ENTER POINT VALUE
? 2



POINTS SO FAR =  26


#13-SIZE OF BUSINESS

LARGE CORPORATION OR COMPANY = 4
MEDIUM SIZE = 2
SMALL = 0

ENTER POINT VALUE
? 4



POINTS SO FAR =  30


#14-EARNINGS AND DIVIDEND RANKING

A+ = 4 POINTS
A  = 3
A- = 3
B+ = 2
B  = 2
B- = 1
C  = 0
D  = 0

ENTER POINT VALUE
? 2



POINTS SO FAR =  32


#15-STOCK MARKET CONDITIONS

UP = 2 POINTS
DOWN OR NO CHANGE = 0

ENTER POINT VALUE
? 2



POINTS SO FAR =  34


FINAL POINT SCORE IS  34


THE STOCK IS ACCEPTABLE

IT IS RECOMMENDED FOR PURCHASE
```

Fig. 27-1—cont. Stock Buying Guide sample run.

```
100    HOME : PRINT "STOCK BUYING GUIDE"
110    PRINT "COPYRIGHT (C) 1980 BY HOWARD BERENBON"
120    PRINT "APPLE II"
130    GOSUB 1710: HOME
140    PRINT "USE THE FOLLOWING QUESTIONNAIRE TO"
150    PRINT "HELP DETERMINE IF A PARTICULAR STOCK"
160    PRINT "WILL BE A GOOD INVESTMENT. THERE ARE
170    PRINT "15 QUESTIONS WITH DIFFERENT POINT"
180    PRINT "VALUES FOR EACH ANSWER. A TOTAL SCORE"
190    PRINT "OF 27 OR BETTER IS A RECOMMENDATION"
200    PRINT "TO INVEST IN THE STOCK. THE PRELIMINARY"
210    PRINT "QUESTION MUST BE ANSWERED WITH A 'NO'"
220    PRINT "TO ALLOW ENTRY INTO THE QUESTIONNAIRE."
230    PRINT
240    PRINT "PRELIMINARY QUESTION"
250    PRINT
260    PRINT "IS THE COMPANY IN A DEFICIT?"
270    PRINT "1-YES  0-NO"
280    INPUT A
290    IF A = 1 THEN 1740
300    IF A = 0 THEN 320
310    GOTO 230
320    HOME
330    PRINT "STOCK BUYING GUIDE"
340    PRINT
350 S1 = 0
360    PRINT "#1-STOCK PRICE"
370    PRINT
380    PRINT "$6 TO 30 = 4 POINTS"
390    PRINT "GREATER THAN $30 = 2 POINTS"
400    PRINT "LESS THAN $6 = 0"
410    GOSUB 1610
420    GOSUB 1660
430    PRINT "#2-PRICE FLUCTUATION"
440    PRINT "(LAST 6 MONTHS)"
450    PRINT
460    PRINT "UP=2 POINTS"
470    PRINT "DOWN = 0"
480    PRINT "NO CHANGE = 1"
490    GOSUB 1610
500    GOSUB 1660
510    PRINT "#3-PE RATIO"
520    PRINT
530    PRINT "4/1 TO 8/1 = 4 POINTS"
540    PRINT "9/1 TO 13/1 = 3"
550    PRINT "14/1 TO 17/1 = 2"
560    PRINT "18/1 TO 24/1 = 1"
570    PRINT "25/1 AND ABOVE = 0"
580    GOSUB 1610
590    GOSUB 1660
600    PRINT "#4-VOLUME SOLD, LAST (HUNDREDS)"
610    PRINT
620    PRINT "0 TO 300 = 0 POINTS"
```

```
630    PRINT "301 TO 600 = 1"
640    PRINT "601 TO 1000 = 2"
650    PRINT "1001 AND GREATER = 3"
660    GOSUB 1610
670    GOSUB 1660
680    PRINT "#5-DIVIDENDS"
690    PRINT
700    PRINT "NONE = 0 POINTS"
710    PRINT "1 TO 2% = 1"
720    PRINT "2.1 TO 3% = 2"
730    PRINT "3.1 TO 6% = 3"
740    PRINT "6.1 TO 12% = 4"
750    PRINT "12.1% AND ABOVE =2"
760    GOSUB 1610
770    GOSUB 1660
780    PRINT "#6-EARNINGS"
790    PRINT
800    PRINT "UP = 2 POINTS"
810    PRINT "DOWN = 0"
820    PRINT "NO CHANGE = 1"
830    GOSUB 1610
840    GOSUB 1660
850    PRINT "#7-RECENT NEWS ABOUT COMPANY"
860    PRINT
870    PRINT "NO NEWS = 1"
880    PRINT "GOOD NEWS =2"
890    PRINT "BAD NEWS = 0"
900    GOSUB 1610
910    GOSUB 1660
920    PRINT "#8-INVESTMENT TYPE"
930    PRINT
940    PRINT "SHORT TERM INVESTMENT = 2"
950    PRINT "LONG TERM INVESTMENT = 1"
960    GOSUB 1610
970    GOSUB 1660
980    PRINT "#9-RECENT SPLITS"
990    PRINT
1000   PRINT "YES = 4"
1010   PRINT "NO = 0"
1020   GOSUB 1610
1030   GOSUB 1660
1040   PRINT "#10-BROKER COMMISSION"
1050   PRINT
1060   PRINT "3% OR LESS = 2 POINTS"
1070   PRINT "3.1 TO 4% = 1"
1080   PRINT "4.1% OR GREATER = 0"
1090   GOSUB 1610
1100   GOSUB 1660
1110   PRINT "#11-EXCHANGE TRADED ON"
1120   PRINT
1130   PRINT "NEW YORK = 4 POINTS"
1140   PRINT "AMERICAN = 2"
1150   PRINT "OTHERS = 0"
```

```
1160   GOSUB 1610
1170   GOSUB 1660
1180   PRINT "#12-NUMBER OF YEARS IN BUSINESS"
1190   PRINT
1200   PRINT "0 TO 6 = 0"
1210   PRINT "7 TO 20 = 1"
1220   PRINT "21 TO 30 = 2"
1230   PRINT "31 TO 40 = 3"
1240   PRINT "41 AND ABOVE = 4"
1250   GOSUB 1610
1260   GOSUB 1660
1270   PRINT "#13-SIZE OF BUSINESS"
1280   PRINT
1290   PRINT "LARGE CORPORATION OR COMPANY = 4"
1300   PRINT "MEDIUM SIZE = 2"
1310   PRINT "SMALL = 0"
1320   GOSUB 1610
1330   GOSUB 1660
1340   PRINT "#14-EARNINGS AND DIVIDEND RANKING"
1350   PRINT
1360   PRINT "A+ = 4 POINTS"
1370   PRINT "A  = 3"
1380   PRINT "A- = 3"
1390   PRINT "B+ = 2"
1400   PRINT "B  = 2"
1410   PRINT "B- = 1"
1420   PRINT "C  = 0"
1430   PRINT "D  = 0"
1440   GOSUB 1610
1450   GOSUB 1660
1460   PRINT "#15-STOCK MARKET CONDITIONS"
1470   PRINT
1480   PRINT "UP = 2 POINTS"
1490   PRINT "DOWN OR NO CHANGE = 0"
1500   GOSUB 1610
1510   GOSUB 1660
1520   PRINT
1530   PRINT "FINAL POINT SCORE IS ";S1
1540   PRINT
1550   IF S1 < 27 THEN 1740
1560   PRINT
1570   PRINT "THE STOCK IS ACCEPTABLE"
1580   PRINT
1590   PRINT "IT IS RECOMMENDED FOR PURCHASE"
1600   END
1610   PRINT
1620   PRINT "ENTER POINT VALUE"
1630   INPUT S
1640 S1 = S + S1: HOME
1650   RETURN
1660   PRINT
1670   PRINT "POINTS SO FAR = ";S1
1680   PRINT
```

```
1690  PRINT
1700  RETURN
1710  FOR A = 1 TO 2043
1720  NEXT A
1730  RETURN
1740  PRINT
1750  PRINT "THE STOCK IS NOT ACCEPTABLE"
1760  PRINT
1770  PRINT "IT IS NOT RECOMMENDED FOR PURCHASE"
1780  GOTO 1600
```

CHAPTER 28

Stock Record Keeper

If you're an investor in the stock market then the Stock Record Keeper can help you. The program allows you to keep a record of each of the stocks in your portfolio, and it gives gain or loss information on your stocks. It's written in BASIC for your microcomputer. See Program 28-1 for the program listing.

THE PROGRAM

The program requires that you enter your stock data in DATA statements beginning at line 1000. Enter the data in the following format:

DATA COMPANY NAME,# OF SHARES,DATE OF PURCHASE,PURCHASE PRICE,RECENT PRICE

or

DATA GM,100,2/1/80,54,55.5

The last DATA statement in your list must be DATA END,0,0,0,0.

The program allows you to list data on one or all of the stocks, including the company name, the number of shares held, the date of purchase (entered MM/DD/YY), the purchase price, and the recent price. It also displays the net worth, gain or loss, and the percent (%) gain or loss for your stocks. Finally, you can display the total gain or loss in your portfolio.

After you run the program, you have the following four options:

1. Enter a 1 to list one stock.
2. Enter a 2 to list all stocks.
3. Enter a 3 to list total gain or loss.
4. Enter a 4 to end the program.

List One Stock

Entering a 1 allows you to list the data on a single stock. The program requests entry of the stock name, and it searches the list for that name. If the name is found, the stock data is displayed. If the name is not found, the computer will display ENTRY NOT FOUND and then allow you to enter into one of the four previously listed options.

List All Stocks

Entering a 2 allows you to list the data on all the stocks in your portfolio. The program will list one stock at a time. After the data for a stock is displayed, enter a 1 to continue to the next stock in your list. When all the stock data has been displayed, the program will allow you to enter into one of the four options listed.

List Total Gain or Loss

Entering a 3 allows you to list the total gain or loss for the stocks in your portfolio. The program lists the total stock costs and their total worth. Then it displays the total (+) gain or (−) loss and the percent (+) gain or (−) loss, and then it allows you to enter into one of the four options listed.

See Fig. 28-1 for a sample run.

ONE LAST NOTE

This program does not take into account the brokerage fees associated with the buying and selling of your stocks. But these fees must be included when calculating your gains or losses for income tax purposes.

```
STOCK RECORD KEEPER                              STOCK DATA
COPYRIGHT (C) 1980 BY HOWARD BERENBON
                                                 STOCK NAME: AMPEX
THIS PROGRAM ALLOWS YOU TO KEEP
A RECORD OF YOUR STOCK PORTFOLIO.                # OF SHARES =  100    DATE OF PURCHASE IS 7/18/80
YOU CAN LIST ONE OR ALL OF YOUR                  PURCHASE PRICE = $ 14.5    TOTAL COST = $ 1450
STOCKS INCLUDING THE NAME, # OF
SHARES, THE DATE OF PURCHASE,                    RECENT PRICE = $ 19.25    NET WORTH = $ 1925
PURCHASE PRICE, AND RECENT PRICE.
IT ALSO DISPLAYS THE NET WORTH, GAIN             (+) GAIN OR (-) LOSS IF SOLD = $ 475
OR LOSS, % GAIN OR LOSS, AND THE                 PERCENT (+) GAIN OR (-) LOSS =  32.75
TOTAL GAIN OR LOSS IN YOUR PORTFOLIO.

ENTER '1' TO CONTINUE
? 1                                              ENTER '1' TO CONTINUE
                                                 ? 1

ENTER YOUR STOCK DATA IN DATA                    ENTER CHOICE
STATEMENTS BEGINNING AT LINE 1000,
IN THE FOLLOWING FORMAT:                         1-LIST ONE STOCK
DATA NAME,# SHARES,PUR DATE,PUR PRICE,REC PRICE  2-LIST ALL STOCKS
DATA GM,100,2/1/80,54,55.5                       3-GIVE TOTAL GAIN OR LOSS
THE LAST STATEMENT IN THE LIST MUST BE:          4-END PROGRAM
DATA END,0,0,0,0                                 ? 3

ENTER '1' TO CONTINUE
? 1




                                                 TOTAL COST = $ 23125    NET WORTH =$ 25600

ENTER CHOICE                                     TOTAL (+) GAIN OR (-) LOSS FOR
                                                 ALL STOCKS IS $ 2475    OR  10.7   PERCENT
1-LIST ONE STOCK
2-LIST ALL STOCKS                                ENTER '1' TO CONTINUE
3-GIVE TOTAL GAIN OR LOSS                        ? 1
4-END PROGRAM                                    ENTER CHOICE
? 1
                                                 1-LIST ONE STOCK
                                                 2-LIST ALL STOCKS
LIST ONE STOCK                                   3-GIVE TOTAL GAIN OR LOSS
                                                 4-END PROGRAM
ENTER STOCK NAME                                 ? 4
? AMPEX
```

Fig. 28-1. Stock Record Keeper sample run.

```
100   HOME : PRINT "STOCK RECORD KEEPER"
110   PRINT "COPYRIGHT (C) 1980 BY HOWARD BERENBON"
120   PRINT "APPLE II"
130   PRINT
140   PRINT "THIS PROGRAM ALLOWS YOU TO KEEP"
150   PRINT "A RECORD OF YOUR STOCK PORTFOLIO."
160   PRINT "YOU CAN LIST ONE OR ALL OF YOUR"
170   PRINT "STOCKS INCLUDING THE NAME, # OF"
180   PRINT "SHARES, THE DATE OF PURCHASE,"
190   PRINT "PURCHASE PRICE, AND RECENT PRICE."
200   PRINT "IT ALSO DISPLAYS THE NET WORTH, GAIN"
210   PRINT "OR LOSS, % GAIN OR LOSS, AND THE"
220   PRINT "TOTAL GAIN OR LOSS IN YOUR PORTFOLIO."
230   GOSUB 710
240   HOME
250   PRINT "ENTER YOUR STOCK DATA IN DATA"
260   PRINT "STATEMENTS BEGINNING AT LINE 1000,"
270   PRINT "IN THE FOLLOWING FORMAT:"
280   PRINT "DATA NAME,# SHARES,PUR DATE,PUR PRICE,  RECENT PRICE"
290   PRINT "DATA GM,100,2/1/80,54,55.5
300   PRINT "THE LAST STATEMENT IN THE LIST MUST BE:"
310   PRINT "DATA END,0,0,0,0"
320   GOSUB 710
330   PRINT "ENTER CHOICE": RESTORE
340   PRINT :P = 0:Q = 0
350   PRINT "1-LIST ONE STOCK"
360   PRINT "2-LIST ALL STOCKS"
370   PRINT "3-GIVE TOTAL GAIN OR LOSS"
380   PRINT "4-END PROGRAM"
390   INPUT B: HOME
400   ON B GOTO 420,530,600,890
410   GOTO 320
420   PRINT "LIST ONE STOCK"
430   PRINT
440   PRINT "ENTER STOCK NAME"
450   INPUT A$
460   READ B$,C,C2$,D,E
470   IF B$ = "END" THEN 690
480   IF B$ = A$ THEN 500
490   GOTO 460
500   GOSUB 740
510   PRINT
520   GOTO 320
530   PRINT "LIST ALL STOCKS"
540   PRINT
550   READ B$,C,C2$,D,E
560   IF B$ = "END" THEN 330
570   GOSUB 750
580   GOSUB 710
590   GOTO 540
600   PRINT :T2 = 0:T5 = 0
610   GOSUB 900
620 Q =  INT ((P * 100 + .5)) / 100
```

```
630 R = (Q / T2) * 100:R =  INT (R * 100) / 100
640  PRINT "TOTAL COST=$";T2;"  NET WORTH=$";T5
650  PRINT
660  PRINT "TOTAL (+) GAIN OR (-) LOSS FOR"
670  PRINT "ALL STOCKS IS $";Q;"  OR ";R;" PERCENT"
680  GOTO 320
690  PRINT "STOCK '";A$;"' NOT FOUND"
700  GOTO 320
710  PRINT : PRINT "ENTER '1' TO CONTINUE"
720  INPUT A
730  RETURN
740  HOME : PRINT "STOCK DATA"
750  PRINT
760  PRINT "STOCK NAME: ";B$
770  PRINT
780  PRINT "# OF SHARES=";C;"  DATE OF PUR IS ";C2$
790  PRINT "PUR PRICE=$";D;"  TOTAL COST=$";C * D
800  PRINT
810  PRINT "RECENT PRICE=$";E;"   NET WORTH=$";C * E
820  PRINT : GOSUB 960
830  PRINT "(+) GAIN OR (-) LOSS IF SOLD = $";T1
840 C2 = C * D
850 R = (T1 / C2) * 100:R =  INT (R * 100) / 100
860  PRINT "PERCENT (+) GAIN OR (-) LOSS = ";R
870  PRINT
880  RETURN
890  END
900  READ B$,C,C2$,D,E
910  IF B$ = "END" THEN 950
920  GOSUB 960
930 P = P + T1
940  GOTO 900
950  RETURN
960 N = C * E:M = C * D
970 T1 = N - M:T2 = T2 + M:T5 = T5 + N
980  RETURN
1000  DATA GM,200,2/11/80,54,55.5
1010  DATA FORD,200,5/23/80,26.5,26
1020  DATA NVF,300,5/23/80,4.75,4.75
1030  DATA CHRYSLER,100,6/20/80,10.75,6.25
1040  DATA SONY,300,6/27/80,10.25,17.75
1050  DATA AMPEX,100,6/18/80,14.5,19.25
1060  DATA END,0,0,0,0
```

CHAPTER 29

Stock Plotter

A third program for the stock investor is the Stock Plotter. It will display a plot, using the TAB function, for any stock with a high price of up to $200, given a series of prices. These prices may be made of daily, weekly, or monthly data on a particular stock. The program is written in BASIC for your microcomputer. See Program 29-1 for the program listing.

THE PROGRAM

The stock price data must be entered into DATA statements beginning at line 810. Enter the data in the following format:

DATA PRICE1,PRICE2,PRICE3,PRICE4, . . . PRICEN

or

DATA 14.5,13.75,14.25,13.75

The last DATA statement in the list must be DATA 9999; this is used to test for the end of the data.

After you run the program, it requests your entry of the type of data plot. Enter a 1 for daily, 2 for weekly, or 3 for monthly. Then it requests an entry of the company name and the starting date of the plot (MM/DD/YY). Finally, enter a 1 to start the plot.

Now the program will find the highest price of the stock. Then it uses this price for scaling the output of the plot. The program will then print the company name, the date of the plot, and whether the plot is for daily, weekly, or monthly data. It then prints a horizontal scale from 0, at the left end, up to 200, at the right end. This scaling is dependent on the high price of the stock. Finally, the program plots each stock price using a plus sign (+) for each point. After all the data points are plotted, the program will display the average price

of the stock over the given number of days, weeks, or months, and print the high price for that period.

See Fig. 29-1 for a sample run.

```
STOCK PLOTTER
COPYRIGHT (C) 1980 BY HOWARD BERENBON

THIS PROGRAM WILL PLOT ANY STOCK,
GIVEN A SERIES OF PRICES FOR
DAILY, WEEKLY, OR MONTHLY DATA.

DATA IS STORED IN DATA STATEMENTS,
BEGINNING AT LINE 810. ENTER IN
THE FOLLOWING FORMAT:
DATA 14.5,13.75,14.25,13.75
THE LAST DATA STATEMENT SHOULD BE
DATA 9999. THIS IS USED TO TEST
FOR THE END OF THE DATA.

ENTER TYPE OF DATA?
1=DAILY  2=WEEKLY  3=MONTHLY
? 3


3

ENTER NAME OF THE COMPANY
? ABC

ENTER THE STARTING DATE OF PLOT
(MM/DD/YY)
? 06/15/80

ENTER A '1' FOR PLOT
? 1




COMPANY=ABC   DATE=06/15/80
MONTH               PRICE
0          12.5        25          37.5          50
++++++++++++++++++++++++++++++++++++++++++++++++++++++++
  1           +
  2             +
  3           +
  4           +
  5             +
  6             +
  7             +
  8               +
  9             +
 10                 +
 11                 +
 12                     +



AVERAGE PRICE OF THE STOCK
ABC, OVER A PERIOD OF  12  MONTHS
IS $ 16.1
HIGH PRICE FOR THAT PERIOD IS $ 25.25
```

Fig. 29-1. Stock Plotter sample run.

```
100    HOME
110    PRINT "STOCK PLOTTER"
120    PRINT "APPLE II"
130    PRINT "COPYRIGHT (C) 1980 BY HOWARD BERENBON"
140    GOSUB 690: HOME
150    PRINT "THIS PROGRAM WILL PLOT ANY STOCK,"
160    PRINT "GIVEN A SERIES OF PRICES FOR"
170    PRINT "DAILY, WEEKLY, OR MONTHLY DATA."
180    PRINT
190    PRINT "DATA IS STORED IN DATA STATEMENTS,"
200    PRINT "BEGINNING AT LINE 810. ENTER IN"
210    PRINT "THE FOLLOWING FORMAT:"
220    PRINT "DATA 14.5,13.75,14.25,13.75"
230    PRINT "THE LAST DATA STATEMENT SHOULD BE"
240    PRINT "DATA 9999. THIS IS USED TO TEST"
250    PRINT "FOR THE END OF THE DATA."
260    PRINT
270    REM  BEGIN PLOT
280    PRINT "ENTER TYPE OF DATA?"
290    PRINT "1=DAILY  2=WEEKLY  3=MONTHLY"
300    INPUT T
310    PRINT
320    PRINT "ENTER NAME OF THE COMPANY"
330    INPUT A$
340    PRINT
350    PRINT "ENTER THE STARTING DATE OF PLOT"
360    PRINT "(MM/DD/YY)"
370    INPUT D$:S = 0
380    GOSUB 620
390    GOSUB 410
400    GOTO 450
410    IF S <  = 10 THEN P = 10:A = 3.5: RETURN
420    IF S <  = 35 THEN P = 35:A = 1: RETURN
430    IF S <  = 100 THEN P = 100:A = .35: RETURN
440    IF S <  = 200 THEN P = 200:A = .175: RETURN
450    PRINT : PRINT "ENTER A '1' FOR PLOT"
460    INPUT J
470    HOME :C = 1
480    PRINT "COMPANY=";A$;"  DATE=";D$
490    IF T = 1 THEN P$ = "DAY"
500    IF T = 2 THEN P$ = "WEEK"
510    IF T = 3 THEN P$ = "MONTH"
520    PRINT P$; TAB( 20)"PRICE"
530    PRINT "0"; TAB( 9);P / 4; TAB( 18);P / 2; TAB( 26);
       INT ((P / 1.3333) * 100) / 100; TAB( 35);P:R = 0
540    PRINT "++++++++++++++++++++++++++++++++++++++++++++"
550    READ D:U =  INT (D * A + .5)
560    IF D = 9999 THEN 720
570 R = R + D
580    PRINT C; TAB( U)"+":C = C + 1
590    FOR B = 1 TO 1500
600    NEXT B
610    GOTO 550
```

```
620   REM  FIND HIGH PRICE
630 S = A
640   READ A: IF A = 9999 THEN 670
650   IF S > (A) THEN 640
660   GOTO 630
670   RESTORE
680   RETURN
690   FOR G = 1 TO 3178
700   NEXT G
710   RETURN
720   GOSUB 690
730 C = C - 1:U = R / C
740 U =   INT (100 * U) / 100
750   PRINT
760   PRINT "AVERAGE PRICE OF THE STOCK"
770   PRINT A$;", OVER A PERIOD OF ";C;" ";P$;"S"
780   PRINT "IS $";U
790   PRINT "HIGH PRICE FOR THAT PERIOD IS $";S
800   END
810   DATA 12.25,13.75,12,13,15.25,14.75
820   DATA 15.25,17.5,15.25,19.75,19.25,25.25
830   DATA 9999
```

SECTION IV

ESP Testing

This section is directed to the study of extrasensory perception, also known as ESP or psi. It consists of two programs that test for ESP. The first program tests the subject for clairvoyance, and the second program tests for precognition.

CHAPTER 30

Parapsychology Test 1: Clairvoyance

Clairvoyance is defined as the ability to perceive things that are not in sight or that cannot be seen. This program tests for clairvoyance using five each of the symbols *, +, −, =, and 0 stored in the computer. The subject will try to guess the symbol card, from the shuffled deck of 25. After the test is completed, a score is given. A score of 6 or more, after at least five consecutive tests, may be an indication of clairvoyance. The program is written in BASIC for your microcomputer. See Program 30-1 for the program listing.

THE PROGRAM

After you run the program, enter your name, or the subject's name, and the date (MM/DD/YY). Then enter a 1 to shuffle the deck. The computer will randomly mix the symbols and store them in array C$(M). After the shuffling is done, the computer will print SHUFFLING COMPLETED. Then the clairvoyance test number is displayed along with the date, the subject's name, and CARD# 1. You are then requested to enter the symbol guess.

Before entering your guess of the symbol, try to imagine yourself looking into the computer's memory and seeing the first symbol which appears in the shuffled deck. This first symbol will be stored in array C$(1), the second will be in C$(2), and so on through the twenty-fifth card. Enter the first symbol that appears in your mind. The program will advance to card No. 2. Continue entering the symbols in this manner until all 25 guesses are entered. You may now take another test by entering a Y, or end the testing with an N.

Entering an N will cause the computer to display your test data, including your score out of 25, for each test, the average score out of G tests taken, and the percent score. Then an analysis is given. If your average score is 6 or above, the program will indicate that there is a possibility that you are clairvoyant. If your average score is 5 or less, the program will indicate that you have an average score and there is no indication of clairvoyance.

It is recommended that at least five tests be taken to ensure an accurate analysis of your test data. The program allows a maximum of 25 consecutive tests.

PLOT

After your test scoring is complete, you may see a plot of the test data. The total score for each test is plotted horizontally, using the TAB function. A period (.) is displayed, along with the test number, at TAB(GG) on the horizontal line, where GG is the test score for each test as taken from the array T(A).

See Fig. 30-1 for a sample run.

```
PARAPSYCHOLOGY TEST 1
CLAIRVOYANCE
COPYRIGHT (C) 1980 BY HOWARD BERENBON

THIS IS A TEST FOR CLAIRVOYANCE. USING
FIVE EACH OF THE SYMBOLS *, +, -, =,
AND 0, THE SUBJECT WILL TRY TO GUESS THE
SYMBOL CARD, FROM THE SHUFFLED DECK,
IN ORDER FROM 1 TO 25. AFTER THE TEST IS
COMPLETED, A SCORE IS GIVEN. A SCORE OF
5 OR LESS IS AVERAGE. A SCORE OF 6 OR
MORE, AFTER AT LEAST 5 TESTS, MAY BE AN
INDICATION OF CLAIRVOYANCE.

ENTER SUBJECT'S NAME
? BRUCE

BRUCE

ENTER DATE (MM/DD/YY)
? 05/07/80

ENTER A '1' TO SHUFFLE THE CARDS
? 1
NOW SHUFFLING


SHUFFLING COMPLETED


CLAIRVOYANCE TEST  1

DATE : 05/07/80
SUBJECT: BRUCE

CARD#  1        TEST  1

ENTER SYMBOL GUESS
(* + - = 0)
? +


CARD#  2        TEST  1

ENTER SYMBOL GUESS
(* + - = 0)
? 0


CARD#  3        TEST  1

ENTER SYMBOL GUESS
(* + - = 0)
? 0



CARD#  4        TEST  1

ENTER SYMBOL GUESS
(* + - = 0)
? 0


CARD#  5        TEST  1

ENTER SYMBOL GUESS
(* + - = 0)
? +



CARD#  24       TEST  1

ENTER SYMBOL GUESS
(* + - = 0)
? =


CARD#  25       TEST  1

ENTER SYMBOL GUESS
(* + - = 0)
? +



ANOTHER TEST?
Y=YES  N=NO
? N


CLAIRVOYANCE TEST SCORING
DATE: 05/07/80
SUBJECT:  BRUCE

CORRECT SCORE OUT OF 25
TEST #  1
  5
AVERAGE SCORE OUT OF  1
TEST(S) IS  5

THAT'S  20  PERCENT CORRECT



YOU HAVE AN AVERAGE SCORE.
AT THIS TIME, THERE IS NO
INDICATION OF CLAIRVOYANCE.
WOULD YOU LIKE A PLOT
OF THE TEST SCORES
Y=YES  N=NO
? Y


PLOT OF CLAIRVOYANCE TEST DATA
SUBJECT:  BRUCE   DATE: 05/07/80

0    5   10  15       25
++++++++++++++++++++++++++
     .  TEST #  1
```

Fig. 30-1. Parapsychology Test 1: Clairvoyance sample run.

```
100    HOME : PRINT "PARAPSYCHOLOGY TEST 1"
110    PRINT "CLAIRVOYANCE"
120    PRINT "APPLE II"
130    PRINT "COPYRIGHT (C) 1980 BY HOWARD BERENBON"
140    PRINT
150    REM    DIM ARRAYS
160    DIM A(25),C$(25),T(25)
170    PRINT "THIS IS A TEST FOR CLAIRVOYANCE. USING"
180    PRINT "FIVE EACH OF THE SYMBOLS *, +, -, =,"
190    PRINT "AND O, THE SUBJECT WILL TRY TO GUESS THE"
200    PRINT "SYMBOL CARD, FROM THE SHUFFLED DECK,"
210    PRINT "IN ORDER FROM 1 TO 25. AFTER THE TEST IS"
220    PRINT "COMPLETED, A SCORE IS GIVEN. A SCORE OF"
230    PRINT "5 OR LESS IS AVERAGE. A SCORE OF 6 OR"
240    PRINT "MORE, AFTER AT LEAST 5 TESTS, MAY BE AN"
250    PRINT "INDICATION OF CLAIRVOYANCE."
260    GOSUB 1260
270    GOSUB 1260
280    PRINT
290    PRINT "ENTER SUBJECT'S NAME"
300    INPUT N$: PRINT
310    PRINT "ENTER DATE (MM/DD/YY)"
320    INPUT D$
330    PRINT
340    HOME :G = 0:T = 0
350    PRINT "ENTER A '1' TO SHUFFLE THE CARDS"
360    INPUT A
370    IF A <  > 1 THEN 340
380    PRINT "NOW SHUFFLING": GOSUB 840
390    PRINT :G = G + 1:T = T + 1
400    PRINT "SHUFFLING COMPLETED"
410    GOSUB 1260
420    GOSUB 1260
430    HOME
440    PRINT "CLAIRVOYANCE TEST ";T
450    PRINT : PRINT "DATA :  ";D$
460    PRINT "SUBJECT: ";N$
470    PRINT
480    FOR A = 1 TO 25
490    PRINT "CARD# ";A,"TEST ";T
500    PRINT
510    PRINT "ENTER SYMBOL GUESS"
520    PRINT "(* + - = O)"
530    INPUT C$: HOME
540    IF C$ = C$(A) THEN T(G) = T(G) + 1
550    NEXT A
560    PRINT
570    PRINT "ANOTHER TEST?"
580    PRINT "Y=YES   N=NO"
590    INPUT A$
600    IF A$ = "Y" THEN 350
610    HOME
620    PRINT "CLAIRVOYANCE TEST SCORING"
```

```
630   PRINT "DATE:  ";D$
640   PRINT "SUBJECT:  ";N$
650   PRINT
660   PRINT "CORRECT SCORE OUT OF 25"
670 J = 0
680   FOR A = 1 TO G
690   PRINT "TEST # ";A
700   PRINT T(A):J = T(A) + J
710   NEXT A
720   GOSUB 1260
730   PRINT "AVERAGE SCORE OUT OF ";G
740   PRINT "TEST(S) IS ";J / G
750   PRINT
760   PRINT "THAT'S ";J / G * 4;" PERCENT CORRECT"
770   GOSUB 1260: GOSUB 1260: GOSUB 1140
780   PRINT "WOULD YOU LIKE A PLOT"
790   PRINT "OF THE TEST SCORES"
800   PRINT "Y-YES  N=NO"
810   INPUT A$
820   IF A$ = "Y" THEN 980
830   END
840   FOR N = 1 TO 25
850 A(N) = 0
860   NEXT N
870   FOR N = 1 TO 25
880 M =  INT ( RND (1) * 25 + 1)
890   FOR A = 1 TO M
900   READ B$
910   NEXT A
920   RESTORE
930   IF A(M) = 1 THEN 880
940 A(M) = 1
950 C$(M) = B$
960   NEXT N
970   RETURN
980   PRINT "PLOT OF CLAIRVOYANCE TEST DATA"
990   PRINT "SUBJECT: ";N$;"   DATE: ";D$
1000  PRINT
1010  PRINT "0    5    10   15        25"
1020  PRINT "+++++++++++++++++++++++++++"
1030  FOR A = 1 TO G
1040 GG = T(A) + 1
1050  PRINT  TAB( GG)".   TEST # ";A
1060  GOSUB 1260
1070  NEXT A
1080  END
1090  DATA "*","*","*","*","*"
1100  DATA "+","+","+","+","+"
1110  DATA "-","-","-","-","-"
1120  DATA "=","=","=","=","="
1130  DATA "0","0","0","0","0"
1140  PRINT
1150  IF J / G > = 6 THEN 1210
```

```
1160   PRINT
1170   PRINT "YOU HAVE AN AVERAGE SCORE."
1180   PRINT "AT THIS TIME, THERE IS NO"
1190   PRINT "INDICATION OF CLAIRVOYANCE."
1200   RETURN
1210   PRINT
1220   PRINT "YOUR SCORE IS ABOVE AVERAGE."
1230   PRINT "THERE IS A POSSIBILITY THAT YOU"
1240   PRINT "ARE CLAIRVOYANT."
1250   RETURN
1260   REM  DELAY
1270   FOR Z = 1 TO 1135
1280   NEXT Z
1290   RETURN
```

CHAPTER 31

Parapsychology Test 2: Precognition

Precognition is defined as the ability to perceive events before they occur. This program tests for precognition using five each of the symbols *, +, −, =, and 0 stored in the computer. The subject will try to guess the symbol card in order from 1 to 25. The deck is shuffled after all 25 guesses are entered. After the test is completed, a score is given. A score of 6 or more, after at least five consecutive tests, may be an indication of precognition. The program is written in BASIC for your microcomputer. See Program 31-1 for the program listing.

THE PROGRAM

After you run the program, enter your name, or the subject's name, and the date (MM/DD/YY). Then the precognition test number is displayed along with the date, the subject's name, and CARD# 1. You are then requested to enter the symbol guess.

Before entering your guess of the symbol, try to imagine yourself looking into the computer's memory at some future time, after the cards have been shuffled (the cards will not be shuffled until all symbol guesses are entered). Imagine seeing the first symbol which will appear in the shuffled deck. This first symbol will be stored in array C$(1), the second will be in C$(2), and so on through the twenty-fifth card. Enter the first symbol that appears in your mind. The program will advance to card No. 2. Continue entering the symbols in this manner until all 25 guesses are entered. Then the cards will be shuffled. You may now take another test, by entering a Y, or end the testing with an N.

Entering an N will cause the computer to display your test data including your score out of 25, for each test, the average score out of G tests taken, and the percent score. Then an analysis is given. If your average score is 6 or above, the program will indicate that there is a possibility that you have precognition abilities. If your average score is 5 or less, the program will indicate that you have an average score and there is no indication of precognition.

It is recommended that at least five tests are taken to ensure an accurate analysis of your test data. The program allows a maximum of 25 consecutive tests.

PLOT

After your test scoring is complete, you may see a plot of the test data. The total score for each test is plotted horizontally, using the TAB function. A period (.) is displayed, along with the test number, at TAB(GG) on the horizontal line, where GG is the test score for each test as taken from the array T(A).

See Fig. 31-1 for a sample run.

```
PARAPSYCHOLOGY TEST 2: PRECOGNITION
COPYRIGHT (C) 1980 BY HOWARD BERENBON

THIS IS A TEST FOR PRECOGNITION. USING
FIVE EACH OF THE SYMBOLS x, +, -, =,
AND 0, THE SUBJECT WILL TRY TO GUESS
THE SYMBOL CARD IN ORDER FROM 1 TO 25.
THE DECK IS SHUFFLED AFTER ALL 25
GUESSES ARE ENTERED. AFTER THE TEST IS
COMPLETED, A SCORE IS GIVEN. A SCORE OF
5 OR LESS IS AVERAGE. A SCORE OF 6 OR
MORE, AFTER AT LEAST 5 TESTS, MAY BE AN
INDICATION THAT THE SUBJECT CAN
PREDICT THE FUTURE.


ENTER SUBJECT'S NAME
? BRUCE

ENTER DATE (MM/DD/YY)
? 05/07/80




PRECOGNITION TEST  1

DATE :  05/07/80
SUBJECT: BRUCE

CARD# 1        TEST 1

ENTER SYMBOL GUESS
(x + - = 0)
? =



CARD# 2        TEST 1

ENTER SYMBOL GUESS
(x + - = 0)
? +



CARD# 3        TEST 1

ENTER SYMBOL GUESS
(x + - = 0)
? x



CARD# 4        TEST 1

ENTER SYMBOL GUESS
(x + - = 0)
? x



CARD# 5        TEST 1

ENTER SYMBOL GUESS
(x + - = 0)
? 0
```

```
CARD# 24       TEST 1

ENTER SYMBOL GUESS
(x + - = 0)
? =




CARD# 25       TEST 1

ENTER SYMBOL GUESS
(x + - = 0)
? -


ENTRY COMPLETED AND RECORDED

STAND BY . . .
THE CARDS ARE BEING SHUFFLED

SHUFFLING COMPLETED



NOW SCORING


TEST  1   SCORE RECORDED

ANOTHER TEST?
Y=YES  N=NO
? N


PRECOGNITION TEST SCORING
DATE: 05/07/80
SUBJECT: BRUCE

CORRECT SCORE OUT OF 25
TEST # 1
 5
AVERAGE SCORE OUT OF  1
TEST(S) IS  5
THAT'S  20  PERCENT CORRECT



YOU HAVE AN AVERAGE SCORE.
AT THIS TIME, THERE IS NO
INDICATION OF PRECOGNITION
ABILITIES.

WOULD YOU LIKE A PLOT
OF THE TEST SCORES
Y=YES  N=NO
? Y



PLOT OF PRECOGNITION TEST DATA
SUBJECT: BRUCE   DATE: 05/07/80

0    5   10  15        25
+++++++++++++++++++++++++++
      .  TEST # 1
```

Fig. 31-1. Parasychology Test 2: Precognition sample run.

```
100   HOME : PRINT "PARAPSYCOLOGY TEST 2: PRECOGNITION"
110   PRINT "APPLE II"
120   PRINT "COPYRIGHT (C) 1980 BY HOWARD BERENBON"
130   PRINT
140   REM  DIM ARRAY
150   DIM A(25),C$(25),T(25),D$(25)
160   PRINT "THIS IS A TEST FOR PRECOGNITION. USING"
170   PRINT "FIVE EACH OF THE SYMBOLS *, +, -, =,"
180   PRINT "AND 0, THE SUBJECT WILL TRY TO GUESS"
190   PRINT "THE SYMBOL CARD IN ORDER FROM 1 TO 25."
200   PRINT "THE DECK IS SHUFFLED AFTER ALL 25"
210   PRINT "GUESSES ARE ENTERED. AFTER THE TEST IS"
220   PRINT "COMPLETED, A SCORE IS GIVEN. A SCORE OF"
230   PRINT "5 OR LESS IS AVERAGE. A SCORE OF 6 OR"
240   PRINT "MORE, AFTER AT LEAST 5 TESTS, MAY BE AN"
250   PRINT "INDICATION THAT THE SUBJECT CAN"
260   PRINT "PREDICT THE FUTURE."
270   GOSUB 1250
280   GOSUB 1250
290   PRINT
300   PRINT "ENTER SUBJECT'S NAME"
310   INPUT N$: PRINT
320   PRINT "ENTER DATE (MM/DD/YY)"
330   INPUT D$
340   HOME :G = 0:T = 0
360 T = T + 1
370   HOME
380   PRINT "PRECOGNITION TEST ";T
390   PRINT : PRINT "DATE :   ";D$
400   PRINT "SUBJECT: ";N$
410   PRINT
420   FOR A = 1 TO 25
430   PRINT "CARD# ";A,"TEST ";T
440   PRINT
450   PRINT "ENTER SYMBOL GUESS"
460   PRINT "(* + - = 0)"
470   INPUT C$: HOME
480 D$(A) = C$
490   NEXT A
500   PRINT : PRINT "ENTERY COMPLETED AND RECORDED"
510   GOSUB 1250: GOSUB 1250
520   GOSUB 1320
530   PRINT "ANOTHER TEST?"
540   PRINT "Y=YES  N=NO"
550   INPUT A$
560   IF A$ = "Y" THEN 360
570   HOME
580   PRINT "PRECOGNITION TEST SCORING"
590   PRINT "DATE:   ";D$
600   PRINT "SUBJECT:   ";N$
610   PRINT
620   PRINT "CORRECT SCORE OUT OF 25"
630 J = 0
```

```
640   FOR A = 1 TO G
650   PRINT "TEST # ";A
660   PRINT T(A):J = T(A) + J
670   NEXT A
680   GOSUB 1250
690   PRINT "AVERAGE SCORE OUT OF ";G
700   PRINT "TEST(S) IS ";J / G
710   PRINT "THAT'S ";(J / G) * 4;" PERCENT CORRECT"
720   GOSUB 1250: GOSUB 1250
730   GOSUB 1250: GOSUB 1250: GOSUB 1100: GOSUB 1250
740   PRINT "WOULD YOU LIKE A PLOT"
750   PRINT "OF THE TEST SCORES"
760   PRINT "Y=YES   N=NO"
770   INPUT A$
780   IF A$ = "Y" THEN 940
790   END
800   FOR N = 1 TO 25
810 A(N) = 0
820   NEXT N
830   FOR N = 1 TO 25
840 M =  INT ( RND (1) * 25 + 1)
850   FOR A = 1 TO M
860   READ B$
870   NEXT A
880   RESTORE
890   IF A(M) = 1 THEN 840
900 A(M) = 1
910 C$(M) = B$
920   NEXT N
930   RETURN
940   HOME : PRINT "PLOT OF PRECOGNITION TEST DATA"
950   PRINT "SUBJECT:  ";N$;"   DATE: ";D$
960   PRINT
970   PRINT "0    5    10   15          25"
980   PRINT "+++++++++++++++++++++++++++"
990   FOR A = 1 TO G
1000 GG = T(A) + 1
1010   PRINT  TAB( GG)".   TEST # ";A
1020   GOSUB 1250
1030   NEXT A
1040   END
1050   DATA "*","*","*","*","*"
1060   DATA "+","+","+","+","+"
1070   DATA "-","-","-","-","-"
1080   DATA "=","=","=","=","="
1090   DATA "0","0","0","0","0"
1100   PRINT
1110   IF J / G  = 6 THEN 1200
1120   IF J / G < 4 THEN 1290
1130   PRINT
1140   PRINT "YOU HAVE AN AVERAGE SCORE."
1150   PRINT "AT THIS TIME, THERE IS NO"
1160   PRINT "INDICATION OF PRECOGNITION"
```

```
1170   PRINT "ABILITIES."
1180   PRINT
1190   RETURN
1200   PRINT "YOUR SCORE IS ABOVE AVERAGE."
1210   PRINT "THERE IS A POSSIBILITY THAT YOU"
1220   PRINT "HAVE PRECOGNITION ABILITIES."
1230   PRINT
1240   RETURN
1250   REM  DELAY
1260   FOR Z = 1 TO 1135
1270   NEXT Z
1280   RETURN
1290   PRINT
1300   PRINT "YOUR SCORE IS LESS THAN AVERAGE."
1310   GOTO 1150
1320   PRINT
1330   PRINT "STAND BY . . ."
1340   PRINT "THE CARDS ARE BEING SHUFFLED"
1350   GOSUB 800
1360   PRINT :G = G + 1
1370   PRINT "SHUFFLING COMPLETED"
1380   GOSUB 1250
1390   PRINT : GOSUB 1250: GOSUB 1250
1400   PRINT "NOW SCORING"
1410   GOSUB 1250: GOSUB 1250
1420   FOR A = 1 TO 25
1430   IF C$(A) = D$(A) THEN T(G) = T(G) + 1
1440   NEXT A
1450   HOME : PRINT "TEST ";T;"  SCORE RECORDED"
1460   GOSUB 1250
1470   PRINT
1480   RETURN
```

SECTION V

A Fantasy Game

This last section includes a complete fantasy game called The Dungeon of Danger. It is the longest program in the book, requiring almost 16K of RAM to run.

Here, you may choose your fantasy character's name and boldly roam the chambers and corridors of the dungeon, with your magic sword, seeking out monsters and gold. Your goal is to find your way out, unharmed, with as much gold as possible. Good luck.

CHAPTER 32

The Dungeon of Danger

The Dungeon of Danger is an adventure fantasy game in which the player must fight monsters as he or she wanders through the chambers and corridors of the dungeon. It's a two-level dungeon, based on the fantasy role-playing game Dungeons and Dragons.* It's written in BASIC for your microcomputer, and it requires 16K of RAM to run. See Program 32-1 for the program listing.

THE PROGRAM

You are given 500 gold pieces and are teleported to a random location in the lower level of this 128-chamber, two-level (64 chambers per level) dungeon. Your goal is to find your way out, with as much gold as possible. Gold pieces are acquired by finding and killing monsters that occupy the dungeon. Each time you kill a monster, you will find a random amount of gold in the chamber. But, monsters fight back, and if you're not careful you can be killed and lose the game. There are other places in the dungeon where gold may be found, but this will be discussed later.

ACTIONS OR MOVES

In your trip through the dungeon you will encounter monsters (up to 37 types), thieves, empty chambers, trap doors, secret doors leading to north-south or east-west corridors, caverns, vials (filled with liquids that can heal), teleportation traps, maps, enchanted keys, and stairways leading up.

See Fig. 32-1 for a sample run.

After you run the program, enter your name or your favorite fantasy character's name, for your

---

* Dungeons and Dragons is a registered trademark of TSR Hobbies, Inc.

trip into the Dungeon of Danger. Then enter the difficulty level; enter a 1 for moderate or a 2 for difficult. The computer will then generate your "hit-point" value for combat. A typical hit-point value for difficulty level 1 is about 26, and for difficulty level 2 is about 15. When fighting, if a monster scores a "hit" on you, then this number is subtracted from your current hit-point value. If your hit-point value is depleted to zero, then you will die and lose the game. Each monster has a different strength, and may be difficult to kill, depending on its hit-point number.

After your hit-point value is generated, you will be teleported to a random location in the lower level of the dungeon.

You now have a choice of eight actions. Enter the letter in parentheses for the following actions or moves in the dungeon:

(N)ORTH movement	(up)
(E)AST movement	(right)
(S)OUTH movement	(down)
(W)EST movement	(left)
(U)P movement	(when at a stairway, and have the enchanted key)
(M)AP display	(if found-when encountering thieves)
(G)OLD pieces left	
(H)IT POINTS left	

North Movement (UP)

Entering an N allows you to move north through the dungeon. You may not move north under the following conditions:

1. If you reach the North Wall, you cannot pass through it.
2. If you enter an east-west corridor (through

```
THE DUNGEON OF DANGER
COPYRIGHT (C) 1980 BY HOWARD BERENBON

A FANTASY GAME




YOU WILL BE TELEPORTED TO . . .

THE DUNGEON OF DANGER

ENTER DIFFICULTY LEVEL?
1=MODERATE  2=DIFFICULT
? 1

ENTER YOUR CHARACTER'S NAME?
? FRODO




YOU CARRY A MAGIC SWORD
AND 500 GOLD PIECES WITH YOU.
YOUR 'HIT-POINT' VALUE IS  21
IF IT REACHES ZERO, YOU WILL DIE
. . . . . . . . SO BE CAREFUL

FRODO . . . YOU ARE ON YOUR WAY




YOU HAVE ARRIVED AT . . . .

THE DUNGEON OF DANGER . . . LEVEL 2

YOU WILL ENCOUNTER MONSTERS AND
THIEVES, AND GOLD . . . GOOD LUCK




YOU ARE IN A DAMP AND MISTY
. . . . . . . EMPTY CHAMBER

FRODO, WHAT IS YOUR ACTION OR MOVE?

(N)ORTH, (E)AST, (S)OUTH, (W)EST
(U)P, (M)AP, (G)OLD, (H)IT POINTS
? N




THERE IS SOMETHING LURKING . . .
. . . . IN THIS CHAMBER . . . .
. . . . . . . . . . . BEWARE

IT IS A . . . . . VAMPIRE BAT . .

WILL YOU (F)IGHT OR (R)UN ?
? F




YOU ATTACK THE . . . VAMPIRE BAT
WITH A SWING OF YOUR SWORD
YOU DO  2  HIT POINT(S) OF DAMAGE

IT HAS . .  4  'HIT-POINT(S)' LEFT


. . . . . . . IT ATTACKS YOU
AND IT DOES  2  'HIT-POINT(S)' OF DAMAGE

YOU HAVE . . .  19  'HIT-POINT(S)' LEFT

WILL YOU (F)IGHT OR (R)UN ?
? F
```

```
YOU ATTACK THE . . . VAMPIRE BAT
WITH A SWING OF YOUR SWORD

YOU HAVE KILLED THE VAMPIRE BAT

YOU SEARCH THE AREA . . . .
AND FIND . . .  229  GOLD PIECES

FRODO,  WHAT IS YOUR ACTION OR MOVE?

(N)ORTH, (E)AST, (S)OUTH, (W)EST
(U)P, (M)AP, (G)OLD, (H)IT POINTS
? E




YOU ENTER AN . . . EAST-WEST CORRIDOR
THRU A . . . . . . . SECRET DOOR

THE DOOR CLOSES AND LOCKS BEHIND YOU

FRODO,  WHAT IS YOUR ACTION OR MOVE?

(N)ORTH, (E)AST, (S)OUTH, (W)EST
(U)P, (M)AP, (G)OLD, (H)IT POINTS
? E




THERE IS A THIEF IN THIS CHAMBER

. . . . . . . HE SURPRISES YOU
AS HE QUICKLY PASSES BY YOU HE
SNATCHES . . .  65  GOLD PIECES

FRODO,  WHAT IS YOUR ACTION OR MOVE?

(N)ORTH, (E)AST, (S)OUTH, (W)EST
(U)P, (M)AP, (G)OLD, (H)IT POINTS
? N




YOU STUMBLED ONTO . . . . .
A HIDDEN CAVERN

YOU LOOK AROUND . . .
ON THE GROUND, AT YOUR FEET, IS A VIAL

YOU PICK UP THE VIAL . . AND SEE THAT
IT CONTAINS . . . A MILKY LIQUID

WOULD YOU LIKE A DRINK?
ENTER (Y)ES  OR  (N)O
? Y




YOU TAKE A DRINK . . .




IT WAS A WHITE MAGIC POTION . . .
WHICH INCREASED YOUR 'HIT-POINTS' BY  12

THE CAVERN SEEMS EMPTY . . .

FRODO,  WHAT IS YOUR ACTION OR MOVE?

(N)ORTH, (E)AST, (S)OUTH, (W)EST
(U)P, (M)AP, (G)OLD, (H)IT POINTS
? W




YOU ARE IN A DAMP AND MISTY
. . . . . . . EMPTY CHAMBER

FRODO,  WHAT IS YOUR ACTION OR MOVE?

(N)ORTH, (E)AST, (S)OUTH, (W)EST
(U)P, (M)AP, (G)OLD, (H)IT POINTS
? W
```

Fig. 32-1. The Dungeon

```
THERE IS SOMETHING LURKING . . .
. . . . IN THIS CHAMBER . . . .
. . . . . . . . . . . BEWARE

IT IS A . . . . . BLACK CAT . .


. . . . . . . . IT ATTACKS YOU
AND IT DOES  2  'HIT-POINT(S)' OF DAMAGE

YOU HAVE . . .  36  'HIT-POINT(S)' LEFT


WILL YOU (F)IGHT OR (R)UN ?
? F




YOU ATTACK THE . . . BLACK CAT
WITH A SWING OF YOUR SWORD

YOU HAVE KILLED THE BLACK CAT

YOU SEARCH THE AREA . . . .
AND FIND . . .  126  GOLD PIECES

FRODO,  WHAT IS YOUR ACTION OR MOVE?

(N)ORTH, (E)AST, (S)OUTH, (W)EST
(U)P, (M)AP, (G)OLD, (H)IT POINTS
? S




THERE IS A THIEF IN THIS CHAMBER

. . . . . . . . HE SURPRISES YOU
AS HE QUICKLY PASSES BY YOU HE
SNATCHES . . .  135  GOLD PIECES

YOU SEARCH THE CHAMBER AND
YOU . . . . . FIND A MAP

FRODO,  WHAT IS YOUR ACTION OR MOVE?

(N)ORTH, (E)AST, (S)OUTH, (W)EST
(U)P, (M)AP, (G)OLD, (H)IT POINTS
? S




YOU ARE AT A STAIRWAY
. . . . . . . GOING UP

FRODO,  WHAT IS YOUR ACTION OR MOVE?

(N)ORTH, (E)AST, (S)OUTH, (W)EST
(U)P, (M)AP, (G)OLD, (H)IT POINTS
? U




YOU WALK UP THE STAIRWAY
THE ENCHANTED KEY . . . OPENS THE LOCK

YOU ARE AT . . . . . LEVEL 1




THERE IS SOMETHING LURKING . . .
. . . . IN THIS CHAMBER . . . .
. . . . . . . . . . . BEWARE

IT IS A . . . . . DEADLY COBRA . .

WILL YOU (F)IGHT OR (R)UN ?
? F




YOU ATTACK THE . . . DEADLY COBRA
WITH A SWING OF YOUR SWORD


YOU HAVE KILLED THE DEADLY COBRA

YOU SEARCH THE AREA . . . .
AND FIND . . .  571  GOLD PIECES

FRODO,  WHAT IS YOUR ACTION OR MOVE?

(N)ORTH, (E)AST, (S)OUTH, (W)EST
(U)P, (M)AP, (G)OLD, (H)IT POINTS
? E




YOU ACTIVATED A . . . TRAP DOOR

BUT . . . YOU CAUGHT YOURSELF
FROM FALLING

FRODO,  WHAT IS YOUR ACTION OR MOVE?

(N)ORTH, (E)AST, (S)OUTH, (W)EST
(U)P, (M)AP, (G)OLD, (H)IT POINTS
? S




THERE IS SOMETHING LURKING . . .
. . . . IN THIS CHAMBER . . . .
. . . . . . . . . . . BEWARE

IT IS A . . . . . BERSERKER . .


. . . . . . . . IT ATTACKS YOU
AND IT DOES  11  'HIT-POINT(S)' OF DAMAGE

YOU HAVE . . .  25  'HIT-POINT(S)' LEFT


WILL YOU (F)IGHT OR (R)UN ?
? F




YOU ATTACK THE . . . BERSERKER
WITH A SWING OF YOUR SWORD

YOU HAVE KILLED THE BERSERKER

YOU SEARCH THE AREA . . . .
AND FIND . . .  126  GOLD PIECES

FRODO,  WHAT IS YOUR ACTION OR MOVE?

(N)ORTH, (E)AST, (S)OUTH, (W)EST
(U)P, (M)AP, (G)OLD, (H)IT POINTS
? N




YOU ARE AT A STAIRWAY
. . . . . . GOING UP

FRODO,  WHAT IS YOUR ACTION OR MOVE?

(N)ORTH, (E)AST, (S)OUTH, (W)EST
(U)P, (M)AP, (G)OLD, (H)IT POINTS
? U




YOU WALK UP THE STAIRWAY
THE ENCHANTED KEY . . . OPENS THE LOCK
YOU FOUND YOUR WAY . . .
. . . . OUT OF THE DUNGEON OF DANGER

YOU HAVE ACQUIRED  2708  GOLD PIECES

GAME RATING IS  556  = WARRIOR

YOU TOOK  48  TURNS TO FIND THE WAY OUT,
AND KILLED  12  MONSTERS.

ANOTHER GAME?
ENTER (Y)ES  OR  (N)O
? Y
```

of Danger sample run.

a secret door), movement north is not allowed.

East Movement (RIGHT)

Entering an E allows you to move east. You may not move east under the following conditions:

1. If you reach the East Wall, you cannot pass through it.
2. If you enter a north-south corridor (through a secret door), movement east is not allowed.

South Movement (DOWN)

Entering an S allows you to move south. You may not move south under the following conditions:

1. If you reach the South Wall, you cannot pass through it.
2. If you enter an east-west corridor (through a secret door), movement south is not allowed.

West Movement (LEFT)

Entering a W allows you to move west. You may not move west under the following conditions:

1. If you reach the West Wall, you cannot pass through it.
2. If you enter a north-south corridor (through a secret door), movement west is not allowed.

Up Movement

Entering a U, when you are at a stairway and have found the Enchanted Key, allows you to go up to the next level. If you haven't found the key or you are not at a stairway, you cannot go up the stairway. To find the Enchanted Key, you must kill a random number of monsters for each level. Also, there is a different key for each level.

Map Display

Entering an M, when you have found a map, will display the map for that level. Each level has a different map, and they may be found when encountering thieves. The 64-chamber dungeon is displayed using the following symbols:

    M = monster
    0 = empty chamber
    ? = unknown contents (either a thief or a trap door)
    C = cavern
  UP = stairway up

NS = north-south corridor (entered through secret doors)

EW = east-west corridor (entered through secret doors)

P 1 = your location in the dungeon

See Fig. 32-2 for a sample map.

```
THE DUNGEON OF DANGER-MAP:  LEV   1

M    EW  NS  M   0   C   M   UP
EW   EW  EW  C   0   M   0   M
NS   EW  EW  ?   0   M   M   UP
M    C   UP  NS  0   NS  C   C
NS   ?   0   ?   0   M   0   NS
?    UP  ?   NS  0   P1  M   0
?    M   NS  NS  0   0   0   M
NS   EW  EW  0   C   0   EW  ?

FRODO,   WHAT IS YOUR ACTION OR MOVE?

(N)ORTH, (E)AST, (S)OUTH, (W)EST
(U)P, (M)AP, (G)OLD, (H)IT POINTS
? N
```

Fig. 32-2. The Dungeon of Danger sample map.

A question mark (?) indicates either a thief or a trap door. There is no way of knowing which is there, unless you enter the chamber. If you encounter a thief, either you surprise him and he drops some of his gold, or he surprises you and steals some of your gold. This is randomly determined, but it's in favor of the thief. After you encounter a thief, the chamber becomes empty.

If you activate a trap door, you can either fall through or catch yourself from falling. If you fall through, you will lose most of your gold pieces, when playing at difficulty level 1 (moderate). But you can die if you are playing at difficulty level 2 (difficult). There is a 25-percent chance that you will fall through, when your difficulty level is 1, and a 50-percent chance when your difficulty is 2. If you are at level two of the dungeon, then you will fall into a deep pit. If you made it up to level one, then you will fall back down to level two. Avoid these traps, if possible.

When displaying the map, your location in the dungeon is identified with the symbol P1.

Gold Pieces Left

Entering a G will display the number of gold pieces you have with you. You will start out with 500 and can gain or lose gold during your trip. The more gold you acquire, the better your game rating will be.

Hit-Points Left

Entering an H will display the number of hit-points you have left. Also, each time you fight a monster, your number of hit-points left is displayed.

When you are entering into a chamber occupied by a monster, the monster may or may not attack you. Then, you have the option of fighting, by entering an F, or running, by entering an R.

Fighting

If you choose to fight, then enter an F. Your character will swing at the monster with his magic sword, always making contact, and damaging it by depleting some of its hit-points. But then the monster will attack you and possibly score a hit, depleting some of your hit-points. There is a chance that the monster will miss you, if you are lucky. You may now continue fighting until the monster is killed, it kills you, or you run out.

Each monster has a different hit-point number, depending on its strength. A weak monster (easy to kill) will have a hit-point value of between 1 and 3. A monster with a hit-point value of 4 or greater is considered strong and more difficult to kill. The stronger the monster, the harder it can hit you. Each of the 37 monsters have two hit-point numbers. The first number is the maximum it can hit you with, at one time, and the second is the number of hit-points required to kill it. The DATA statements in program lines 3720 through 4050 hold the names and hit-points of most of the monsters in the dungeon. This data may be changed, or modified, for different monsters with different strengths. The last four monsters in the data list are the corridor monsters. They are the weakest and easiest to kill.

Each hit on a monster will deplete its hit-point value, until it reaches zero, then it is killed. Each time you kill a monster, you will find a random amount of gold in the chamber, and then the chamber becomes empty.

Running

When fighting a monster, you have the option of running away, by entering an R. This option should be used if your hit-point value is low and you may not survive the next attack. This choice depends on the strength of the monster. Use your own judgment. Entering an R will send you back to the chamber that you previously occupied, but the monster can attack you, with one or two hit-points, as you leave.

Your Strength at Different Levels

The number of hit-points that you deplete from a monster increases with the number of monsters you have killed. So, generally, the more monsters you kill, the easier it will be to kill the next monster that you encounter.

Generally, monsters are more difficult to kill at level one of the dungeon. But if you have killed a large number in finding your way up from level two to level one, then they should be easier to kill, due to your experience. Also, your reward for killing a monster at level one is generally higher than at level two.

CAVERNS

There are several things that can happen to you when you enter into a cavern. Often you will find vials filled with liquids. These liquids can heal wounds, two-thirds of the time, by increasing your hit-point value after you drink them. But sometimes the liquids have no effect, or even decrease your hit-point value slightly. It is recommended that you drink the liquid, if your hit-point value is low.

You may run into giant spiders or the Dark Wizards. They can hit hard and are difficult to kill, so be careful. But fortunately there are the Ancient Wizards that you may encounter. They will increase your hit-point value and give you gold.

Pools of Water

On the lower level of the dungeon (level two), there are pools of water that you may fall into. The following three things can happen when you fall into a pool:

1. You may be attacked by a Gill Monster; and he's not easy to kill.
2. The water will feel warm and soothing; and nothing happens.
3. The water will be steaming hot; and you will lose a random number of gold pieces in the pool.

NORTH-SOUTH AND EAST-WEST CORRIDORS

North-south and east-west corridors may be entered from any direction (through secret doors), but will limit your next move to the direction displayed.

Three things can happen when entering into a corridor:

1. You can activate a teleportation trap and be teleported to an unknown location (at your present level) in the dungeon.
2. You can encounter corridor monsters that may or may not attack you.

3. Or, the corridor can be empty.

There are four types of monsters that you may encounter in the corridors. They are among the weakest of the monsters in the dungeon and can be killed quite easily. They are as follows:

1. Gelatinous Cube
2. Giant Centipede
3. Giant Rat
4. Shadow

No other monsters can appear in the corridors.

WINNING

To win the game you must sucessfully make it up through the two levels and then exit the dungeon.

LOSING

You will lose the game if your hit-point value is depleted to 0. But in some cases (about 50 percent of the time) you will get a second chance. Your hit-points will be restored, and then you will be allowed a random number of moves (based on the number of monsters previously killed) to find your way out. If you die again, you won't get another chance.

GAME RATING

After you complete the game, a game rating is displayed along with the number of gold pieces acquired, the number of monsters killed, and the number of turns (moves) taken. The rating is a number from approximately −600 to +2000, depending on the statistics above. The higher the rating number, the better is the game rating.

Along with the number rating, there is a title rating. The following is a list of ten possible title ratings, and their scores:

−401 or less	Incompetent Serf
−101 to −400	Weakling
−100 to −1	Apprentice
0 to 99	Halfling
100 to 199	Foot Soldier
200 to 599	Warrior
600 to 899	Great Warrior
900 to 1499	Swordsman
1500 to 2499	Magic Swordsman
2500 and above	Dungeon Master

After the game is completed, you may play another game by entering a Y for yes, or end the game by entering an N for no.

THE MONSTER LIST

The following is a list of monsters that appear in the dungeon, with their hit-point values. The first number is used to generate its hit on you. The second number is its strength:

Monster		
Gill Monster	8	14
Dark Wizard	8	14
Giant Spider	6	12
Large Dragon	6	12
Hideous Ghoul	5	10
Lizard Man	4	8
Manticore	6	12
Purple Worm	6	12
Deadly Cobra	5	10
Mad Elf	5	10
Clay Man	4	8
Hairy Beast	5	10
Mad Dwarf	4	8
Zombie	4	8
Berserker	5	10
Giant Scorpion	6	12
Giant Cockroach	4	8
Doppleganger	5	10
Giant Fire Beetle	1	2
Giant Ant	1	2
Giant Tick	2	4
Mummy	3	6
Nasty Orc	2	4
Skeleton	1	2
Troll	3	6
Goblin	3	6
Vampire Bat	3	6
Creeping Blob	3	6
Mad Dog	2	4
Large Spider	3	6
Black Cat	2	4
Man-Eating Plant	1	2
Hydra	3	6
Gelatinous Cube	2	4
Giant Centipede	1	2
Giant Rat	2	4
Shadow	2	4

```
100   HOME
110 : PRINT "THE DUNGEON OF DANGER"
120   PRINT "APPLE II"
130   PRINT "COPYRIGHT (C) 1980 BY HOWARD BERENBON"
140   PRINT
150   PRINT "A FANTASY GAME"
160 BB = 2
170   GOSUB 470
180   HOME : DIM A(9,9,2)
190   PRINT "YOU WILL BE TELEPORTED TO . . . "
200   PRINT
210   PRINT "THE DUNGEON OF DANGER"
220   PRINT :DY = 0:MD = 1
230   GOSUB 5530
240 MA = 0:CA = 0:G = 500:M1 = 1:K = 0:HI = 20 +  INT ( RND (1) * 15 + 1):
      HI =  INT (HI / PL)
250 H1 = HI: PRINT "ENTER YOUR CHARACTER'S NAME?"
260   INPUT A$
270   GOSUB 460
280   PRINT : PRINT "YOU CARRY A MAGIC SWORD"
290   PRINT "AND 500 GOLD PIECES WITH YOU."
300   PRINT "YOUR 'HIT-POINT' VALUE IS ";H1: GOSUB 460
310   PRINT "IF IT REACHES ZERO, YOU WILL DIE"
320   PRINT ". . . . . . . . . SO BE CAREFUL"
330   PRINT : GOSUB 460: PRINT A$;" . . . YOU ARE ON YOUR WAY"
340 BB = 5: GOSUB 470
350   GOSUB 500
360   HOME
370   PRINT "YOU HAVE ARRIVED AT . . . ."
380   PRINT
390   PRINT "THE DUNGEON OF DANGER . . . LEVEL 2"
400   PRINT
410   PRINT "YOU WILL ENCOUNTER MONSTERS AND"
420   PRINT "THIEVES, AND GOLD . . . GOOD LUCK"
430 BB = 6
440   GOSUB 470
450   GOTO 1030
460 BB = 1
470   FOR ZZ = 1 TO 909 * BB
480   NEXT ZZ
490   RETURN
500   FOR X = 1 TO 8
510   FOR Y = 1 TO 8
520   FOR Z = 1 TO 2
530 A(X,Y,Z) =  INT ( RND (1) * 7 + 1)
540   NEXT Z
550   NEXT Y
560   NEXT X
570 H =  INT ( RND (1) * 3 + 1)
580   FOR A = 1 TO 2
590   FOR N = 1 TO H
600 X =  INT ( RND (1) * 8 + 1)
610 Y =  INT ( RND (1) * 8 + 1)
```

```
620 A(X,Y,A) = 8
630  NEXT N
640  NEXT A
650 S =  INT ( RND (1) * 4 + 1) + 2
660  FOR A = 1 TO 2
670  FOR N = 1 TO S
680 X =  INT ( RND (1) * 8 + 1)
690 Y =  INT ( RND (1) * 8 + 1)
700 A(X,Y,A) = 9
710  NEXT N
720  NEXT A
730  RETURN
740 L1 = L1 - 1
750  PRINT "YOU WALK UP THE STAIRWAY"
760  GOSUB 460
770  PRINT "THE ENCHANTED KEY . . . OPENS THE LOCK"
780  GOSUB 460
790  IF L1 = 0 THEN 890
800 MA = 0:K = 0:K4 =  INT ( RND (1) * 4 + 1) + 1: IF H1 < HI THEN 820
810  GOTO 850
820 H1 = HI
830  PRINT "YOU FEEL STRONGER . . . . .": GOSUB 460
840  PRINT "YOUR 'HIT-POINTS' ARE RESTORED TO ";HI
850  PRINT :CB = CA + K4
860  PRINT "YOU ARE AT . . . . . LEVEL 1"
870 BB = 4: GOSUB 470
880  GOTO 1070
890  PRINT "YOU FOUND YOUR WAY . . . "
900  PRINT ". . . OUT OF THE DUNGEON OF DANGER"
910  PRINT
920  PRINT "YOU HAVE ACQUIRED ";G;" GOLD PIECES"
930  GOSUB 950
940  GOTO 1810
950 GG = G + 1
960 R =  INT ((GG * CA - 7000 + 1) / M1)
970  PRINT
980  PRINT "GAME RATING IS ";R;" = ";: GOSUB 5620
990  PRINT : IF G <  = 0 THEN 3210
1000  PRINT "YOU TOOK ";M1;" TURNS TO FIND THE WAY OUT,"
1010  PRINT "AND KILLED ";CA;" MONSTERS."
1020  RETURN
1030 C =  INT ( RND (1) * 8 + 1)
1040 D =  INT ( RND (1) * 8 + 1)
1050 A(C,D,2) = 1
1060 L1 = 2:K4 =  INT ( RND (1) * 4 + 1) + 1
1070 F$ = " ": HOME
1080 A = A(C,D,L1)
1090  GOSUB 460
1100  ON A GOSUB 2100,4060,3580,3580,2210,2510,2560,2610,2870
1110  IF TE = 1 THEN TE = 0: GOTO 1070
1120  PRINT : IF H1 <  = 0 THEN 1700
1130  IF DY = 1 THEN MD = MD - 1
1140  IF DY = 1 AND MD = 0 THEN 1700
```

```
1150   IF F$ = "R" THEN 1070
1160   PRINT A$;",  WHAT IS YOUR ACTION OR MOVE?"
1170   PRINT
1180   PRINT "(N)ORTH, (E)AST, (S)OUTH, (W)EST"
1190   PRINT "(U)P, (M)AP, (G)OLD, (H)IT POINTS"
1200   INPUT M1$
1210 M1 = M1 + 1:TL = 0
1220 C1 = C:D1 = D
1230   IF M1$ = "N" THEN 1320
1240   IF M1$ = "E" THEN 1360
1250   IF M1$ = "S" THEN 1400
1260   IF M1$ = "W" THEN 1440
1270   IF M1$ = "U" THEN 1480
1280   IF M1$ = "M" THEN 1570
1290   IF M1$ = "G" THEN 1600
1300   IF M1$ = "H" THEN 3280
1310   PRINT : GOTO 1120
1320   IF A = 7 THEN 1620
1330   IF (D - 1) = 0 THEN 1880
1340 D = D - 1
1350   GOTO 1070
1360   IF A = 6 THEN 1660
1370   IF (C + 1) = 9 THEN 1930
1380 C = C + 1
1390   GOTO 1070
1400   IF A = 7 THEN 1620
1410   IF (D + 1) = 9 THEN 1950
1420 D = D + 1
1430   GOTO 1070
1440   IF A = 6 THEN 1660
1450   IF (C - 1) = 0 THEN 1970
1460 C = C - 1
1470   GOTO 1070
1480   HOME : IF A < > 9 THEN 1540
1490   IF K = 1 THEN 740
1500   PRINT
1510   PRINT "YOU CANNOT GO UP THE STAIRWAY"
1520   PRINT "YOU DON'T HAVE THE KEY"
1530   GOSUB 460: PRINT : GOTO 1120
1540   PRINT "YOU ARE NOT AT A STAIRWAY"
1550   GOSUB 460: GOTO 1120
1560   GOTO 1120
1570   HOME : IF MA = 1 THEN 1990
1580   PRINT "YOU DON'T HAVE THE MAP"
1590   PRINT : GOSUB 460: GOTO 1120
1600   HOME : PRINT "YOU HAVE ";G;" GOLD PIECES WITH YOU"
1610   PRINT : GOTO 1120
1620   PRINT
1630   HOME : PRINT "YOU ARE IN AN EAST-WEST CORRIDOR"
1640   PRINT "YOU CAN ONLY GO EAST OR WEST"
1650   PRINT : GOTO 1120
1660   PRINT
1670   HOME : PRINT "YOU ARE IN A NORTH-SOUTH CORRIDOR"
```

```
1680   PRINT "YOU CAN ONLY GO NORTH OR SOUTH"
1690   GOTO 1650
1700 BB = 2: GOSUB 470: HOME : IF DY = 1 THEN 5510
1710   PRINT "YOUR 'HIT-POINTS' HAVE BEEN DEPLETED,"
1720   PRINT :G = O: PRINT "AND UNFORTUNATELY . . . YOU JUST DIED"
1730 BB = 5: GOSUB 470
1740   PRINT :W =  INT ( RND (1) * 6 + 1): IF DY = O AND W >  = 3 THEN 5370
1750   HOME : PRINT "YOU LOST ALL YOUR GOLD AND YOU WERE"
1760   PRINT ". . . UNABLE TO MEET THE DEMANDS OF"
1770   PRINT ". . . . . THE DUNGEON OF DANGER"
1780   PRINT : PRINT
1790   PRINT "BETTER LUCK NEXT TIME"
1800   GOSUB 950
1810   PRINT
1820   PRINT "ANOTHER GAME?"
1830   PRINT "ENTER (Y)ES  OR  (N)O"
1840   INPUT F$
1850   IF F$ = "Y" THEN 1870
1860   END
1870   HOME : GOTO 210
1880   HOME : PRINT "YOU ARE AT THE NORTH WALL"
1890   PRINT "YOU CANNOT PASS THROUGH"
1900   PRINT
1910   PRINT "TRY ANOTHER DIRECTION?"
1920   GOTO 1120
1930   HOME : PRINT "YOU ARE AT THE EAST WALL"
1940   GOTO 1890
1950   HOME : PRINT "YOU ARE AT THE SOUTH WALL"
1960   GOTO 1890
1970   HOME : PRINT "YOU ARE AT THE WEST WALL"
1980   GOTO 1890
1990   HOME : PRINT "THE DUNGEON OF DANGER-MAP:  LEV   ";L1
2000   PRINT
2010   FOR Q = 1 TO 8
2020   FOR N = 1 TO 8
2030   IF C = N AND D = Q THEN  PRINT "P1  ";: GOTO 2060
2040 S1 = A(N,Q,L1)
2050   ON S1 GOSUB 2910,2970,2930,2930,2950,2990,3010,3030,3040
2060   NEXT N
2070   PRINT
2080   NEXT Q
2090   GOTO 1120
2100 W =  INT ( RND (1) * 2 + 1): IF W = 2 THEN 2160
2110   PRINT
2120   PRINT "YOU ARE IN A COLD AND DARK"
2130   PRINT " . . . . . . EMPTY CHAMBER"
2140   PRINT
2150   RETURN
2160   PRINT
2170   PRINT "YOU ARE IN A DAMP AND MISTY"
2180   PRINT ". . . . . . . EMPTY CHAMBER"
2190   PRINT
2200   RETURN
```

```
2210  HOME : PRINT "THERE IS A THIEF IN THIS CHAMBER"
2220 A(C,D,L1) = 1
2230  GOSUB 460
2240 G4 =  INT ( RND (1) * 500 / L1 + 1): IF (G - G4) < 0 THEN G4 = G
2250 Y =  INT ( RND (1) * 8 + 1)
2260  IF Y < = 3 THEN 2420
2270  PRINT
2280  PRINT ". . . . . . . HE SURPRISES YOU"
2290  GOSUB 460
2300  PRINT "AS HE QUICKLY PASSES BY YOU HE"
2310  PRINT "SNATCHES . . . ";G4;" GOLD PIECES": PRINT
2320 G = G - G4
2330  IF MA = 1 THEN  RETURN
2340 MA =  INT ( RND (1) * 4 + 1): IF MA < = 2 THEN MA = 1
2350  IF MA = 1 THEN 2380
2360  RETURN
2370  GOSUB 460
2380  PRINT "YOU SEARCH THE CHAMBER AND"
2390  GOSUB 460
2400  PRINT "YOU . . . . . FIND A MAP"
2410  RETURN
2420  PRINT : PRINT "YOU SURPRISED THE THIEF . . . ."
2430  GOSUB 460
2440  PRINT "AS HE RUNS OUT HE DROPS . . . ."
2450 G4 =  INT ( RND (1) * 400 / L1 + 1): PRINT " . . . ";G4;" GOLD PIECES."
2460  PRINT "YOU PICK UP THE GOLD PIECES":G = G + G4
2470  PRINT : IF MA = 1 THEN  RETURN
2480 MA =  INT ( RND (1) * 4 + 1): IF MA < = 2 THEN MA = 1
2490  IF MA = 1 THEN 2380
2500  RETURN
2510  HOME : PRINT
2520  PRINT "YOU ENTER A . . . NORTH-SOUTH CORRIDOR"
2530  PRINT "THRU A . . . . . . . SECRET DOOR"
2540  PRINT : GOSUB 3240
2550  RETURN
2560  HOME : PRINT
2570  PRINT "YOU ENTER AN . . . EAST-WEST CORRIDOR"
2580  PRINT "THRU A . . . . . . . SECRET DOOR"
2590  PRINT : GOSUB 3240
2600  RETURN
2610  PRINT "YOU ACTIVATED A . . . TRAP DOOR"
2620  GOSUB 460
2630 TD =  INT ( RND (1) * 4 + 1) * PL: IF TD > 4 THEN  PRINT "YOU FELL THRU . . .":
      GOSUB 460: GOTO 1720
2640  IF TD = 4 THEN 2690
2650  PRINT
2660  PRINT "BUT . . . YOU CAUGHT YOURSELF"
2670  PRINT "FROM FALLING"
2680  RETURN
2690  IF L1 = 2 THEN 2800
2700 L1 = L1 + 1: PRINT :K = 1
2710  PRINT "YOU FELL THRU TO LEVEL 2 . . . AND"
2720 G = 0
```

```
2730   GOSUB 460
2740   PRINT
2750   PRINT "YOU . . . . . . . . LOST"
2760   PRINT "ALL OF YOUR GOLD PIECES"
2770   PRINT : IF PT = 1 THEN PT = 0: RETURN
2780   PRINT "BUT . . . YOU STILL HAVE YOUR KEY"
2790   RETURN
2800   PRINT "YOU FELL INTO A DEEP . . . PIT":PT = 1
2810   GOSUB 460
2820   PRINT "LUCKILY . . YOU DIDN'T GET HURT"
2830   PRINT
2840   GOSUB 460
2850   PRINT "BUT IN CLIMBING OUT . . ."
2860   GOTO 2720
2870   PRINT "YOU ARE AT A STAIRWAY"
2880   PRINT " . . . . . . GOING UP"
2890   PRINT
2900   RETURN
2910   PRINT "O    ";
2920   RETURN
2930   PRINT "M    ";
2940   RETURN
2950   PRINT "?    ";
2960   RETURN
2970   PRINT "C    ";
2980   RETURN
2990   PRINT "NS   ";
3000   RETURN
3010   PRINT "EW   ";
3020   RETURN
3030   GOTO 2950
3040   PRINT "UP   ";
3050   RETURN
3060 H = 1:O = 9:W = 8
3070 B = 0:E = 5:R = 14
3080 C = 0:PR = 0
3090   GOTO 1030
3100   RETURN
3110   GOSUB 460
3120 K = 1
3130   PRINT : PRINT "YOU LOOK TO THE GROUND . . . . . ."
3140   PRINT "AND FIND THE ENCHANTED KEY"
3150   GOSUB 460
3160   RETURN
3170   GOSUB 3120
3180   GOTO 1230
3190   IF CA = CB THEN 3110
3200   RETURN
3210   PRINT "YOU KILLED ";CA;" MONSTERS "
3220   PRINT ". . . . . IN ";M1;" TURNS."
3230   RETURN
3240   PRINT "THE DOOR CLOSES AND LOCKS BEHIND YOU": GOSUB 460
3250 W =  INT ( RND (1) * 8 + 1): IF W > = 7 THEN 3300
```

```
3260 W =  INT ( RND (1) * 8 + 1): IF W = 8 THEN 3390
3270  RETURN
3280  HOME : PRINT "YOU HAVE ";H1;" 'HIT-POINT(S)' LEFT"
3290  GOTO 1120
3300 W =  INT ( RND (1) * 4 + 1) + 30
3310  FOR AA = 1 TO W
3320  READ MS$,HP,HM
3330  NEXT AA
3340  RESTORE
3350  PRINT
3360  PRINT "THERE IS SOMETHING LURKING"
3370  PRINT "IN THIS CORRIDOR . . .": GOSUB 460
3380  PRINT : GOTO 3680
3390 TE = 1:TL = 1
3400  IF K = 1 THEN 3460
3410 K = 1: PRINT : PRINT "YOU NOTICE A SHINY OBJECT . . . ."
3420  PRINT ". . . . AT YOUR FEET": GOSUB 460
3430  PRINT "YOU PICK IT UP AND FIND THAT . . ."
3440  PRINT "IT IS THE ENCHANTED KEY . . . . . .": GOSUB 460
3450  PRINT : PRINT "BUT YOU WEREN'T CAREFUL . . . .": GOSUB 460
3460  PRINT "YOU ACTIVATED SOME SORT OF TRAP . . .": GOSUB 460
3470 C =  INT ( RND (1) * 8 + 1):D =  INT ( RND (1) * 8 + 1):BB = 5: GOSUB 470: HOME
3480  PRINT "SUDDENLY YOU FEEL DIZZY, AND PASS OUT"
3490  PRINT :BB = 2: GOSUB 470: GOSUB 3540
3500  PRINT "WHEN YOU WAKE UP . . . YOU FIND"
3510  PRINT "THAT YOU WERE . . . . TELEPORTED"
3520  PRINT "TO AN UNKNOWN LOCATION . . . ."
3530 BB = 5: GOSUB 470: RETURN
3540  FOR AA = 1 TO 300
3550  PRINT "*         %";
3560  NEXT AA
3570  GOSUB 460: HOME : RETURN
3580  IF A = 4 THEN 3600
3590 W =  INT ( RND (1) * 15 + 1): GOTO 3610
3600 W =  INT ( RND (1) * 15 + 1) + 15
3610  FOR AA = 1 TO W
3620  READ MS$,HP,HM
3630  NEXT AA
3640  RESTORE
3650  PRINT
3660  PRINT "THERE IS SOMETHING LURKING . . . "
3670  PRINT ". . . . IN THIS CHAMBER . . . .": GOSUB 460
3680  PRINT ". . . . . . . . . . . BEWARE": GOSUB 460
3690  PRINT
3700  PRINT "IT IS A . . . . . ";MS$;" . . ": GOSUB 460
3710  GOTO 4510
3720  DATA "LARGE DRAGON",6,12
3730  DATA "HIDEOUS GHOUL",5,10
3740  DATA "LIZARD MAN",4,8
3750  DATA "MANITCORE",6,12
3760  DATA "PURPLE WORM",6,12
3770  DATA "DEADLY COBRA",5,10
3780  DATA "MAD ELF",5,10
```

```
3790  DATA "CLAY MAN",4,8
3800  DATA "HAIRY BEAST",5,10
3810  DATA "MAD DWARF",4,8
3820  DATA "ZOMBIE",4,8
3830  DATA "BERSERKER",5,10
3840  DATA "GIANT SCORPION",6,12
3850  DATA "GIANT COCKROACH",4,8
3860  DATA "DOPPLEGANGER",5,10
3870  DATA "GIANT FIRE BEETLE",1,2
3880  DATA "GIANT ANT",1,2
3890  DATA "GIANT TICK",2,4
3900  DATA "MUMMY",3,6
3910  DATA "NASTY ORC",2,4
3920  DATA "SKELETON",1,2
3930  DATA "TROLL",3,6
3940  DATA "GOBLIN",3,6
3950  DATA "VAMPIRE BAT",3,6
3960  DATA "CREEPING BLOB",3,6
3970  DATA "MAD DOG",2,4
3980  DATA "LARGE SPIDER",3,6
3990  DATA "BLACK CAT",2,4
4000  DATA "MAN EATING PLANT",1,2
4010  DATA "HYDRA",3,6
4020  DATA "GELATINOUS CUBE",2,4
4030  DATA "GIANT CENTIPEDE",1,2
4040  DATA "GIANT RAT",2,4
4050  DATA "SHADOW",2,4
4060  PRINT "YOU STUMBLED ONTO . . . . ."
4070  PRINT "A HIDDEN CAVERN": GOSUB 460
4080  PRINT : GOSUB 4210: IF H1 < = 0 THEN  RETURN
4090  W =  INT ( RND (1) * 9 + 1)
4100  GOSUB 460: IF W > 3 THEN  PRINT : PRINT "THE CAVERN SEEMS EMPTY . . .": RETURN
4110 BB = 2: GOSUB 470: GOSUB 4500
4120  GOSUB 460: PRINT "BUT WAIT . . BEFORE YOU PROCEED": GOSUB 460: PRINT
4130  PRINT "YOU HEAR A NOISE OFF IN THE DISTANCE"
4140 BB = 3: GOSUB 470
4150  PRINT "CAUTIOUSLY YOU WALK TOWARDS THE SOUND"
4160 BB = 3: GOSUB 470:W =  INT ( RND (1) * 4 + 1): IF HI < H1 THEN 4180
4170  IF W = 1 THEN 5040
4180  IF W = 2 THEN 5170
4190  IF W = 4 AND L1 = 2 THEN 5720
4200  GOTO 5230
4210  PRINT : PRINT "YOU LOOK AROUND . . . ": GOSUB 460
4220 V =  INT ( RND (1) * 7 + 1)
4230  IF V > = 5 THEN 4250
4240  RETURN
4250  PRINT "ON THE GROUND, AT YOUR FEET, IS A VIAL"
4260  PRINT :BB = 2: GOSUB 470
4270  PRINT "YOU PICK UP THE VIAL . . AND SEE THAT"
4280  PRINT "IT CONTAINS . . . A MILKY LIQUID"
4290  PRINT
4300  PRINT "WOULD YOU LIKE A DRINK?"
4310  PRINT "ENTER (Y)ES OR  (N)O":DL =  INT ( RND (1) * 6 + 1)
```

```
4320   INPUT D$
4330   IF D$ = "Y" THEN 4350
4340   RETURN
4350   PRINT : PRINT "YOU TAKE A DRINK . . .":BB = 2: GOSUB 470: HOME
4360   IF DL >  = 3 THEN 4440
4370   IF DL = 2 THEN 4480
4380 H3 =  INT ( RND (1) * 6 + 1) * PL:H1 = H1 - H3
4390   PRINT "YOU FEEL A LITTLE FUNNY . . .": GOSUB 460: GOSUB 460
4400   IF H1 <  = 0 THEN  RETURN
4410   PRINT : PRINT "IT WAS A BLACK MAGIC POTION . . ."
4420   PRINT "WHICH DECREASED YOUR 'HIT-POINTS' BY";H3
4430   RETURN
4440 H3 =  INT ( RND (1) * 10 / PL + 1) + (6 / PL):H1 = H1 + H3
4450   PRINT "IT WAS A WHITE MAGIC POTION . . ."
4460   PRINT "WHICH INCREASED YOUR 'HIT-POINTS' BY ";H3
4470   RETURN
4480   PRINT "THE LIQUID HAD NO EFFECT ON YOU"
4490   RETURN
4500   GOSUB 460: PRINT : RETURN
4510   PRINT :W =  INT ( RND (1) * 4 + 1)
4520   IF W <  = 2 THEN 4540
4530   GOSUB 460: GOSUB 4780
4540   IF H1 <  = 0 THEN  RETURN
4550   PRINT : PRINT "WILL YOU (F)IGHT OR (R)UN ?"
4560   INPUT F$: HOME
4570   IF F$ = "F" THEN 4600
4580   IF F$ = "R" THEN 4700
4590   GOTO 4540
4600   HOME : PRINT : GOSUB 460
4610   PRINT "YOU ATTACK THE . . . ";MS$: GOSUB 460
4620   PRINT "WITH A SWING OF YOUR SWORD"
4630 N =  INT ( RND (1) * 5 + 1) +  INT ( RND (1) * CA / 2 + 1):HM = HM - N
4640   IF HM <  = 0 THEN 4890
4650   PRINT "YOU DO ";N;" HIT POINT(S) OF DAMAGE"
4660   PRINT : GOSUB 460
4670   PRINT "IT HAS . . ";HM;" 'HIT-POINT(S)' LEFT"
4680   PRINT : GOSUB 460
4690   GOTO 4530
4700 W =  INT ( RND (1) * 4 + 1):C = C1:D = D1
4710   PRINT "YOU QUICKLY RUN OUT . . .": IF TL = 1 THEN 5560
4720 N =  INT ( RND (1) * 2 + 1):BB = 2: GOSUB 470: IF W >  = 3 THEN 5330
4730 H1 = H1 - N
4740   PRINT "AS YOU LEAVE, THE ";MS$;" ATTACKS": GOSUB 460
4750   IF H1 <  = 0 THEN  RETURN
4760   PRINT "AND IT DOES ";N;" 'HIT-POINT(S)' OF DAMAGE"
4770 BB = 3: GOSUB 470: RETURN
4780   PRINT :W =  INT ( RND (1) * 7 + 1)
4790   PRINT ". . . . . . . . IT ATTACKS YOU": IF W <  = 2 THEN 5350
4800 W =  INT ( RND (1) * 6 + 1): IF W >  = 3 THEN 4830
4810 N =  INT ( RND (1) * HP / L1 + 1) +  INT ( RND (1) * HP / L1 + 1)
4820   GOTO 4840
4830 N =  INT ( RND (1) * HP * PL + 1)
4840   IF HM <  = 2 THEN N = 1
```

```
4850 H1 = H1 - N: GOSUB 460: IF H1 < = 0 THEN  RETURN
4860  PRINT "AND IT DOES ";N;" 'HIT-POINT(S)' OF DAMAGE"
4870  PRINT : PRINT "YOU HAVE . . . ";H1;" 'HIT-POINT(S)' LEFT"
4880  PRINT : RETURN
4890  PRINT : GOSUB 460
4900  PRINT "YOU HAVE KILLED THE ";MS$
4910  PRINT
4920  IF A(C,D,L1) > = 6 THEN 4950
4930  IF A(C,D,L1) = 2 THEN 4950
4940 A(C,D,L1) = 1
4950 G8 = 500: IF A(C,D,L1) > = 6 THEN G8 = 250
4960 G4 =  INT ( RND (1) * G8 / L1 + 1) + 75: IF A = 2 THEN G4 = G4 * 2
4970 G = G + G4: GOSUB 460
4980  PRINT "YOU SEARCH THE AREA . . . ."
4990  GOSUB 460: PRINT "AND FIND . . . ";G4;" GOLD PIECES"
5000 CA = CA + 1: IF K = 1 THEN  RETURN
5010  IF L1 = 1 THEN 3190
5020  IF CA = K4 THEN 3110
5030  RETURN
5040  GOSUB 460: GOSUB 460
5050  GOSUB 5290
5060  PRINT "HALT . . . I AM THE ANCIENT WIZARD"
5070  PRINT "I WILL NOT HARM YOU . . . . . .": GOSUB 460: GOSUB 460
5080  PRINT :G4 =  INT ( RND (1) * 300 + 1) + 100:G = G + G4: PRINT
5090  PRINT "I GIVE YOU . . . ";G4;" GOLD PIECES"
5100  PRINT "OUT OF GOOD WILL AND FRIENDSHIP"
5110  PRINT
5120 H4 =  INT ( RND (1) * 10 / PL + 1) + (6 / PL):H1 = H1 + H4
5130  PRINT "ALSO, I WILL INCREASE . . . ."
5140  PRINT "YOUR 'HIT-POINTS' BY . . . ";H4
5150  GOSUB 460
5160  RETURN
5170  GOSUB 5290
5180 MS$ = "GIANT SPIDER":HP = 6:HM = 12
5190  PRINT "IT'S A HUGE MAN-SIZED CRAWLING"
5200  PRINT ". . . . . . . SPIDER . . .": GOSUB 460
5210  PRINT ". . . . . AND . . . . ."
5220  GOTO 4530
5230  GOSUB 5290
5240 MS$ = "DARK WIZARD":HP = 8:HM = 14: HOME
5250  PRINT "DO NOT PASS . . . I AM THE ";MS$: GOSUB 460
5260  PRINT "AND I WILL HACK YOU TO PIECES . . ."
5270 BB = 2: GOSUB 470
5280  GOTO 4530
5290  HOME : PRINT "SUDDENLY . . . SOMETHING JUMPS . . ."
5300  PRINT "IN FRONT OF YOU . . . . . . ."
5310 BB = 3: GOSUB 470: HOME
5320  RETURN
5330  GOSUB 460: PRINT "AS YOU LEAVE . . . "
5340  PRINT "THE ";MS$;" ATTACKS . .": GOSUB 460
5350  GOSUB 460: PRINT "BUT . . . . . . . . IT MISSES":BB = 2: GOSUB 470
5360  RETURN
5370 BB = 2: GOSUB 470: GOSUB 3540:DY = 1:H1 = HI
```

```
5380   PRINT "YOU HAVE ENTERED . . A ZONE"
5390   PRINT "BETWEEN . . LIFE AND DEATH"
5400   PRINT :BB = 3: GOSUB 470
5410   PRINT : PRINT "I . . . . THE ANCIENT WIZARD"
5420   PRINT "WILL RESTORE YOUR 'HIT-POINTS' TO ";HI
5430   PRINT "AND . . . . YOU HAVE ONE MORE"
5440   PRINT "CHANCE IN THE DUNGEON"
5450   PRINT :MD =  INT ( RND (1) * 15 + 1) * CA + 10:H1 = HI
5460   PRINT "YOU SHALL HAVE ";MD;" MOVES"
5470   PRINT "LEFT TO FIND YOUR WAY OUT"
5480   PRINT "OF THE DUNGEON OF DANGER"
5490 BB = 9: GOSUB 470
5500   GOSUB 3540: GOTO 1110
5510   PRINT A$;", YOU HAVE DEPLETED YOUR MOVES"
5520   GOTO 1720
5530   PRINT "ENTER DIFFICULTY LEVEL?"
5540   PRINT "1=MODERATE  2=DIFFICULT"
5550   INPUT PL: PRINT : RETURN
5560 TL = 0:BB = 2: GOSUB 470
5570   PRINT "YOU REACTIVATED THE TELEPORTATION TRAP"
5580 BB = 2: GOSUB 470: GOSUB 3540
5590   PRINT "YOU END UP BACK IN THE AREA WHERE"
5600   PRINT ". . . YOU LAST TELEPORTED FROM": GOSUB 460
5610 BB = 2: GOSUB 470: RETURN
5620   IF R <  - 400 THEN  PRINT "INCOMPETENT SERF": RETURN
5630   IF R <  - 100 THEN  PRINT "WEAKLING": RETURN
5640   IF R < 0 THEN  PRINT "APPRENTICE": RETURN
5650   IF R < 100 THEN  PRINT "HALFLING": RETURN
5660   IF R < 200 THEN  PRINT "FOOT SOLDIER": RETURN
5670   IF R < 600 THEN  PRINT "WARRIOR": RETURN
5680   IF R < 900 THEN  PRINT "GREAT WARRIOR": RETURN
5690   IF R < 1500 THEN  PRINT "SWORDSMAN": RETURN
5700   IF R < 2500 THEN  PRINT "MAGIC SWORDSMAN": RETURN
5710   IF R >  = 2500 THEN  PRINT "DUNGEON MASTER": RETURN
5720   HOME : PRINT "YOU FALL INTO A DEEP . . DARK": GOSUB 460
5730   PRINT ". . . POOL . . OF MURKY WATER":BB = 4: GOSUB 470
5740 W =  INT ( RND (1) * 6 + 1): PRINT : IF W >  = 5 THEN 5780
5750   IF W >  = 3 THEN 5860
5760   PRINT "IT IS WARM AND SOOTHING . .AND":BB = 2: GOSUB 470
5770   PRINT "YOU CLIMB OUT . . FEELING RELAXED": PRINT : RETURN
5780 MS$ = "GILL MONSTER":HP = 8:HM = 12: HOME
5790   PRINT "THE WATER IS . . . ICY COLD":BB = 5: GOSUB 470: PRINT
5800   PRINT "SUDDENLY . . YOU FEEL SOMETHING WARM"
5810   PRINT " . . . RUB AGAINST YOUR LEGS . . . .":BB = 4: GOSUB 470: PRINT
5820   PRINT "IT THEN SURFACES NEXT TO YOU . . ."
5830   PRINT " AND YOU SEE THAT IT IS A SLIMY . ."
5840   PRINT ". . . ";MS$;" . . READY TO ATTACK":BB = 2: GOSUB 470
5850   PRINT : PRINT "AS YOU CLIMB OUT . . .": GOSUB 460: GOTO 4530
5860   PRINT "THE WATER IS STEAMING . . . . HOT":BB = 3: GOSUB 470
5870   PRINT : PRINT "AS YOU QUICKLY JUMP OUT . . . ."
5880 G4 =  INT ( RND (1) * 500 + 1) + 100: IF (G - G4) < 0 THEN G4 = G
5890 G = G - G4: PRINT "YOU DROP . . . ";G4;" GOLD PIECES"
5900   PRINT "WHICH FALL INTO THE POOL . . LOST":BB = 5: GOSUB 470: RETURN
```

NOTES

NOTES

NOTES

NOTES

TO THE READER

Sams Computer books cover Fundamentals — Programming — Interfacing — Technology written to meet the needs of computer engineers, professionals, scientists, technicians, students, educators, business owners, personal computerists and home hobbyists.

Our Tradition is to meet your needs and in so doing we invite you to tell us what your needs and interests are by completing the following:

1. I need books on the following topics:

2. I have the following Sams titles:

3. My occupation is:

_____ Scientist, Engineer	_____ D P Professional
_____ Personal computerist	_____ Business owner
_____ Technician, Serviceman	_____ Computer store owner
_____ Educator	_____ Home hobbyist
_____ Student	Other _____________________

Name (print)_______________________________________

Address____

City ____________________ State __________ Zip __________

Mail to: **Howard W. Sams & Co., Inc.**
       Marketing Dept. #CBS1/80
       4300 W. 62nd St., P.O. Box 7092
       Indianapolis, Indiana 46206